# The Agricultural Economics of the 21$^{st}$ Century

Vítor João Pereira Domingues Martinho
Editor

# The Agricultural Economics of the 21st Century

Springer

*Editor*
Vítor João Pereira Domingues Martinho
Viseu
Portugal

ISBN 978-3-319-09470-0 ISBN 978-3-319-09471-7 (eBook)
DOI 10.1007/978-3-319-09471-7
Springer Cham Heidelberg New York Dordrecht London

Library of Congress Control Number: 2014953908



Printed on acid-free paper

Springer is part of Springer Science+Business Media (www.springer.com)

*A special thanks to my wife, Lúcia, and my two daughters, Inês and Isabel.*

# Acknowledgement

I would like to thank "Roccio Torregrosa", "Irene Barrios-Kežić" and "Sylvia Schneider" frcm Springer editorial and Vinodhini Gejendran from SPi global for their cooperation in completing this book.

# Contents

# Chapter 1
# Introduction

**Vítor João Pereira Domingues Martinho**

This publication is intended to be a contribution (considering approaches among many others) towards the understanding of the evolution of agricultural economics over recent years and around the world. In this way we analyzed several variables related to the economic performance of the farming sector and associated to it the relationship between agriculture and other sectors, the dynamics of rural areas, multifunctional aspects, the environment, and sustainability.

This handbook was divided, apart from this first chapter for the introduction and the last chapter for the conclusion, into nine more chapters that investigate these questions in the European Union, USA, BRICS countries, and in Portugal. In the following paragraphs what was intended and considered in each one of the nine chapters will be outlined.

Beginning with the second chapter, in this part of the handbook, the aim was to analyze the interrelation between the agricultural output and other variables associated with it, in the context of the USA, from 1961 to 2012, with data from the World Bank, using time series econometric instruments, through the Stata software and taking into account the Cobb–Douglas function of production in a linear format as a base model.

The third chapter analyzes the performance of some variables related to agricultural economics in the former twenty seven European Union countries and their influence in the agricultural production, with statistical data that was obtained via European Union statistics, for the period 1973–2013, that were analyzed though cross-sectional estimations and with spatial econometric instruments, considering the GeoDa software.

The performance of the manufacturing sector, was the objective in the fourth chapter, namely that based on agriculture and fishery, in the first 27 countries of the European Union, through the Verdoorn law extended with new variables (the wages

V.J.P.D. Martinho (✉)
Agricultural School, Polytechnic Institute of Viseu, 3500 Viseu, Portugal
e-mail: vdmartinho@esav.ipv.pt


V.J.P.D. Martinho (ed.), *The Agricultural Economics of the 21$^{st}$ Century*,
DOI 10.1007/978-3-319-09471-7_1

and salaries, number of people employed per enterprise, share of employment in manufacturing total, investment per person employed, and the share of R&D employment in the number of people), from 1996 to 2008, and with data which was obtained from Eurostat.

The fifth chapter aims to analyze some economic, social, and environmental causes of the agricultural output in some European Union countries, analyzing data from the World Bank and considering time series econometric instruments. Some influential countries, such as Spain, France, Italy, Germany, and UK were also considered along with the three countries (Portugal, Ireland, and Greece) that have received financial assistance from International Institutions.

Not forgetting the emerging economies, with data from the World Bank, for the period 1961–2012, and considering the traditional function of production, the contextual agricultural economics within BRICS countries were also analyzed in the sixth chapter through time series econometric techniques.

In the seventh chapter the objective was to analyze the demographic, scientific, and social sustainability of the economic growth in Portuguese sectors, with data for the Portuguese NUTs II (seven), obtained via Eurostat for the period 1995–2010 and with panel data econometric instruments, based on the Keynesian models.

Considering the period 2004–2011, in the eighth chapter we investigated the influence of the environmental variables within Portuguese economic growth, specifically in the manufacturing sector, including those having the agricultural sector as a base, taking into account the Keynesian models, for the Portuguese regions (NUTs III), and the data (in panel) available for the Statistics of Portugal.

In the ninth chapter we analyzed the influence of other sectors related to the farming sector in the performance of some indicators in agriculture, namely the output, using statistical information from the Statistics of Portugal for the year of 2009 and considering cross-sectional estimations through several tests and techniques, including those related to spatial econometrics.

The tenth chapter intends to identify and find the objectives and priorities of the Azorean dairy farmer's decision making. The proposed methodology is based on multicriteria models, by simulation of the dairy farmers' behavior through data of the Farm Accountancy Data Network.

# Chapter 2
# An Approach to the Determinants of the Agricultural Output Dynamics in the USA

Vítor João Pereira Domingues Martinho

## 1 Introduction

The USA, indeed, has a different reality across its whole economy and in its agricultural economics being different in several aspects to that of others countries, namely in the European Union and in the BRICS.

For example, in some European Union countries the extension services for agriculture were reduced or closed whereas for the USA, Schimmelpfennig et al. (2006) found that the extension as well the social science research and agricultural R&D have had a considerable impact on agricultural efficiency.

Nowadays, climate change in the USA and food security are the main concerns in policy design (Mukherjee et al. 2013). Water quality is another preoccupation for the USA, but, also, within the European Union. Water quality is affected by economic factors, a lack of good water management systems, agricultural practices, and urban expansion (Zia et al. 2013). Today, with precision agriculture it is possible to manage several variables, using advanced technologies. Maintaining a farm's economic viability while simultaneously preserving the environment, namely the water quality, is a challenge for the USA (Ghebremichael et al. 2013). The paradigm of agricultural practices changed from the twentieth to the twenty-first century; now society is interested in sustainable economic activities that do not damage health or quality of life (Bowman and Zilberman 2013). The interactions between agriculture and the forest can help in the explanations of some environmental problems, namely those related with the greenhouse gas effects in the USA (Latta et al. 2013). The impact of agriculture on air quality is, also, a concern in the USA, for policy makers (Zhang and Wu 2013).

The academy can aid in adjustments to the changes in society. In this way, academics from several areas were mobilized in the 1930s by the Agricultural

V.J.P.D. Martinho (✉)
Agricultural School, Polytechnic Institute of Viseu, 3500, Viseu, Portugal
e-mail: vdmartinho@esav.ipv.pt



V.J.P.D. Martinho (ed.), *The Agricultural Economics of the 21st Century*,
DOI 10.1007/978-3-319-09471-7_2

Department in the USA to help in the economic, social, and cultural changes of rural areas (Jewett 2013).

Sometimes, the policies designed for agriculture can have indirect effects within the sector and within society. For example, the agricultural policies in the USA have influenced caloric ingestion, but that effect has decreased over the last few years (Rickard et al. 2013). Another example is the fact that subsidies for agricultural production and export, in the USA and in the European Union, create some distortions in the international trade of agricultural products (Bruno et al. 2012).

Taking into account the influence of the US economy on the emergent world, it seems important to present this original study in order to raise understanding about the USA's agricultural dynamics and about the interrelationship between agricultural output and other sustainable, social and economic variables. For that, the World Bank database (2014) was considered and we used time series econometric instruments, through the Stata (2014) software and taking into account as a base model the Cobb and Douglas (1928) function of production.

## 2 Data Description

The percentage of land for agriculture in the USA decreased continuously from 49 % in 1961 to about 45 % (Fig. 2.1). This is a phenomena verified in many developed countries where the agricultural sector reduced the percentage of area, due to the increase of the weight of other sectors and because of improvements made to the efficiency of the sector.

On the other hand, the area used for forest increased its weight slightly in the last two decades, from about 32 % in 1990 to around 33 % in 2011 (Fig. 2.2).

Figure 2.3 confirms what was referred to previously in Fig. 2.1. Indeed, the agricultural productivity, at 2005 constant prices, increased from about US$10,000 in 1980 to US$60,000 per worker in 2009 and 2010. This is a significant improvement in the performance in the dynamics of the USA's agricultural economics.

The fossil fuel energy consumption weighed against the total of energy consumed (Fig. 2.4) decreased by about 12 % from 1961 to 2012, from around 96 % to 84 %.

The $CO_2$ emissions increased slightly in the 1970s and decreased slightly towards the end of the last decade (Fig. 2.5), but, in general, more or less about 20 metric tons per capita.

The percentage of methane emissions (Fig. 2.6) and nitrous oxide emissions (Fig. 2.7) from agriculture increased by about 10 % in both cases, from 1990 to 2010. This again, seems to be in unison with the reduction in land for agriculture and with the rise in agricultural productivity at constant prices.

The rise in the percentage of population in urban clusters, from 1961 to 2012, was of about 10 %, from 40 % to 50 % (Fig. 2.8). The increase in population in large urban centers can help the economic dynamics in some cases, through the number of producers (New Economic Geography) and improvements to the scales of firms (Keynesian theory), but can also be the origin of problems such as urban congestion and regional asymmetries. So, this is a question that requires more careful analysis.

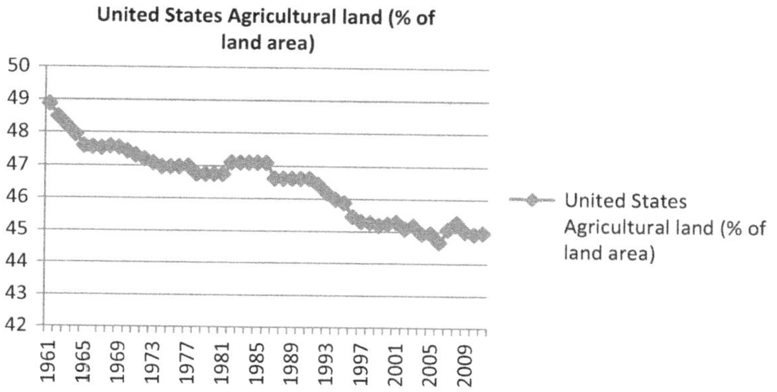


Fig. 2.1 Agricultural land (% of land area) in the USA

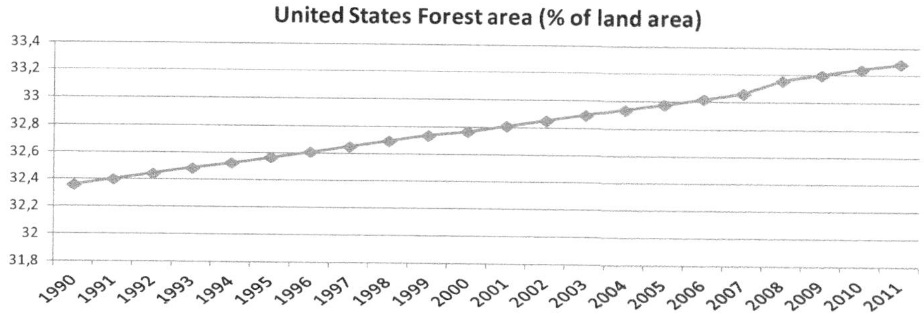


Fig. 2.2 Forest area (% of land area) in the USA

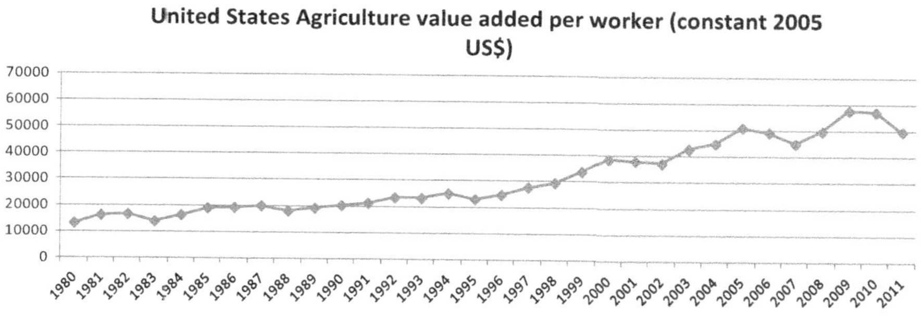


Fig. 2.3 Agriculture value added per worker (constant 2005 US$) in the USA

Again, the percentage of annual freshwater withdrawals for agriculture, which increased about 20 % in the period 1982–2011, seems to confirm the rise in intensity of USA agriculture over the last decades (Fig. 2.9).

Inflation (Fig. 2.10) presented some problems in the 1970s and 1980s, but over the last few years had values of around 2 and 4 %. The lending interest rates

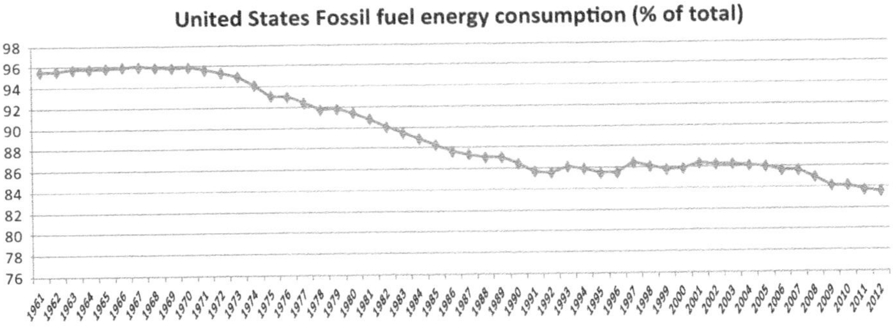


**Fig. 2.4** Fossil fuel energy consumption (% of total) in the USA

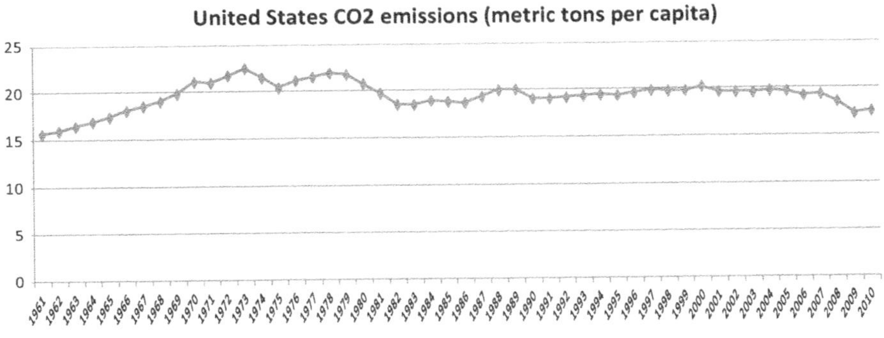


**Fig. 2.5** $CO_2$ emissions (metric tons per capita) in the USA

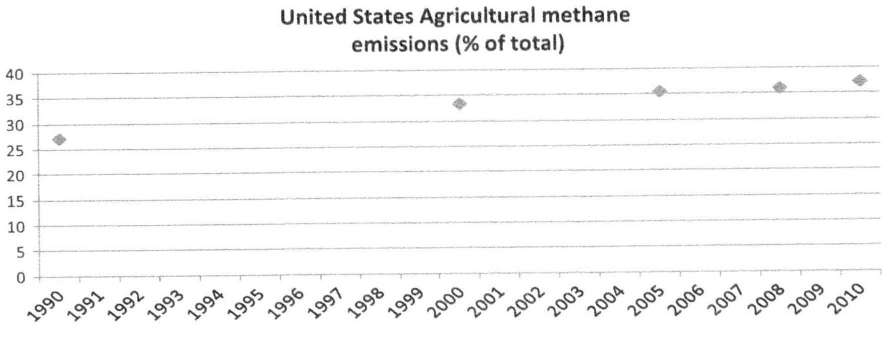


**Fig. 2.6** Agricultural methane emissions (% of total) in the USA

(Fig. 2.11) return in 2009, 2010, 2011, and 2012 to the values of the beginning of the 1960s at about 4 %.

The central government debt in percentage of the GDP increased drastically from about 30 % in 2001 to 80 % in 2011 (Fig. 2.12). In reality, the financial crisis

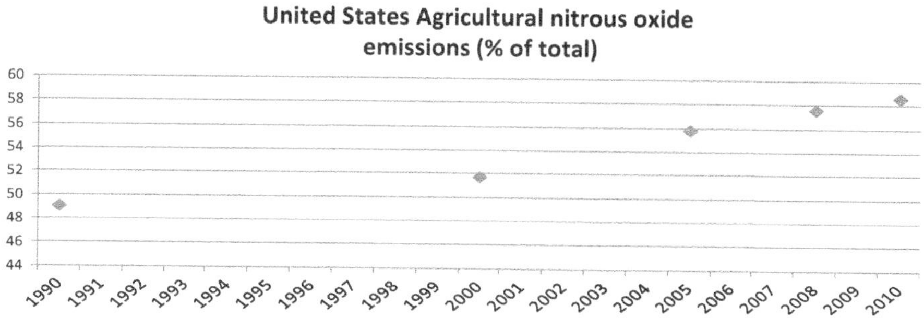


**Fig. 2.7** Agricultural nitrous oxide emissions (% of total) in the USA

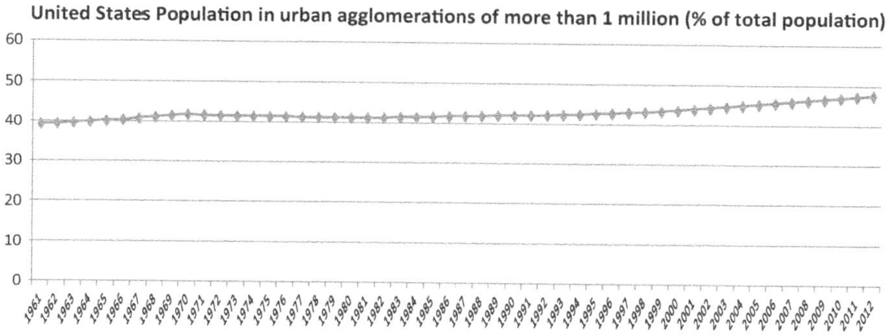


**Fig. 2.8** Population in urban agglomerations of more than one million (% of total population) in the USA

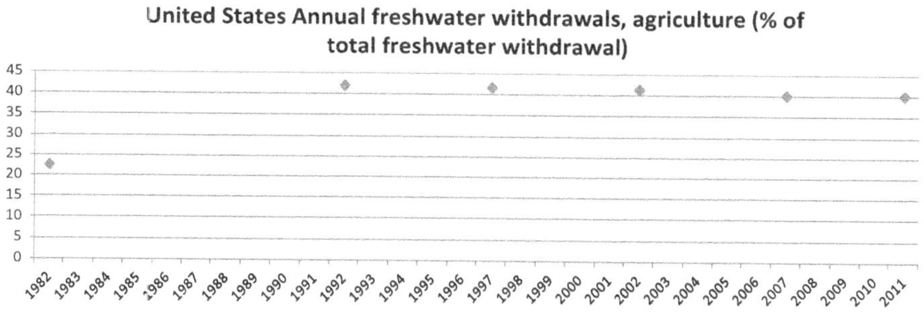


**Fig. 2.9** Annual freshwater withdrawals, agriculture (% of total freshwater withdrawal) in the USA

of 2008 in the USA leaves its mark in many economic and social indicators and in many countries, not only in the USA.

Curiously, or not, the number of motor vehicles per 1,000 persons diminished from 2008, from about 820 in 2007 to about 800 in 2010 (Fig. 2.13).

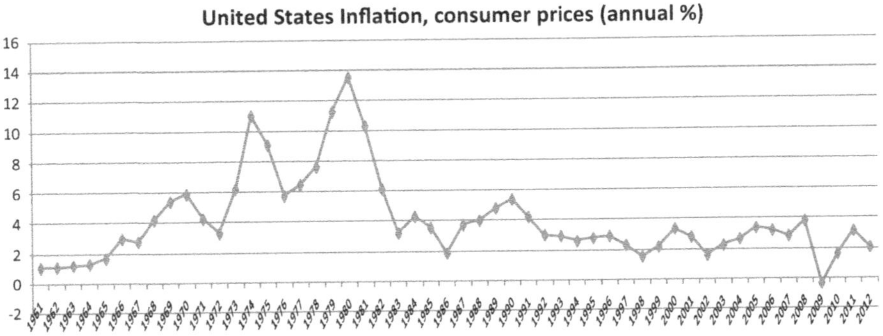


**Fig. 2.10** Inflation, consumer prices (annual %) in the USA

**Fig. 2.11** Lending interest rate (%) in the USA

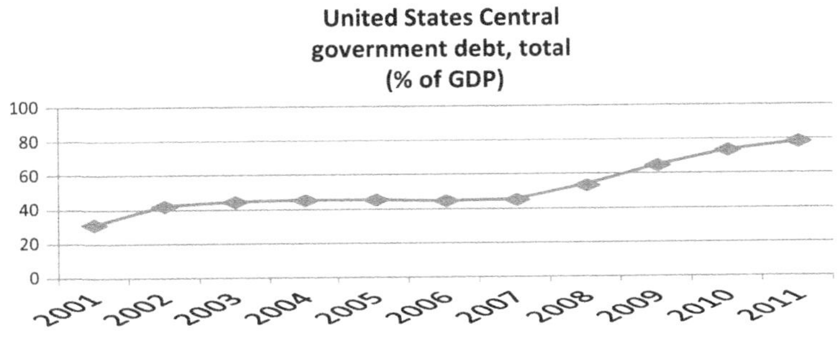


**Fig. 2.12** Central government debt, total (% of GDP) in the USA

The percentage of exports relative to the GDP increased significantly, in the period 1961–2012, from around 5 % in 1961 to about 14 % in 2012 (Fig. 2.14). This shows great economic dynamics and great perspectives for the future, considering that the external demand is one the most important engines for the economy (Keynesian theory).

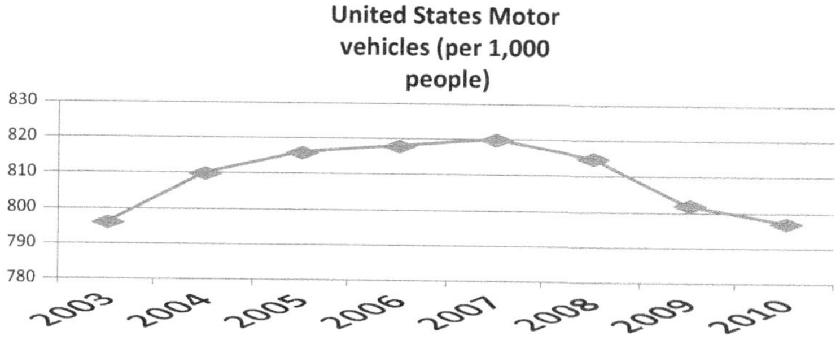


**Fig. 2.13** Motor vehicles (per 1,000 people) in the USA

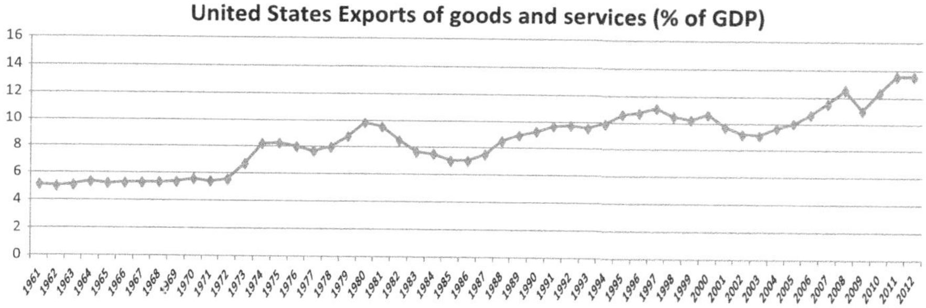


**Fig. 2.14** Exports of goods and services (% of GDP) in the USA

The investment in percentage of the GDP has been more or less situated in the interval of around 20–25 % since the 1960s until 2012 (Fig. 2.15). The financial crisis of 2008 also had an influence on the performance for investment in percentage of the GDP.

The weight of the value added from agriculture to the GDP diminished from about 3.5 % in the 1970s to around 1 % in 2011 (Fig. 2.16). This loss of weight in the contribution of agriculture to the GDP was common in many developed countries, because of improvements in the dynamics of other sectors.

The evolution of industry's contribution to the GDP follows, more or less, the pattern for agriculture and decreased its percentage from about 35 to 20 % (Fig. 2.17).

On the other hand, the weight of services rose considerably from more or less 60 to 80 % (Fig. 2.18), in the period considered (1970–2011). This is a phenomenon which has also been verified in several developed countries.

The evolution of the GDP growth rates, from 1961 to 2012, was extremely volatile, but in 2010, 2011, and 2012 was situated in values around the 2 % mark, which is a good sign of recuperation from the financial crisis verified in 2008 (Fig. 2.19).

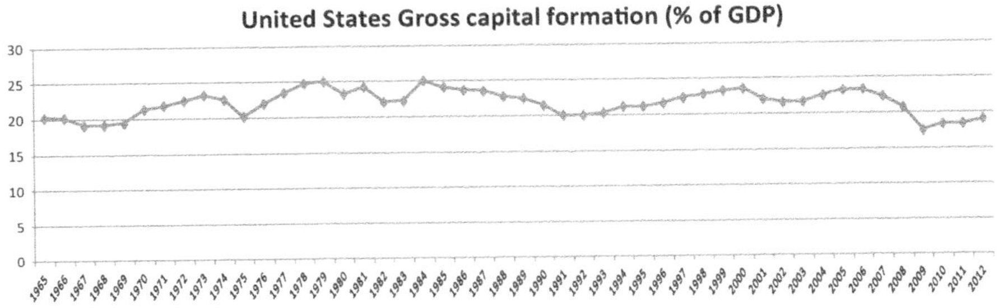


**Fig. 2.15** Gross capital formation (% of GDP) in the USA

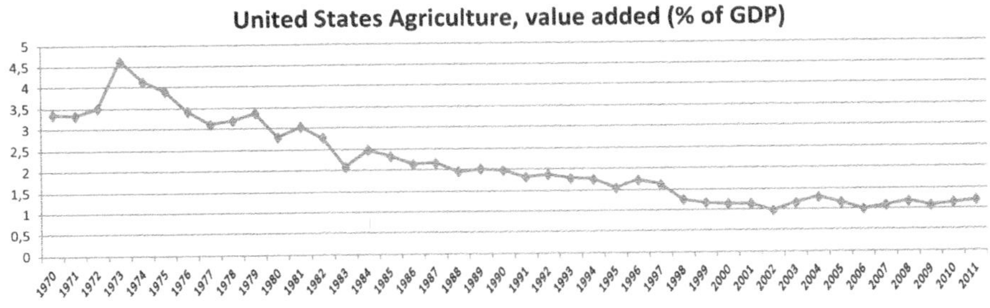


**Fig. 2.16** Agriculture, value added (% of GDP) in the USA

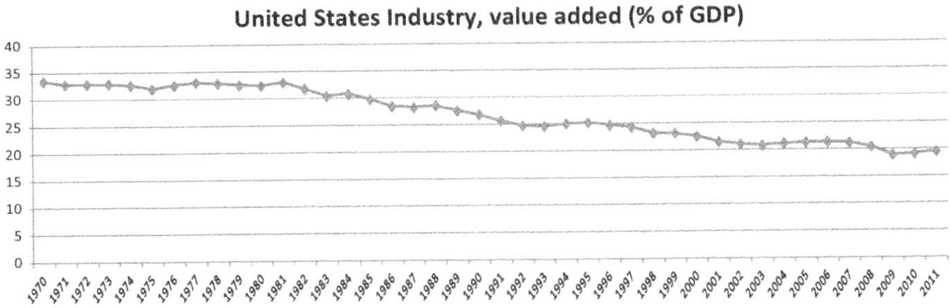


**Fig. 2.17** Industry, value added (% of GDP) in the USA

The GDP per capita, at current prices, rose continuously in the last five decades (Fig. 2.20). These values need other approaches, because of the effects of inflation upon this evolution.

The weight of employment in agriculture decreased significantly in the last three decades, from about 3.5 % in 1980 to 1.5 % in 2010 (Fig. 2.21). This is in concordance with other previous analysis for others variables.

The unemployment rates changed after the financial crisis of 2008 from about 4–6 % in the previous decade to about 8–10 % (Fig. 2.22).

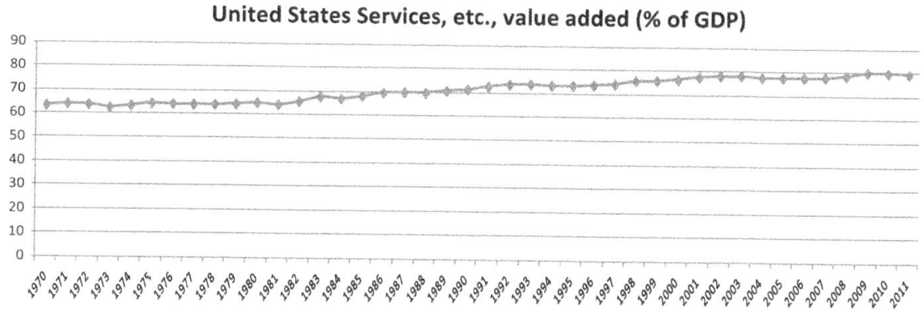


**Fig. 2.18** Services, etc., value added (% of GDP) in the USA

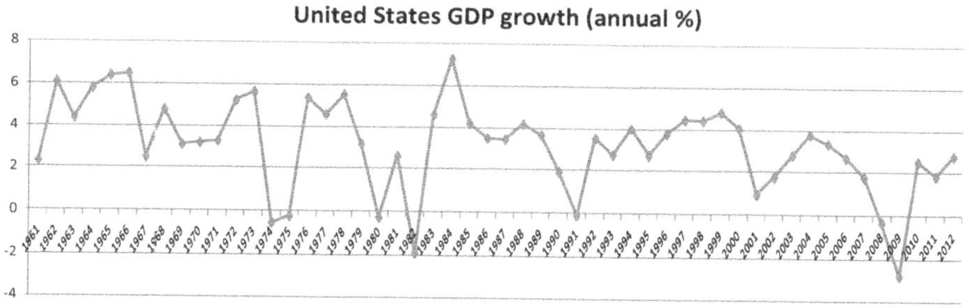


**Fig. 2.19** GDP growth (annual %) in the USA

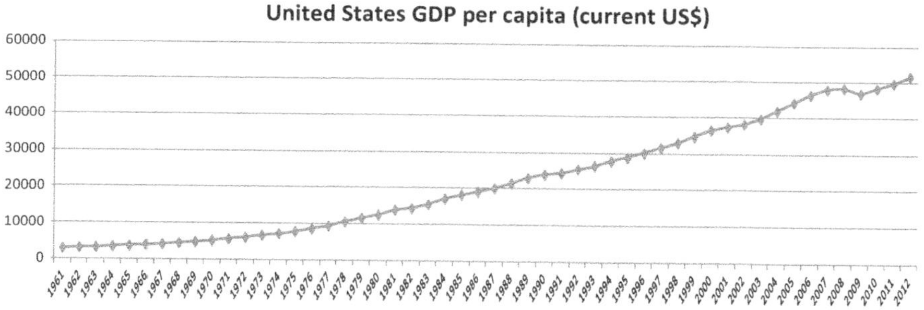


**Fig. 2.20** GDP per capita (current US$) in the USA

The rural population changed from 30 % in 1961 to about 15 % in 2012. This is an expected evolution, considering the reduction of employment in agriculture and the increase in the weight of services (Fig. 2.23).

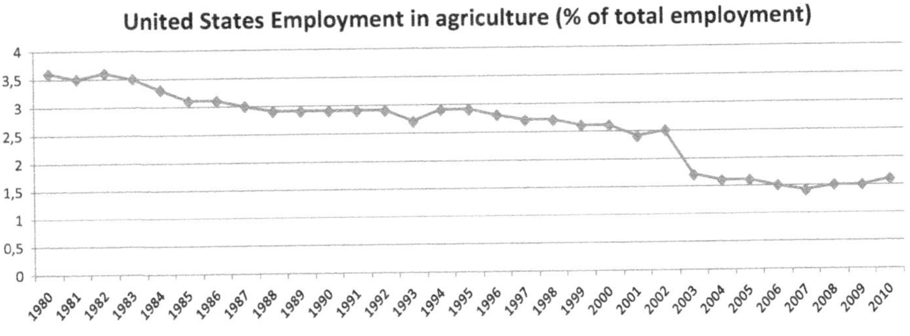


**Fig. 2.21** Employment in agriculture (% of total employment) in the USA

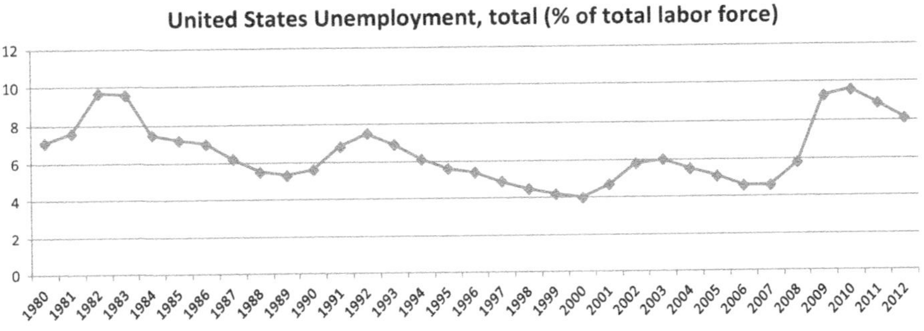


**Fig. 2.22** Unemployment, total (% of total labor force) in the USA

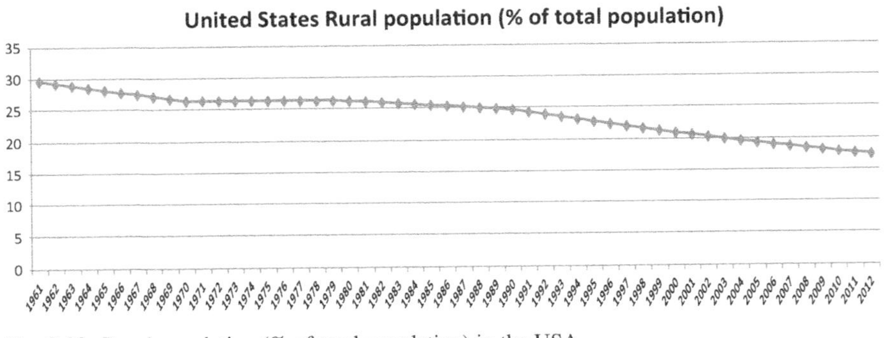


**Fig. 2.23** Rural population (% of total population) in the USA

# 3 Results

The results presented in Table 2.1, about the correlation among the variables considered, namely those with a sufficient number of observations to run a statistically acceptable analysis, show that there are negative and strong correlations between the dependent variable (the agricultural output represented by the

**Table 2.1** Correlate matrix between the variables considered, from 1961 to 2012

| | Agriculture, value added (% of GDP) | Agriculture value added per worker (constant 2005 US$) | Employment in agriculture (% of total employment) | Inflation, consumer prices (annual %) | Agricultural land (% of land area) | Fossil fuel energy consumption (% of total) | $CO_2$ emissions (metric tons per capita) | Population in urban agglomerations of more than one million (% of total population) | Lending interest rate (%) | Exports of goods and services (% of GDP) | Gross capital formation (% of GDP) | GDP growth (annual %) | GDP per capita (current US$) | Rural population (% of total population) |
|---|---|---|---|---|---|---|---|---|---|---|---|---|---|---|
| Agriculture, value added (% of GDP) | 1.000 | | | | | | | | | | | | | |
| Agriculture value added per worker (constant 2005 US$) | −0.913 | 1.000 | | | | | | | | | | | | |
| Employment in agriculture (% of total employment) | 0.771 | −0.905 | 1.000 | | | | | | | | | | | |
| Inflation, consumer prices (annual %) | 0.636 | −0.504 | 0.342 | 1.000 | | | | | | | | | | |
| Agricultural land (% of land area | 0.920 | −0.933 | 0.796 | 0.509 | 1.000 | | | | | | | | | |
| Fossil fuel energy consumption (% of total) | 0.742 | −0.725 | 0.600 | 0.618 | 0.725 | 1.000 | | | | | | | | |
| $CO_2$ emissions (metric tons per capita) | −0.141 | 0.039 | 0.062 | 0.214 | −0.232 | 0.005 | 1.000 | | | | | | | |
| Population in urban agglomerations of more than 1 million (% of total population) | −0.877 | 0.967 | −0.945 | −0.484 | −0.893 | −0.693 | −0.102 | 1.000 | | | | | | |
| Lending interest rate (%) | 0.667 | −0.720 | 0.653 | 0.715 | 0.613 | 0.713 | 0.243 | −0.708 | 1.000 | | | | | |

(continued)

**Table 2.1** (continued)

| | Agriculture, value added (% of GDP) | Agriculture value added per worker (constant 2005 US$) | Employment in agriculture (% of total employment) | Inflation, consumer prices (annual %) | Agricultural land (% of land area) | Fossil fuel energy consumption (% of total) | $CO_2$ emissions (metric tons per capita) | Population in urban agglomerations of more than one million (% of total population) | Lending interest rate (%) | Exports of goods and services (% of GDP) | Gross capital formation (% of GDP) | GDP growth (annual %) | GDP per capita (current US$) | Rural population (% of total population) |
|---|---|---|---|---|---|---|---|---|---|---|---|---|---|---|
| Exports of goods and services (% of GDP) | −0.633 | 0.673 | −0.550 | −0.251 | −0.792 | −0.700 | 0.154 | 0.679 | −0.340 | 1.000 | | | | |
| Gross capital formation (% of GDP) | 0.289 | −0.297 | 0.245 | 0.399 | 0.275 | 0.632 | 0.391 | −0.356 | 0.646 | −0.500 | 1.000 | | | |
| GDP growth (annual %) | 0.397 | −0.391 | 0.355 | 0.033 | 0.330 | 0.264 | 0.042 | −0.402 | 0.275 | −0.299 | 0.366 | 1.000 | | |
| GDP per capita (current US$) | −0.945 | 0.964 | −0.869 | −0.566 | −0.952 | −0.839 | 0.113 | 0.939 | −0.718 | 0.745 | −0.383 | −0.389 | 1.000 | |
| Rural population (% of total population) | 0.928 | −0.982 | 0.907 | 0.537 | 0.949 | 0.728 | −0.000 | −0.984 | 0.707 | −0.726 | 0.345 | 0.394 | −0.970 | 1.000 |

**Table 2.2** Results obtained with time series econometric techniques, based on the function of production model (linear model obtained with logarithms), for agricultural output in the period 1961–2012

| Model | Prais–Winsten |
|---|---|
| Constant | 9.626* (5.570) [0.000] |
| Agriculture value added per worker (constant 2005 US$) | −0.870* (−5.770) [0.000] |
| Employment in agriculture (% of total employment) | |
| Augmented Dickey–Fuller test for unit root | −6.311* [0.000] |
| EG-ADF test for co-integration | −1.809 [0.376] |
| Portmanteau test for white noise for autocorrelation | 224.764* [0.000] |
| Durbin's alternative test for autocorrelation | 0.342 [0.558] |
| Breusch–Godfrey LM test for autocorrelation | 0.388 [0.533] |
| Breusch–Pagan/Cook–Weisberg test for heteroskedasticity | 0.710 [0.398] |
| Ramsey RESET test using powers of the fitted values | 3.720* [0.024] |
| LM test for autoregressive conditional heteroskedasticity (ARCH) | 1.362 [0.243] |

*Note*: *Statistically significant at 5 %

agricultural value added in percentage of the GDP), farming productivity (Agriculture value added per worker at constant 2005 prices), the population in urban agglomeration, and the GDP per capita. On the other hand, there is a strong, positive relationship between the dependent variable and, namely, the agricultural land percentage and the weight of the rural population.

The results obtained in Table 2.2 with the econometric time series estimations show that there is, indeed, a negative and strong, statistically significant, relationship between agricultural output and farming productivity. Considering the form as the values of the variables presented (the output in the percentage relative to others sectors) and the productivity in absolute values, these results only mean that the improvements in productivity were not enough to reduce the decrease in the weight of the agricultural GDP in the whole US economy. The results for the several tests considered to evaluate the autocorrelation, the co-integration of the variables, and the heteroskedasticity confirm the absence of these statistic infractions. The Ramsey RESET test, using powers of the fitted values, shows a lack of variables and because of this finding the model was again estimated with other variables,

**Table 2.3** Results obtained with time series econometric techniques, considering the function of production model extended with others variables (linear model obtained with logarithms), for the agricultural output in the period 1961–2012

| Model | Prais–Winsten |
|---|---|
| Constant | 6.425*<br>(3.390)<br>[0.002] |
| Agriculture value added per worker (constant 2005 US$) | −0.598*<br>(−3.650)<br>[0.001] |
| Employment in agriculture (% of total employment) | |
| Inflation, consumer prices (annual %) | 0.172*<br>(2.870)<br>[0.008] |
| Breusch–Pagan/Cook–Weisberg test for heteroskedasticity | 0.010<br>[0.909] |
| Ramsey RESET test using powers of the fitted values | 3.240*<br>[0.040] |
| LM test for autoregressive conditional heteroskedasticity (ARCH) | 0.732<br>[0.392] |

*Note*: *Statistically significant at 5 %

extending the original model base in the well-known Cobb–Douglas function of production.

Table 2.3 reveals that from all the additional independent variables, despite agricultural employment and productivity, only the inflation of consumer price rates improve the model and show a positive influence towards agricultural output, with a coefficient statistically significant of 0.172. This shows the interrelationship between all the economies of the USA. All the results of the statistical tests reveal that there are no problems with the autocorrelation and with the heteroskedasticity, but the Ramsey RESET test, using powers of the fitted values, maintains evidence of a lack in independent variables, which may be an interesting finding for future research.

Finally, referring that all the results presented in the three tables are in agreement with each other and with the data description made in the previous section.

**Conclusions**

The preoccupation with climate changes, the environment, sustainability, water management, the consequences of agricultural policies in society, the changes in social patterns, and the design of adjusted agricultural policies are the order of the day in many countries, namely in developed countries, when we speak about the agricultural economics in the context of globalized

(continued)

economies, where the pressures of the rules from the negotiations of the World Trade Organization are a reality.

From the data description it was possible to conclude that in agriculture, despite the increase in productivity, this was not sufficient to avoid the reduction in the weight of the farming output in the economy. On the other hand, as expected, the percentage of agricultural employment in farming diminished. This is a tendency verified by many developed countries, namely in North America and in West Europe. The reduction in fossil fuel energy consumption reveals concerns with the environment and sustainability. There are, however, some environmental problems in agriculture, because the levels of methane and nitrous oxide are emitted by this sector. The percentage augmentation of population in urban agglomerations and the reduction of the rural population need microanalysis, because this can be good for economic dynamics and/or bad for regional asymmetries, for example. The performance of exports seems to confirm these apparently good economic dynamics. However, the financial crisis of 2008 had consequences in many economic indicators such as the central government debt in percentage of the GDP, the investment in percentage of the GDP, and the GDP growth rates.

The econometric results reveal that there are negative and strong correlations between the percentage of agricultural output, the agricultural productivity, the population in large urban centers, and the gross domestic product per capita. On the other hand, there is a positive a strong relationship between the level of agricultural output and the percentage of agricultural land and rural population. The results obtained from the estimations confirm these findings and show that despite agricultural productivity, in the USA, the inflation of consumer price rates, also, influences the percentage of the agricultural output. All statistic tests reveal an absence of problems with the autocorrelation, the co-integration of the variables, and the heteroskedasticity. The Ramsey RESET test, using powers of the fitted values, shows a lack of variables in all models. This may be an interesting finding to develop in future research related with these issues.

## References

Bowman, M. S., & Zilberman, D. (2013). Economic factors affecting diversified farming systems. *Ecology and Society, 18*(1), 33.

Bruno, F. M. R., Azevedo, A. F. Z., & Massuquetti, A. (2012). The agricultural subsidies in international trade: The policies adopted by the European Union and the United States of America. *Ciência Rural, 42*(4), 757–764.

Cobb, C. W., & Douglas, P. H. (1928). A theory of production. *American Economic Review, 18* (Suppl), 139–165.

Ghebremichael, L. T., Veith, T. L., & Hamlett, J. M. (2013). Integrated watershed- and farm-scale modeling framework for targeting critical source areas while maintaining farm economic viability. *Journal of Environmental Management, 114*, 381–394.

Jewett, A. (2013). The social sciences, philosophy, and the cultural turn in the 1930s USDA. *Journal of the History of the Behavioral Sciences, 49*(4), 396–427.

Latta, G. S., Baker, J. S., Beach, R. H., Rose, S. K., & McCarl, B. A. (2013). A multi-sector intertemporal optimization approach to assess the GHG implications of U.S. forest and agricultural biomass electricity expansion. *Journal of Forest Economics, 19*, 361–383.

Mukherjee, D., Bravo-Ureta, B. E., & Vries, A. D. (2013). Dairy productivity and climatic conditions: econometric evidence from South-eastern United States. *The Australian Journal of Agricultural and Resource Economics, 57*, 123–140.

Rickard, B. J., Okrent, A. M., & Alston, J. M. (2013). How have agricultural policies influenced caloric consumption in the United States? *Health Economics, 22*, 316–339.

Schimmelpfennig, D. E., O'Donnell, C. J., & Norton, G. W. (2006). Efficiency effects of agricultural economics research in the United States. *Agricultural Economics, 34*, 273–280.

Stata. (2014). *Statistics/Data analysis*. StataCorp, LP.

World Bank (2014). *Several statistics*. Washington, DC: World Bank.

Zhang, Y., & Wu, S.-Y. (2013). Fine scale modeling of agricultural air quality over the South-eastern United States using two air quality models. Part II. Sensitivity studies and policy implications. *Aerosol and Air Quality Research, 13*, 1475–1491.

Zia, H., Harris, N. R., Merrett, G. V., Rivers, M., & Coles, N. (2013). The impact of agricultural activities on water quality: A case for collaborative catchment-scale management using integrated wireless sensor networks. *Computers and Electronics in Agriculture, 96*, 126–138.

# Chapter 3
# Cross-section and Spatial Approaches for the Agricultural Contexts in the 27 Countries of the European Union

Vítor João Pereira Domingues Martinho

## 1 Introduction

The European Union began in 1957/1958, through the Treaty of Rome, with the name European Economic Community and founded by six countries (France, Belgium, Luxembourg, Netherlands, Italy, and the Federal Republic of Germany).

The European Economic Community changed its name to European Union in 1992, through the Maastricht Treaty, and currently has 28 countries. The largest process of adhesion was in 2004 with the entrance of ten countries from Eastern Europe.

The entrance into the European Union by several countries had many impacts upon the domestic economic sectors, namely in those more exposed to international competition (Asaftei and Parmeter 2010).

In this way, the European Union agricultural policies, for example, when designed should have taken into account the specific contexts of farming production in each region and country. If not, the expected effects are seldom obtained (Winter 2000).

The specifics and impacts, at different levels, of several agricultural productions are very distinct and these particularities conduct us towards divergent answers as to the external impact (from internal policies, external pressures, etc.).

For example, the sheep and goat activities contributed to sustainability in many European countries, but new scenarios can appear with new policies from the Common Agricultural Policy and with the international developments from the World Trade Organization (Dýrmundsson 2006).

The Common Agricultural Policy has suffered many alterations since its creation, but concerns with the environment and sustainability are a constant in recent instruments, namely those related with organic farming (Haring 2003).

V.J.P.D. Martinho (✉)
Agricultural School, Polytechnic Institute of Viseu, 3500 Viseu, Portugal
e-mail: vdmartinho@esav.ipv.pt



V.J.P.D. Martinho (ed.), *The Agricultural Economics of the 21st Century*,
DOI 10.1007/978-3-319-09471-7_3

In these scenarios, it would appear to be important to analyze the evolution and the interrelationship of some variables related with the agricultural economic contexts. In this line, considering the former 27 countries of the European Union, the main propose of this research is to analyze the evolution of the statistical information associated to some variables related with the agricultural sector, through description of the data (obtained from Eurostat 2014), and investigating the interaction among these variables, through cross-section and spatial autocorrelation analysis, using GeoDa software (2014).

## 2 Data Description

The first six figures presented below show the evolution of the values associated to some variables related to the farming sector. The database considered provides statistical information for some of these variables for the period 1990–2007 and data for others for the period 1973–2013.

Figure 3.1 presents the values for the agricultural area utilized by several of the former 27 countries of the European Union. The countries with more detached utilized agricultural area, from 1990 to 2007, are, respectively, France, Spain, Germany, United Kingdom, Poland, Romania, and Italy. Italy is the country where this variable decreased the most, namely after 1997 (this may be an interesting question to be developed in future research). In the remainder of the group of countries, Hungary and the Ireland are where the utilized agricultural area is also significant.

The countries with more employment in agriculture (AWU—Annual Work Unit) are, respectively (Fig. 3.2), Romania (decreased drastically after 2003), Poland (increased after the entrance into the European Union in 2004), Italy (diminishing significantly after 1997, for utilized agricultural area), and Spain (with a downward tendency, as all countries in general). The decreasing tendency in the evolution of farming employment is expected, considering the improvements in technology used in agriculture which allow for the delivery of workforce to other sectors with more performance in economic scale. On the other hand, the agricultural policies of extensification from the Common Agricultural Policy, after the 1992 Reform, also contributed to this evolution.

The evolution of the number of holdings follows more or less that referred to for agricultural employment (Fig. 3.3). Maybe, the data for more recent years show a different tendency, because the perception in some countries is that the financial and economic crisis in some European Union countries, as the consequent increase in unemployment, led to more population returning to agriculture, raising employment in this sector, as well the amount of area used and the number of holdings. Moreover, comparing the area utilized and other variables (farming employment and the number of holdings), it seems that there are some structural adjustments.

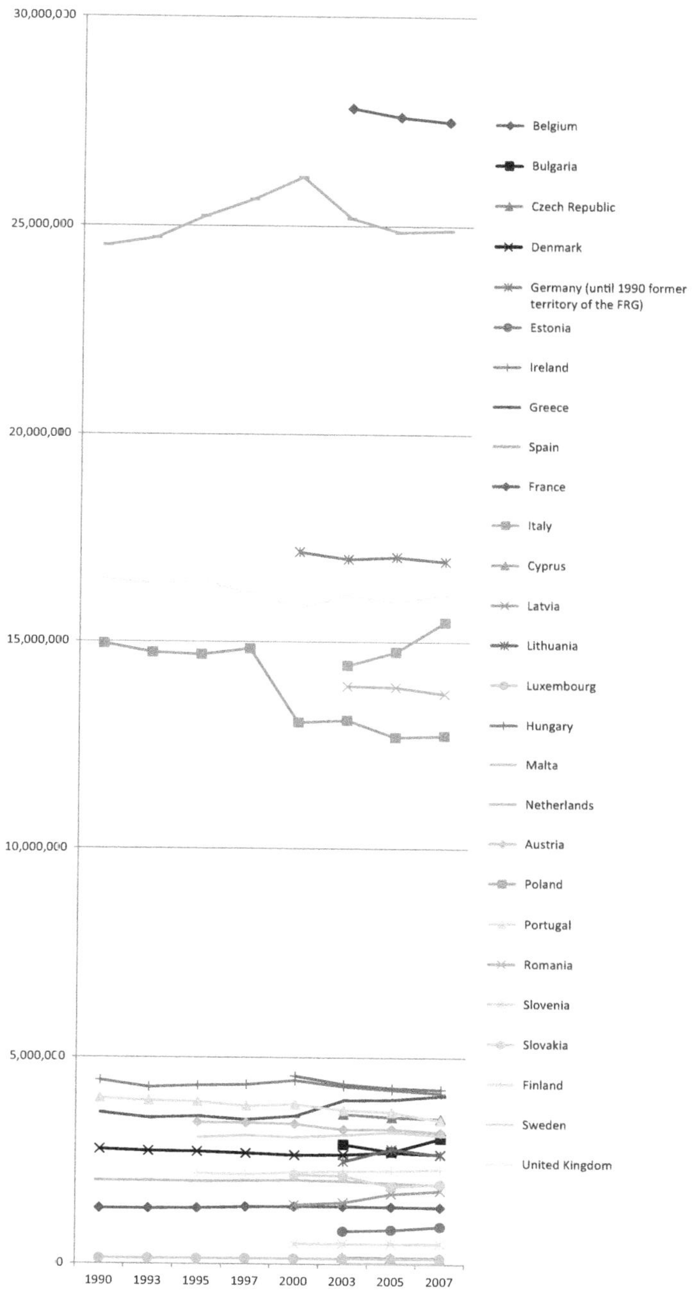


**Fig. 3.1** Utilized agricultural area (ha) among European Union countries

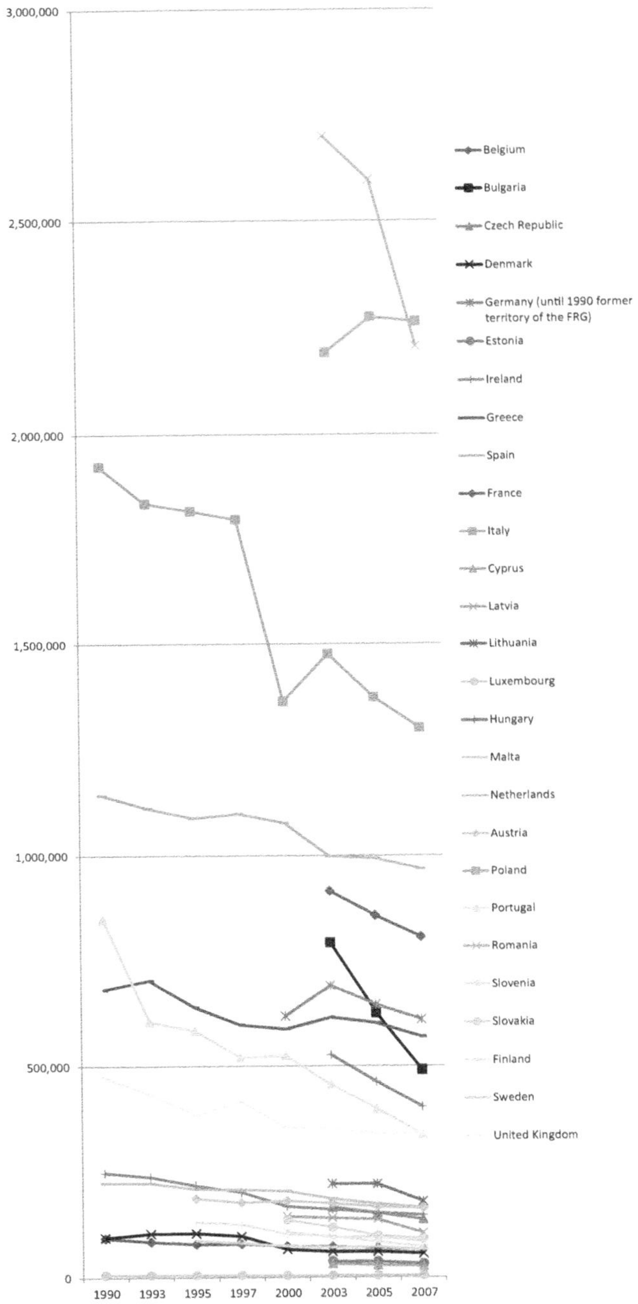


**Fig. 3.2** AWU Labour force—directly employed by the holding among European Union countries

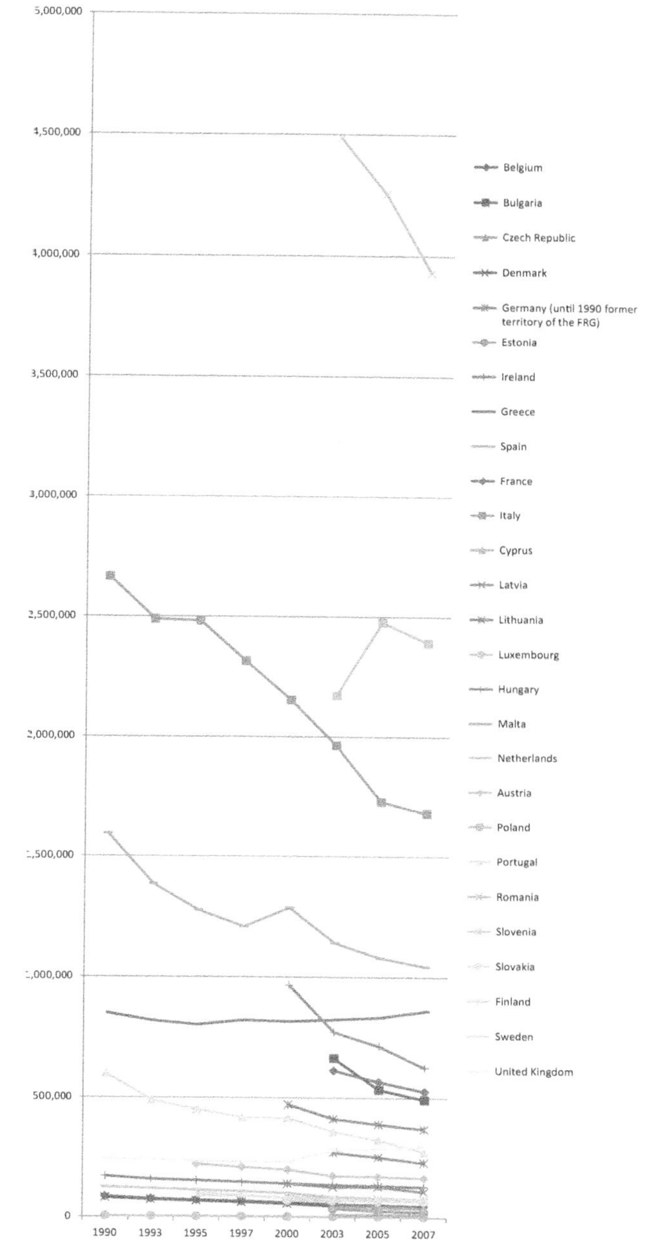


**Fig. 3.3** Number of holdings among European Union countries

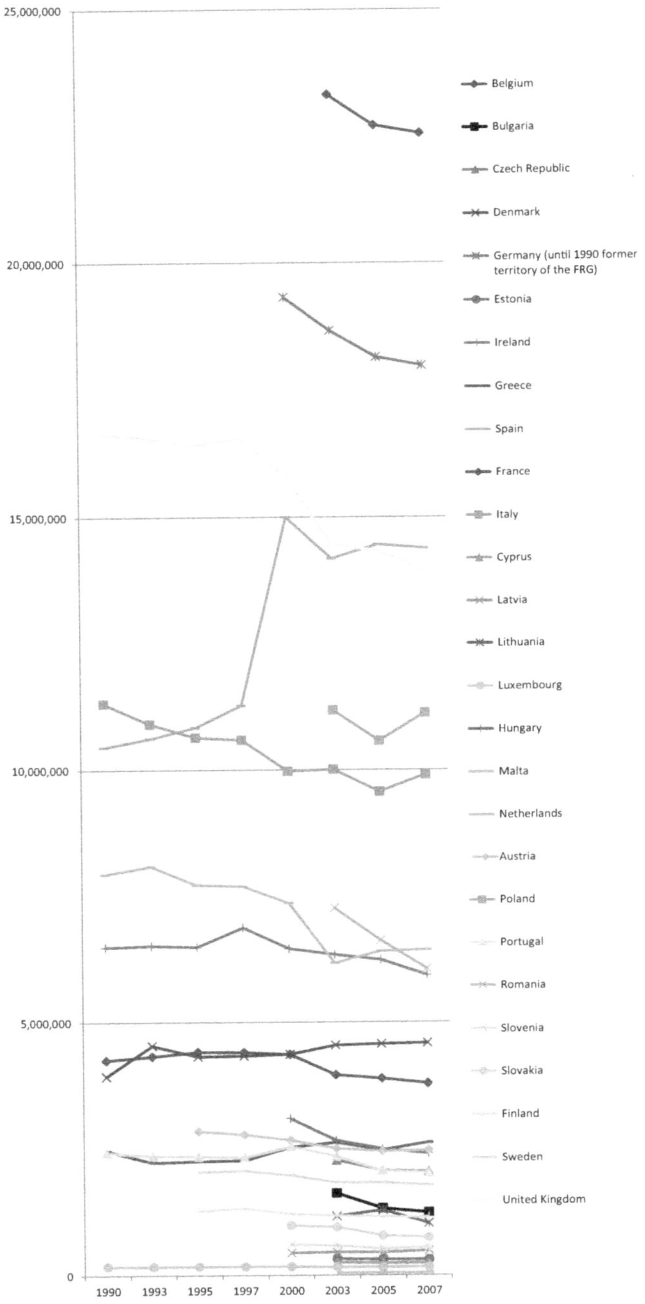


**Fig. 3.4** LSU livestock among European Union countries

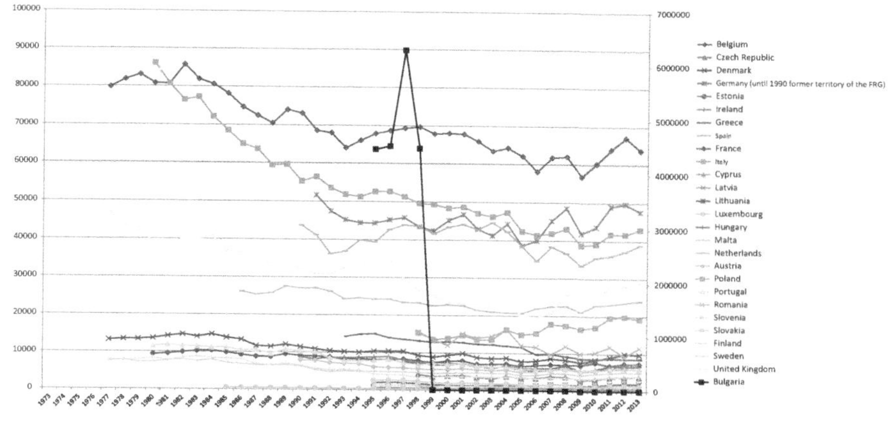


Fig. 3.5 Production value at basic price (millions of euro, base year: 2005 = 100)

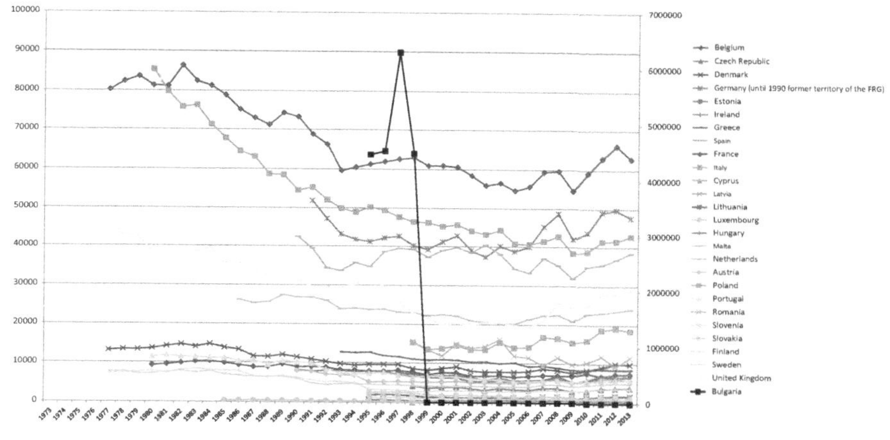


Fig. 3.6 Production value at producer price (millions of euro, base year: 2005 = 100)

The countries with more animal production (Fig. 3.4) are, in this decreasing order, France, Germany, United Kingdom, Spain, Poland, and Italy. The country where the livestock units increased significantly was clearly Spain after 1997.

From Figs. 3.5 and 3.6 it is possible to observe that the countries with more production value at basic price or at producer price (millions of euro, base year: 2005 = 100) are France, Italy, Germany, Spain, United Kingdom, Netherlands, Poland, Romania, etc. Comparing these values, with the values of the variables presented in the former four figures, it is possible to note that there are significant differences in terms of dimension and efficiency in the farming sector between the several countries of the European Union. On the other hand, there is, too, a falling tendency in the agricultural output of the diverse countries and this seems to confirm some of the consequences of the instruments designed in the context of

**Fig. 3.7** Logarithm of the average utilized agricultural area (ha) among European Union countries

**Fig. 3.8** Logarithm of the average AWU Labour force—directly employed by the holding among European Union countries

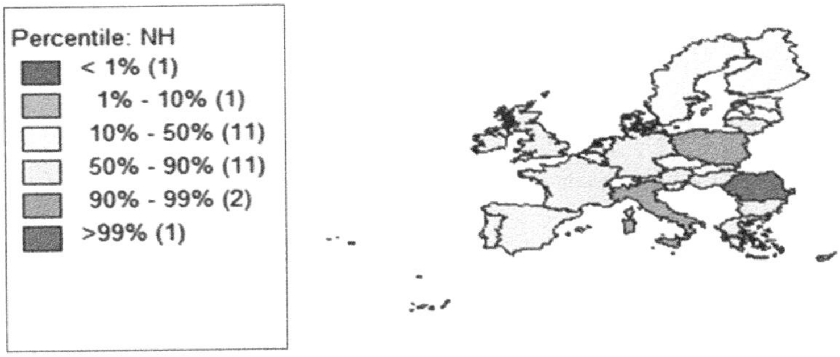


**Fig. 3.9** Logarithm of the average number of holdings among European Union countries

the Common Agricultural Policy. The values for Bulgaria seem strange and need more careful analysis in future research.

Figures 3.7, 3.8, 3.9, 3.10, 3.11, and 3.12 present the same data shown in the previous six figures, but now in average and in the logarithm for the period 1990–2007 (the coincident period for all the variables). These figures confirm the aforementioned for each single variable analyzed.

**Fig. 3.10** Logarithm of the average LSU livestock among European Union countries

**Fig. 3.11** Logarithm of the average production value at basic price (base year: 2005 = 100)

**Fig. 3.12** Logarithm of the average production value at producer price (base year: 2005 = 100)

The following six figures (Figs. 3.13, 3.14, 3.15, 3.16, 3.17, and 3.18) present the values of Moran's I statistics for the global spatial autocorrelation (for the 27 countries considered). When the value of the Moran's I is positive/negative, this signifies that the values of the variable considered in a determined location (in this case country) are positively/negatively correlated with the values of the same variable for neighboring locations (countries). If, the Moran's I statistics are zero, there isn't spatial autocorrelation for the variable among the neighbors' locations. To measure the proximity between neighboring countries, in this study we considered a matrix of queen contiguity, considering only one neighbor country in all directions

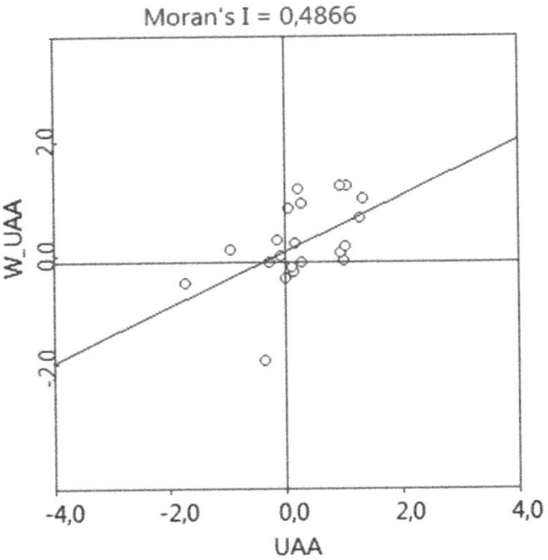


**Fig. 3.13** Global spatial autocorrelation (one neighbor in a queen contiguity matrix) for the logarithm of the average utilized agricultural area (ha) among European Union countries

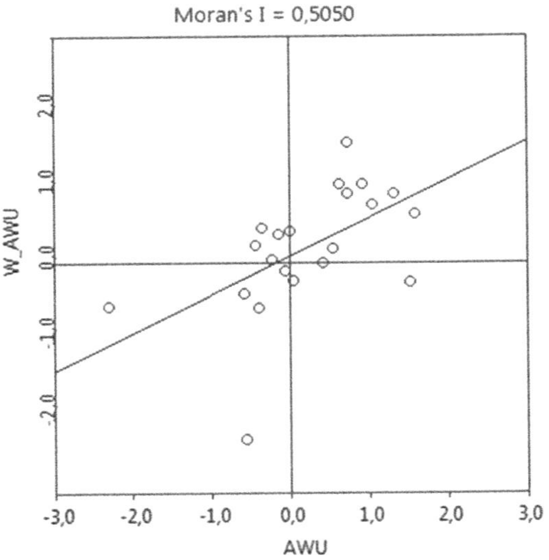


**Fig. 3.14** Global spatial autocorrelation (one neighbor in a queen contiguity matrix) for the logarithm of the average AWU Labour force—directly employed by the holding among European Union countries

Fig. 3.15 Global spatial autocorrelation (one neighbor in a queen contiguity matrix) for the logarithm of the average number of holdings among European Union countries

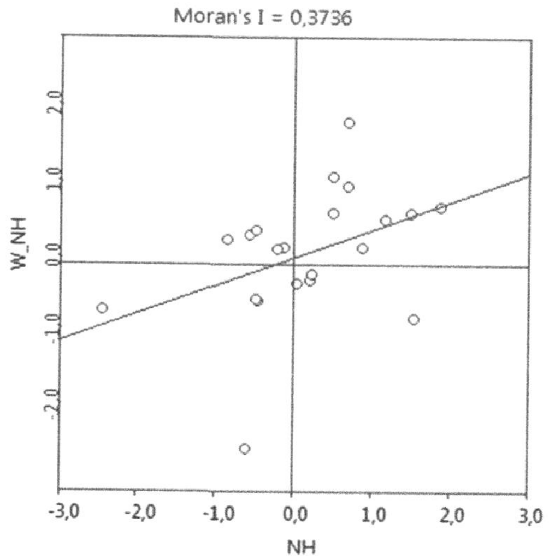


Fig. 3.16 Global spatial autocorrelation (one neighbor in a queen contiguity matrix) for the logarithm of the average LSU livestock among European Union countries

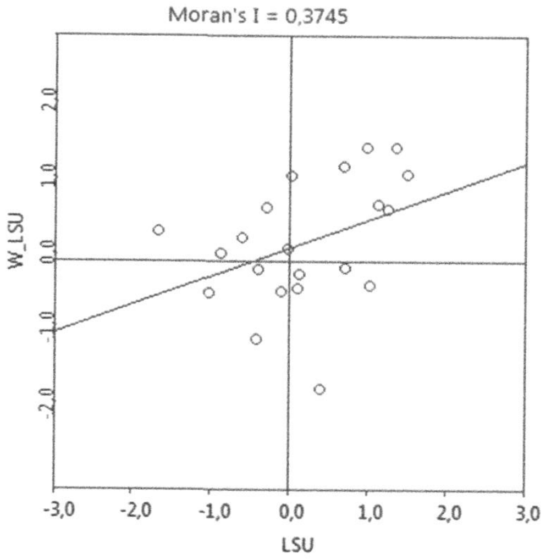


(because with more than one neighbor the value of Moran's I became negative). In analyzing the following six figures, it is possible to conclude that there is positive global spatial autocorrelation, considering one neighbor country in all directions, in all variables, but the stronger value being for agricultural employment (this shows the importance of this variable for agriculture in Europe).

Figures 3.19, 3.20, 3.21, 3.22, 3.23, and 3.24 reveal the values of Moran's I for the local autocorrelation (for each individual European Union country). The values high–high and low–low represent positive spatial autocorrelation for the countries

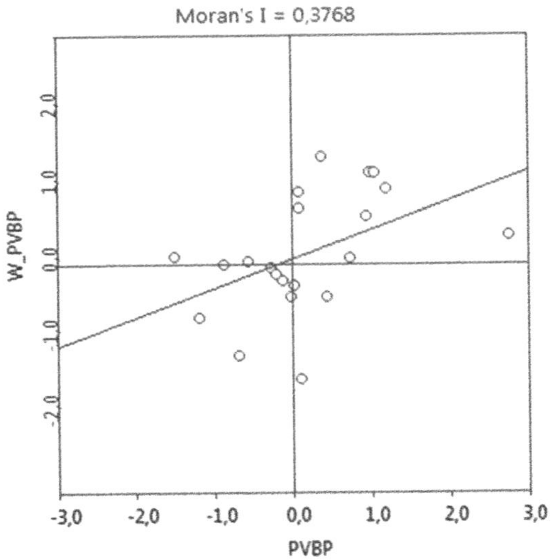


**Fig. 3.17** Global spatial autocorrelation (one neighbor in a queen contiguity matrix) for the logarithm of the average production value at basic price (millions of euro, base year: 2005 = 100)

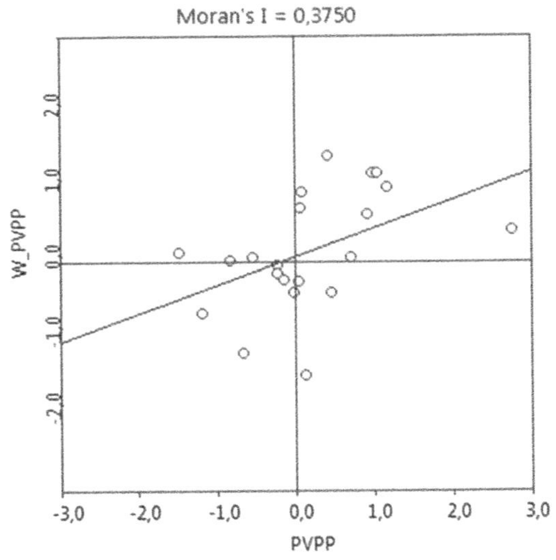


**Fig. 3.18** Global spatial autocorrelation (one neighbor in a queen contiguity matrix) for the logarithm of the average production value at producer price (millions of euro, base year: 2005 = 100)

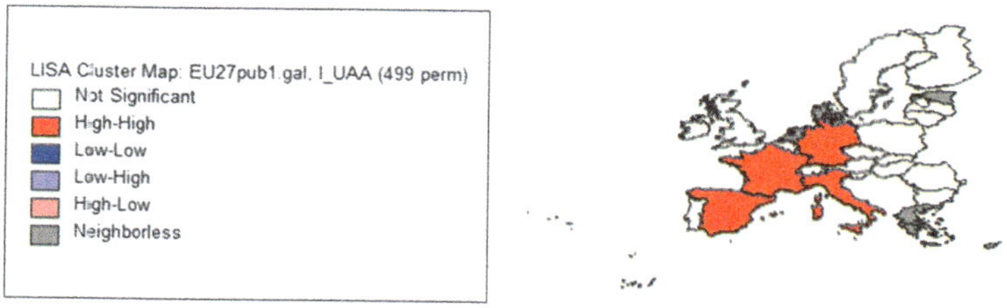


**Fig. 3.19** Local spatial autocorrelation (one neighbor in a queen contiguity matrix) for the logarithm of the average utilized agricultural area (ha) among European Union countries

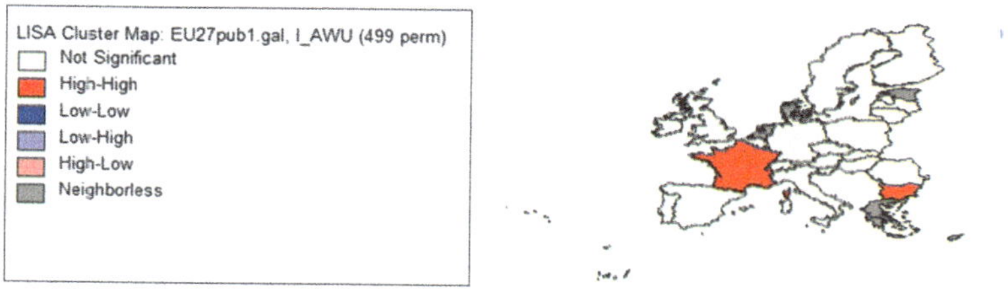


**Fig. 3.20** Local spatial autocorrelation (one neighbor in a queen contiguity matrix) for the logarithm of the average AWU Labour force—directly employed by the holding among European Union countries

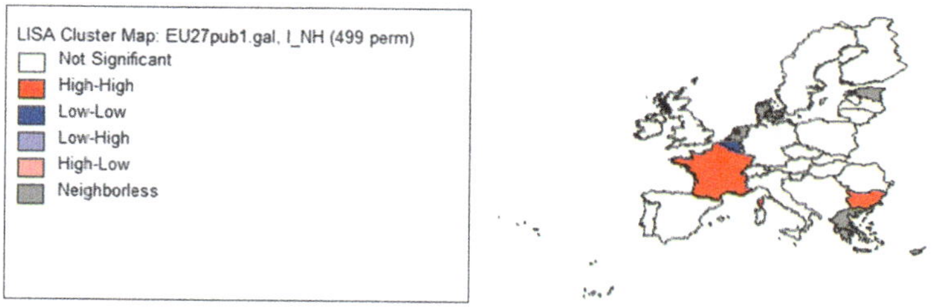


**Fig. 3.21** Local spatial autocorrelation (one neighbor in a queen contiguity matrix) for the logarithm of the average number of holdings among European Union countries

with high values and low values, respectively, for the variable considered. The values high–low and low–high represent negative local spatial autocorrelation. The figures show namely positive local spatial autocorrelation for high values where France appears in all figures, as a country that is positively influenced by high values for neighboring countries. In Fig. 3.21 (for the variable number of holdings) Belgium is positively autocorrelated for low values with neighboring countries. This analysis of global and local spatial autocorrelation may prove to be an important information for the design of future policies.

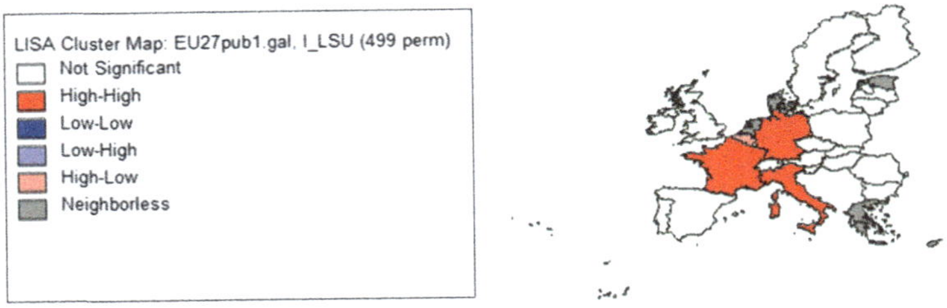


**Fig. 3.22** Local spatial autocorrelation (one neighbor in a queen contiguity matrix) for the logarithm of the average LSU livestock among European Union countries

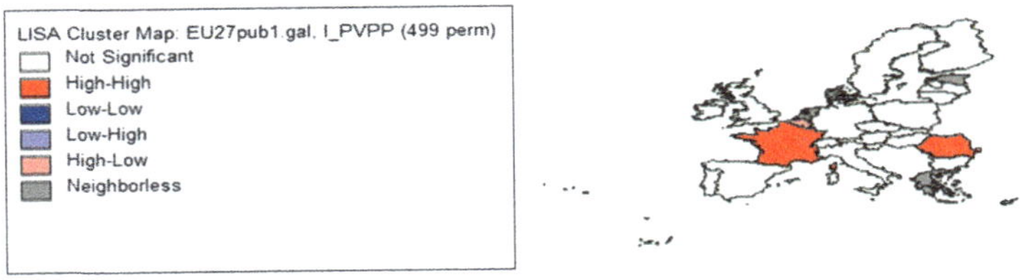


**Fig. 3.23** Local spatial autocorrelation (one neighbor in a queen contiguity matrix) for the logarithm of the average production value at basic price (millions of euro, base year: 2005 = 100)

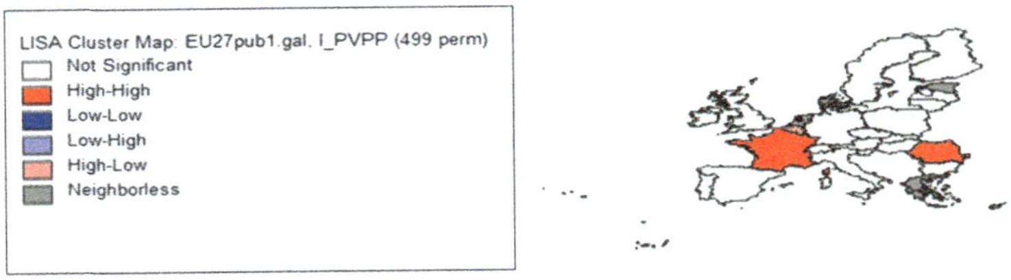


**Fig. 3.24** Local spatial autocorrelation (one neighbor in a queen contiguity matrix) for the logarithm of the average production value at producer price (millions of euro, base year: 2005 = 100)

# 3 Results

In the following two tables are presented the results obtained with cross-section regressions, considering the agricultural output at basic prices (Table 3.1) and the agricultural output at producer prices (Table 3.2) as dependent variables. The other variables were tested as independent variables and the best statistic results were obtained for the model with agricultural employment as an independent variable. The consideration of the two prices (basic and producer prices) was to analyze the influence of tax and subsides, removed from basic prices, in the value of agricultural production and in the dynamics of the agricultural sector.

The values of the statistic tests confirm the robustness of the results obtained. On the other hand, the values of the tests for spatial autocorrelation (Moran's I and LM) reveal an absence of spatial autocorrelation problems in the regression.

**Table 3.1** Results obtained with cross-section econometric techniques, considering the agricultural output (at basic price, base year: 2005 = 100) in average from 1990 to 2007 as dependent variable

| Model | |
|---|---|
| Constant | 10.936*<br>(5.620)<br>[0.000] |
| AWU Labour force—directly employed by the holding | 0.954*<br>(6.020)<br>[0.000] |
| Breusch–Pagan/Cook–Weisberg test for heteroskedasticity | 2.690<br>[0.100] |
| Ramsey RESET test using powers of the fitted values | 1.740<br>[0.188] |
| Moran's I (error) | 0.281<br>[0.778] |
| Robust LM (lag) | 0.001<br>[0.970] |
| Robust LM (error) | 0.001<br>[0.967] |

*Note*: *Statistically significant at 5 %

**Table 3.2** Results obtained with cross-section econometric techniques, considering the agricultural output (at producer price, base year: 2005 = 100) in average from 1990 to 2007 as dependent variable

| Model | |
|---|---|
| Constant | 10.763*<br>(5.480)<br>[0.000] |
| AWU Labour force—directly employed by the holding | 0.962*<br>(6.020)<br>[0.000] |
| Breusch–Pagan/Cook–Weisberg test for heteroskedasticity | 2.430<br>[0.118] |
| Ramsey RESET test using powers of the fitted values | 1.640<br>[0.208] |
| Moran's I (error) | 0.248<br>[0.803] |
| Robust LM (lag) | 0.013<br>[0.909] |
| Robust LM (error) | 0.000<br>[0.997] |

*Note*: *Statistically significant at 5 %

The LM tests (Lagrange Multiplier) are usually used to analyze the spatial autocorrelation that come from the dependent variable in neighboring locations (LM lag) and from random effects in neighboring spatial units (LM error).

**Conclusions**

The evolution of the European Union since the beginning in 1957/1958, designated at the time as the European Economic Community, was not only extraordinary at a geographical level, but also in institutional, social, and economic dimensions. With the adhesion of several countries there were several transformations and changes, namely in the agricultural sector, specifically with the entrance of ten countries from Eastern Europe in 2004. These ten countries had an important tradition in the farming sector.

The description of the data shows that France, Spain, Germany, United Kingdom, Poland, Romania, and Italy are the leader countries in terms of agricultural area used and livestock units. However, Romania, Poland, Italy, and Spain are the countries with a higher level of employment in agriculture and the number of holdings. On the other hand, France, Italy, Germany, Spain, United Kingdom, Netherlands, Poland, and Romania are the countries with more production value both at basic and producer prices. These values reveal the importance of some countries in the European Union agricultural economic context and the structural efficiency in some countries, namely in the French agricultural sector. The Netherlands is a country that appears here with great production value, showing significant agricultural economic performance.

The spatial autocorrelation analysis confirms the importance of taking into account this statistical infraction in future analysis with these variables among European Union countries and in the design of new agricultural policies. On the other hand, this analysis also reveals the importance of agricultural employment in the dynamics of the European farming sector and the influence of France (and the direct neighboring countries) in these contexts and performances.

The econometric estimations show that, indeed, agricultural employment plays a determining role in the agricultural conjuncture of the European Union countries and explains a significant part of the farming output in Europe.

## References

Asaftei, G., & Parmeter, C. F. (2010). Market power, EU integration and privatization: The case of Romania. *Journal of Comparative Economics, 38*, 340–356.

Dýrmundsson, Ó. R. (2006). Sustainability of sheep and goat production in North European countries—From the Arctic to the Alps. *Small Ruminant Research, 62*, 151–157.

Eurostat. (2014). *Several statistics*. Luxembourg: Statistics of the European Union.

GeoDa. (2014). *Informatic software*. http://geodacenter.asu.edu/

Haring, A. M. (2003). Organic dairy farms in the EU: Production systems, economics and future development. *Livestock Production Science, 80*, 89–97.

Winter, M. (2000). Strong policy or weak policy? The environmental impact of the 1992 reforms to the CAP arable regime in Great Britain. *Journal of Rural Studies, 16*, 47–59.

# Chapter 4
# The Performance of Manufacturing in the European Union in the Context of Agricultural Economics

Vítor João Pereira Domingues Martinho

## 1 Introduction

In this current context of crisis across many European countries, it is pertinent to analyze the economic performance for present members of the European Union. In economic literature there are many authors that defend the manufacturing sector as the determinant segment for economic growth, namely those related with the Keynesian theory and with the New Economic Geography, but in different ways. The Keynesian theory in terms of increasing returns to scale which derives from the dimension of the industrial firms and the New Economic Geography in terms of the number of firms. In both cases spillover effects are generated which are able to induce circular and cumulative processes with advantages for the more developed regions and sectors.

In this process the Keynesian theory, namely by Kaldor (1966, 1967, 1970, 1975, 1981) through its three laws, defends that the manufacturing sector is the engine of the economy, because the growth rate of the manufacturing output induces: the growth rate of the economy, the growth rate of manufacturing labor productivity, and the growth rate of nonmanufacturing productivity (Mamgain 1999).

The relationship between the growth rates of labor productivity in manufacturing as dependent upon the growth rate of the output in that sector is known as the Verdoorn (1949) law or second Kaldor law. The Verdoorn law captures increasing returns to scale derived from learning by doing effects and from the endogeneity of the factors. This relation can be mathematically formalized in a linear equation between the two variables and the coefficient, regression being the Verdoorn coefficient. Following the studies of Kaldor for the UK, it is expected that a value for the coefficient of Verdoorn positive and less than the unity is around 0.5. Values

V.J.P.D. Martinho (✉)
Agricultural School, Polytechnic Institute of Viseu, 3500 Viseu, Portugal
e-mail: vdmartinho@esav.ipv.pt



V.J.P.D. Martinho (ed.), *The Agricultural Economics of the 21$^{st}$ Century*,
DOI 10.1007/978-3-319-09471-7_4

above 0.5 signify larger increasing returns to scale and values below reflect lower scale economies.

In this context the aim of the study presented here is to analyze the performance of manufacturing, namely its capacity to capture the economic dynamics related to the spillover effects, the endogeneity and with the increasing returns to scale, and other factors which can affect this evolution, through the Verdoorn law extended (with new variables based on the Keynesian theory), over the period 1996–2008, using data from Eurostat (European Union statistics) and for the first 27 European Union countries. Relevance was given to the manufacture of food, beverages, and tobacco, mainly because this sector has much potential for growth, and actually presents interesting signs of growth in many countries, being a sector that has its importance for the upstream sector (agriculture) and represented in production value, in 2007, 13.54 % of the total manufacturing and 13.61 % in terms of share of employment. We cannot forget the importance of agriculture, the food industry, and tourism for many regions in several countries of the European Union, mainly those which are more disadvantaged. Therefore, this original study is an important contribution towards European Union economic understanding.

## 2 Literature Review

The Verdoorn law has been applied in many countries and in many different ways: with more aggregated/disaggregated data; for the manufacturing sector/all economic sectors; original simple equation/extended equation with other variables (considering in some cases other theories). For example, Fase and Van Den Heuvel (1988) analyzed the Verdoorn law in the manufacturing sector. Leon-Ledesma (1999) tested this law, in 17 Spanish regions, over the period 1962–1991, for the manufacturing sector and confirmed the presence of increasing returns to scale. Some years later León-Ledesma (2002) tested the Verdoorn law again for a set of OECD countries over the period 1965–1994, considering effects from innovation and catching up. On the other hand, Harris and Liu (1999) studied this law and the increasing returns for 62 countries, in the period 1965–1990, based on the co-integration approach. The results also support the hypothesis of increasing returns to scale in the majority of countries. Later, based on this law Dall'Erba et al. (2008) applied a model, considering spatial autocorrelation effects, on the manufacturing sector of the 244 European Union regions, of 25 countries, from 1991 to 2003, and found four different clubs of convergence. These authors considered a Verdoorn equation augmented with variables according to the regional population density, the technological gap, labor productivity, the spatial autocorrelation effects, the urbanization rate, and the geographical distance from Luxembourg (the central location for Europe). In the same line, yet for the European regions, in the period from 1991 to 2002, Angeriz et al. (2009) estimated, also, the Verdoorn law, with spatial autocorrelation effects, for the manufacturing sector. They considered other variables in the Verdoorn equation, such as the density of industrial output, the degree of specialization of the industries, and spatial variables, and confirmed the presence of the dynamic Verdoorn law. This author, one year before Angeriz et al. (2008), had already analyzed this law for the European regional manufacturing, in the period 1986–2002, considering spatial autocorrelation effects, and found, again, robust conclusions about this law. More recently, Alexiadis and Tsagdis (2010) tested the Verdoon law, with several specifications, accounting for variables such as the manufacturing agglomeration and the spatial interaction, in 109 regions of 12 European Union countries, across the period 1977–2005. The results confirm the existence of circular and cumulative processes. Some years before, Alexiadis and Tsagdis (2006) analyzed this law in the Greek regions, with different specifications, namely to capture spatial effects, and found results that support the Verdoorn relationship.

In another perspective, considering the Verdoorn law with other regularities, in the context of the Kaldor laws, there are, also many studies. Drakopoulos and Theodossiou (1991) analyzed the Kaldor theory in the Greek economy, from 1967 to 1988, and the results are consistent with the theory. Pons-Novell and Viladecans-Marsal (1999), considering the Kaldor laws, tested the Verdoorn law in the European regions over the period 1984–1992, accounting for the spatial autocorrelation aspects. The results are consistent with the previsions of these laws. Considering cross-country data for developing countries, in the period 1960–1994, Necmi (1999) analyzed the Kaldor laws with supporting results. In a similar way, Pieper (2003) found several results for 30 developing countries that support the Kaldor interpretation of the growth processes, using time series data disaggregated at a sectorial level. In another economy and context, Wells and Thirlwall (2003) tested these laws across 45 African countries, during the period 1980–1996 and concluded the presence of these laws. Juarez and Leobardo (2011) applied the Kaldor theory in the Mexican regions, namely from 1993 to 2010, and concluded about the importance of the manufacturing sector. McCausland and Theodossiou (2012) testing the Kaldor laws found that the increasing returns appear more in the manufacturing sector and less in the services sector. Recently, Katrakilidis et al. (2013) analyzed these laws in the Greek economy over the period 1970–2006 and their conclusions validated the three laws.

Other studies aim to find relationships between the Verdoorn law and other theories. For example, Erixon (2005) analyzed the relationship between Schumpeterian and Keynesian economics. Ryzhenkov (2009) studied the relation between the Verdoorn law and the Ricardian relationship between employment and returns. Kosfeld and Dreger (2006) analyzed the Verdoorn and the Okun laws for Unified Germany, considering spatial autocorrelation aspects, during the 1990s. Fase and Winder (1999) analyzed the Verdoorm and Baumol laws for the manufacturing and services sectors of the Netherlands, in the period 1956–1993, considering other variables such as employment, the wage rate, and the unit labor cost. The results are more consistent with the Baumol law than with the Verdoorn law.

Finally, some studies, such as that of McCombie and Roberts (2007), investigated the static (constant returns to scale)-dynamic (increasing returns to scale)

**Table 4.1** Literature review summarized about the Verdoorn law

| Authors | Sectors considered | Countries | Relationships | New variables |
|---|---|---|---|---|
| Fase and Van Den Heuvel (1988) | Manufacturing | | Verdoorn law | |
| Leon-Ledesma (1999) | Manufacturing | Spanish regions | | |
| León-Ledesma (2002) | | OECD countries | | Innovation and catching-up |
| Harris and Liu (1999) | | 62 countries | | Cointegration approach |
| Dall'Erba et al. (2008) | Manufacturing | 244 regions, 25 EU countries | | Regional population density, the technological gap, in terms of labor productivity, the spatial autocorrelation effects, the urbanization rate, and the geographical distance from the Luxembourg (the central location of the Europe) |
| Angeriz et al. (2009) | Manufacturing | European Union regions | | Density of industrial output, the degree of specialization of the industries and spatial variables |
| Angeriz et al. (2008) | Manufacturing | European regions | | Spatial autocorrelation effects |
| Alexiadis and Tsagdis (2010) | | 109 regions of 12 - European Union countries | | Manufacturing agglomeration and the spatial interaction |
| Alexiadis and Tsagdis (2006) | | Greek regions | | Spatial effects |
| McCombie and Roberts (2007) | Manufacturing | | | |
| Drakopoulos and Theodossiou (1991) | | Greek economy | Kaldor laws | |
| Pons-Novell and | | European regions | | Spatial autocorrelation aspects |

(continued)

**Table 4.1** (continued)

| Authors | Sectors considered | Countries | Relationships | New variables |
|---|---|---|---|---|
| Viladecans-Marsal (1999) | | | | |
| Necmi (1999) | | Developing countries | | Instrumental variables techniques |
| Pieper (2003) | All sectors | 30 developing countries | | Employment and value added |
| Wells and Thirlwall (2003) | | 45 African countries | | |
| Juarez and Leobardo (2011) | | Mexican regions | | |
| McCausland and Theodossiou (2012) | | | | |
| Katrakilidis et al. (2013) | | Greek economy | | |
| Erixon (2005) | | | Schumpeterian and Keynesian economics | |
| Ryzhenkov (2009) | | Italy | Verdoorn law and the Ricardian relationship between the employment and returns | Capital–output ratio, employment ratio, relative labor compensation and the profit rate |
| Kosfeld and Dreger (2006) | | Unified Germany | Verdoorn and the Okun laws | Spatial autocorrelation aspects |
| Fase and Winder (1999) | Manufacturing and services sectors | Netherland | Verdoorm and Baumol laws | Employment, the rate wage and the unit labor cost |

Verdoorn law paradox and demonstrated the preference for the dynamic relationship, because of the existence of the spatial aggregation bias in the static analysis.

This review of literature about the Verdoorn law made before is summarized in Table 4.1, in order to better understand the following sections, namely that related with the model built and the options for the new variables considered in the Verdoorn equation.

## 3 The Model

The model considered in this study is based on the Verdoorn relationship extended with new variables considering the Keynesian theory and the literature review carried out beforehand and summarized in Table 4.1. Usually the related studies try to develop a model considering variables from other theories, from a perspective of linking different approaches. However, in this study variables are taken into account, related to the Keynesian theory that captures the endogeneity of the factors, effects of learning by doing and increasing returns to scale. It is considered that variables such as the wages and salaries [endogeneity of the factors and salary of efficiency—Fase and Winder (1999) and Ryzhenkov (2009)], number of persons employed per enterprise [endogeneity of the factors—Pieper (2003)], share of employment in manufacturing total [endogeneity of the factors—Alexiadis and Tsagdis (2010) and Angeriz et al. (2009)], investment per person employed [investment, capital, and learning by doing—León-Ledesma (2002)], and the share of R&D employment in the number of persons [capital and learning by doing—León-Ledesma (2002)] can capture these effects. If everything goes as expected by theory and these variables pick increasing returns to scale, a positive effect from everyone is expected. The model is presented as follows:

$$p_{it} = a + bq_{it} + c\mathrm{WS}_{it} + d\mathrm{PEE}_{it} + e\mathrm{SEM}_{it} + f\mathrm{IPE}_{it} + g\mathrm{SRE}_{it}$$

where $p$ is the growth rate of labor productivity and $q$ is the growth rate of the product. The variables WS, PEE, SEM, IPE, and SRE are, respectively, the wages and salaries, number of people employed per enterprise, share of employment in manufacturing total, investment per person employed, and the share of R&D employment in the number of people. The indexes $i$ and $t$ represent the countries and the years and $a$, $b$, $c$, $d$, $e$, $f$, and $g$ are coefficients of estimation.

## 4 The Data

The data is relative to the output, to the number of people employed and to the wages and salaries, number of people employed per enterprise, share of employment in manufacturing total, investment per person employed, and the share of R&D employment in the number of people. This data was obtained from Eurostat (2013) and are disaggregated for the current 27 European Union countries and for the period from 1996 to 2008.

Figure 4.1 presents the productivity of the labor growth rate (%) in averages (for the period considered and for the several forms of manufacturing sectors) for the current several countries of the European Union.

From Fig. 4.1 it is possible to observe that countries such as France, Luxembourg, and Slovenia present a negative average labor productivity growth rate.

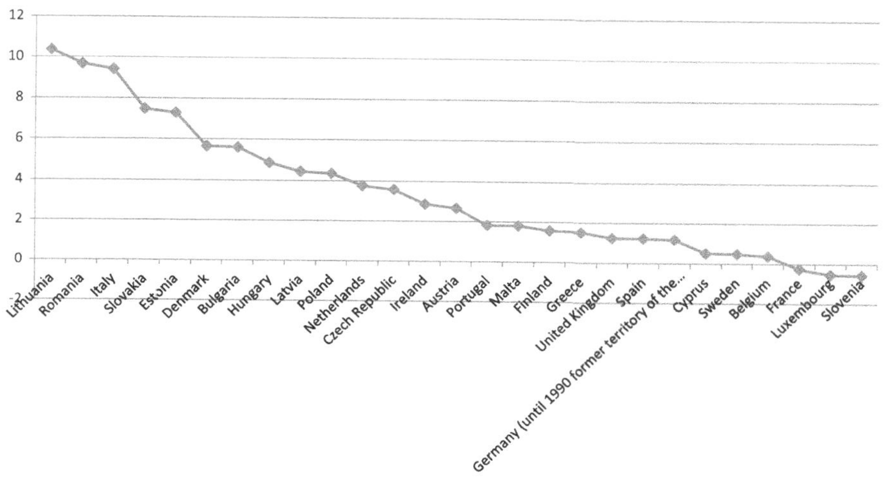


**Fig. 4.1** Productivity of labor (Production value/number of persons employed) growth rate (%) in averages (over the period 1996–2008 and over the different forms of the manufacturing sector considered) for the current several countries of the European Union

Lithuania, Romania, Italy, and Slovakia are the countries with the greatest average labor productivity growth rate.

The figure shows the productivity of labor growth rate (%), also, in averages for the several forms of the manufacturing sector considered.

Observing Fig. 4.2, the manufacture of tobacco products (between the manufacture of food products, beverages and tobacco) possesses the greatest average labor productivity growth rate. On the other hand, the processing and preserving of fish and fish products show negative values for this variable.

# 5 Results

Table 4.2 presents the results obtained with the estimations made with panel data (27 European Union countries and the period 1996–2008) in the Stata software program. The econometric estimations are realized first with fixed and random effects methods and after, if necessary, taking into account some statistic tests, with the ordinary least square. The options for each one of these econometric methods are effectuated considering the several statistic tests presented in Table 4.2 and are the most used in these models.

From Table 4.2 it is possible to conclude that the manufacturing sector across the current 27 European Union countries presents strong increasing returns to scale, considering the value of the Verdoorn coefficient (0.945) for the fixed effects econometric method (considering that the Hausman test (13.310) reject the random effects). On the other hand, the coefficient of the constant does not present statistic

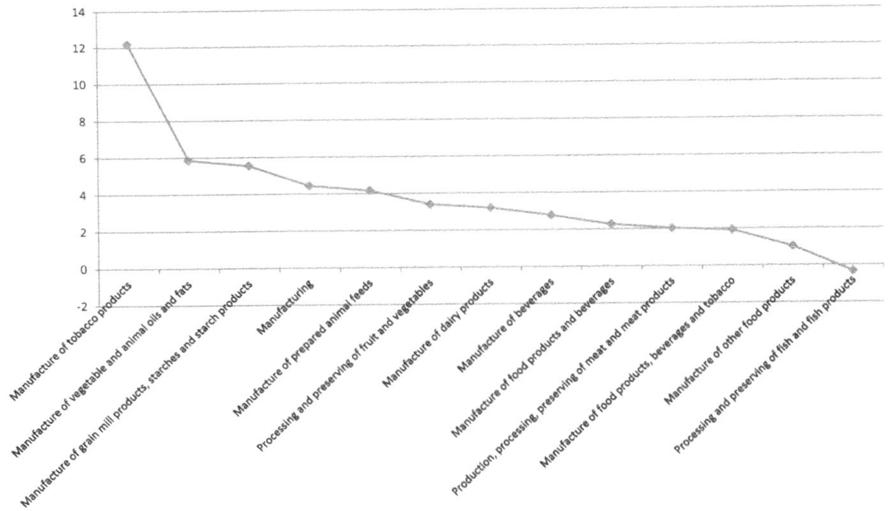


**Fig. 4.2** Productivity of labor (Production value/number of persons employed) growth rate (%) in averages (over the period 1996–2008 and over the differing current countries of the European Union) for the several forms of the manufacturing sector considered

significance. Relative to the other variables, only the coefficient associated with the share of R&D employment in the number of people presents a positive statistic significance, although residual (0.018). For the entire manufacturing sector, considering what was mentioned before and the $R^2$ value, it would seem that the original Verdoorn relationship is the more robust.

The manufacture of food products, beverages, and tobacco is not affected by fixed or random effects (the ordinary least square is the more adjusted method), considering the $F$ tests for these effects. The Verdoorn coefficient is relatively lower (0.896) than that of the whole manufacturing sector and the constant coefficient has statistical significance, but presents a residual value (0.052). In this sector the new variables, number of people employed per enterprise, share of employment in manufacturing total, investment per person employed, all show statistical significance, but the coefficients are close to zero. The first new variable presents a positive effect and the last two, negative effects. This means that the share of employment in the manufacturing total and the investment per person employed did not have, in the period considered, for the current 27 countries of the European Union, an endogenous positive effect upon the labor productivity growth rate and consequently did not help in the improvement of the increasing returns to scale in this sector.

The manufacture of food products and beverages shows a Verdoorn coefficient which is excessively high, because it is close to 1, but higher than 1, because values lower than 1 are expected. This happens in some cases and is explained as a sign of strong increasing returns to scale.

**Table 4.2** Estimations results of the Verdoorn equation extended, with panel data, for the several forms of the manufacturing sector considered, over the period 1996–2008 and over the differing current countries of the European Union

| | Const.[a] | Coef.[b] | Coef.[c] | Coef.[d] | Coef.[e] | Coef.[f] | Coef.[g] | F/Wald (mod.)[h] | F (Fe_OLS)[i] | Corr (u_i)[j] | F (Re_OLS)[k] | Hausman[l] | $R^2$ [m] | N. O.[n] |
|---|---|---|---|---|---|---|---|---|---|---|---|---|---|---|
| Manufacturing | | | | | | | | | | | | | | |
| FE[o] | −0.055 (−1.590) | 0.945* (23.250) | 0.000 (0.050) | 0.001 (1.060) | – | 0.000 (0.680) | 0.018* (1.990) | 117.540* | 2.040* | −0.389 | – | – | 0.846 | 136 |
| RE[p] | 0.008 (0.770) | 0.913* (24.600) | 0.000 (0.800) | 0.000 (0.580) | – | −0.000 (−0.270) | −0.001 (−0.440) | – | – | – | 5.310* | 13.310* | 0.888 | 136 |
| OLS | – | – | – | – | – | – | – | – | – | – | – | – | – | – |
| Manufacture of food products, beverages, and tobacco | | | | | | | | | | | | | | |
| FE[o] | −0.052 (−0.570) | 0.870* (14.000) | −0.000 (−0.080) | 0.002** (1.700) | 0.003 (0.550) | −0.000** (−1.780) | 0.035 (1.440) | 37.350* | 0.790 | −0.418 | – | – | 0.711 | 120 |
| RE[p] | 0.052* (3.180) | 0.896* (16.280) | −0.000 (−0.490) | 0.001* (2.270) | −0.002* (−2.930) | −0.000* (−2.540) | 0.008 (0.940) | – | – | – | 0.000 | 3.430 | 0.896 | 120 |
| OLS | 0.052* (3.180) | 0.896* (16.280) | −0.000 (−0.490) | 0.001* (2.270) | −0.002* (−2.930) | −0.000* (−2.540) | 0.008 (0.940) | 61.560* | – | – | – | – | 0.753 | 120 |
| Manufacture of food products and beverages | | | | | | | | | | | | | | |
| FE[o] | 0.454* (3.300) | 1.221* (12.230) | −0.000 (−1.410) | −0.001 (−0.720) | −0.015** (−1.930) | −0.000 (−1.620) | −0.034 (−0.560) | 32.660* | 1.980* | −0.966 | – | – | 0.827 | 63 |
| RE[p] | 0.027 (0.890) | 1.066* (12.490) | −0.000 (−0.230) | 0.001 (0.950) | −0.000 (−0.140) | −0.000** (−1.730) | 0.015 (0.910) | – | – | – | 0.030 | 1.550 | 0.796 | 63 |
| OLS | 0.026 (0.970) | 1.059* (12.320) | −0.000 (−0.390) | 0.001 (1.330) | −0.001 (−0.450) | −0.000 (−1.460) | 0.010 (0.680) | 36.590* | – | – | – | – | 0.775 | 63 |
| Production, processing, preserving of meat and meat products | | | | | | | | | | | | | | |
| FE[o] | 0.279* (2.630) | 0.999* (16.970) | −0.000 (1.040) | 0.000 (0.340) | −0.107* (−2.040) | −0.000* (−2.450) | 0.026 (1.540) | 51.700* | 0.890 | −0.605 | – | – | 0.760 | 128 |
| RE[p] | 0.059* (2.370) | 0.959* (18.000) | 0.000 (0.250) | 0.000 (0.370) | −0.009 (−1.240) | −0.000* (−2.900) | 0.016 (1.080) | – | – | – | 0.000 | 7.410 | 0.850 | 128 |
| OLS | 0.059* (2.370) | 0.959* (18.000) | 0.000 (0.250) | 0.000 (0.370) | −0.009 (−1.240) | −0.000* (−2.900) | 0.016 (1.080) | 60.150* | – | – | – | – | 0.736 | 128 |

(continued)

**Table 4.2** (continued)

| | Const.[a] | Coef.[b] | Coef.[c] | Coef.[d] | Coef.[e] | Coef.[f] | Coef.[g] | F/Wald (mod.)[h] | F (Fe_OLS)[i] | Corr (u_i)[j] | F (Re_OLS)[k] | Hausman[l] | $R^2$ [m] | N. O.[n] |
|---|---|---|---|---|---|---|---|---|---|---|---|---|---|---|
| Processing and preserving of fish and fish products | | | | | | | | | | | | | | |
| FE[o] | 0.020 (0.260) | 0.519* (7.310) | 0.000 (0.990) | −0.000 (−0.310) | −0.043 (−1.350) | 0.000 (0.190) | −0.014 (−0.260) | 9.660* | 0.980 | −0.731 | – | – | 0.475 | 88 |
| RE[p] | −0.003 (−0.100) | 0.499* (9.440) | 0.000 (0.150) | 0.000 (0.670) | 0.012 (1.520) | 0.000 (0.120) | −0.019 (−0.660) | – | – | – | 0.000 | 5.660 | 0.818 | 88 |
| OLS | −0.003 (−0.100) | 0.499* (9.440) | 0.000 (0.150) | 0.000 (0.670) | 0.012 (1.520) | 0.000 (0.120) | −0.019 (−0.660) | 16.150* | – | – | – | – | 0.511 | 88 |
| Processing and preserving of fruit and vegetables | | | | | | | | | | | | | | |
| FE[o] | 0.184* (2.630) | 0.618* (13.750) | 0.000 (1.180) | 0.004* (4.160) | −0.421* (−5.080) | −0.000 (−0.210) | 0.034 (1.280) | 40.410* | 2.730* | −0.923 | – | – | 0.725 | 122 |
| RE[p] | 0.058* (2.680) | 0.600* (13.230) | −0.000 (−1.450) | 0.000 (0.450) | −0.012 (−0.900) | −0.000** (−1.940) | −0.008 (−0.500) | – | – | – | 0.000 | 36.770* | 0.708 | 122 |
| OLS | – | – | – | – | – | – | – | – | – | – | – | – | – | – |
| Manufacture of vegetable and animal oils and fats | | | | | | | | | | | | | | |
| FE[o] | 0.447* (2.660) | 0.711* (6.120) | −0.000 (−1.570) | −0.006* (−4.070) | −0.565 (−1.140) | 0.000* (2.570) | −0.004 (−0.170) | 10.840* | 2.300* | −0.894 | – | – | 0.516 | 86 |
| RE[p] | 0.071 (1.430) | 0.473* (4.250) | −0.000 (−0.290) | −0.001 (−1.190) | −0.074 (−0.960) | 0.000** (1.780) | −0.017 (−1.090) | – | – | – | 0.000 | 20.200* | 0.303 | 86 |
| OLS | – | – | – | – | – | – | – | – | – | – | – | – | – | – |
| Manufacture of dairy products | | | | | | | | | | | | | | |
| FE[o] | 0.223** (1.970) | 0.794* (7.800) | −0.000 (−0.020) | −0.000 (−0.880) | −0.124** (−1.900) | −0.000 (0.750) | −0.021 (−0.590) | 12.210* | 0.760 | −0.824 | – | – | 0.430 | 126 |
| RE[p] | 0.069* (3.160) | 0.833* (9.210) | −0.000 (−1.630) | 0.000 (1.580) | −0.020* (−2.480) | −0.000 (−1.440) | 0.010 (0.430) | – | – | – | 0.000 | 5.550 | 0.828 | 126 |
| OLS | 0.069* (3.160) | 0.833* (9.210) | −0.000 (−1.630) | 0.000 (1.580) | −0.020* (−2.480) | −0.000 (−1.440) | 0.010 (0.430) | 18.500* | – | – | – | – | 0.457 | 126 |
| Manufacture of grain mill products, starches, and starch products | | | | | | | | | | | | | | |
| FE[o] | 0.085 (0.990) | 0.685* (11.780) | 0.000** (1.730) | −0.002 (−0.850) | −0.285* (−2.100) | 0.000 (1.060) | −0.001 (−0.080) | 32.630* | 2.280* | −0.748 | – | – | 0.718 | 106 |
| RE[p] | 0.038 (1.030) | 0.697* (12.290) | −0.000* (−3.290) | 0.001* (2.050) | −0.044 (−0.820) | 0.000* (2.930) | −0.041* (−4.170) | – | – | – | 1.130 | 16.960* | 0.660 | 106 |

| | | | | | | | | | | | | | | |
|---|---|---|---|---|---|---|---|---|---|---|---|---|---|---|
| OLS | – | – | – | – | – | – | – | – | – | – | – | – | – | – |
| Manufacture of prepared animal feeds | | | | | | | | | | | | | | |
| FE[o] | 0.181* (2.390) | 0.771* (16.180) | 0.000 (1.330) | 0.005* (2.570) | −0.749* (−4.380) | −0.000* (−2.270) | 0.032 (1.540) | 46.230* | 2.400* | −0.763 | – | – | 0.770 | 112 |
| RE[p] | 0.062* (1.960) | 0.748* (15.870) | −0.000 (−0.710) | 0.001 (1.470) | −0.089** (−1.750) | −0.000 (−1.630) | 0.014 (0.840) | – | – | – | 0.540 | 17.230* | 0.726 | 112 |
| OLS | – | – | – | – | – | – | – | – | – | – | – | – | – | – |
| Manufacture of other food products | | | | | | | | | | | | | | |
| FE[o] | −0.113 (−1.510) | 0.644* (9.340) | −0.000 (−0.210) | 0.003** (1.900) | 0.000 (0.020) | 0.000* (2.450) | 0.018 (0.860) | 17.740* | 1.050 | −0.632 | – | – | 0.526 | 126 |
| RE[p] | 0.008 (0.510) | 0.660* (10.680) | −0.000 (−1.570) | 0.001* (2.540) | −0.004* (−2.460) | 0.000 (1.170) | −0.002 (−0.160) | – | – | – | 0.000 | 5.580 | 0.758 | 126 |
| OLS | 0.008 (0.510) | 0.660* (10.680) | −0.000 (−1.570) | 0.001* (2.540) | −0.004* (−2.460) | 0.000 (1.170) | −0.002 (−0.160) | 25.590* | – | – | – | – | 0.541 | 126 |
| Manufacture of beverages | | | | | | | | | | | | | | |
| FE[o] | 0.089 (1.190) | 0.758* (11.200) | 0.000 (1.220) | −0.001 (−0.420) | −0.043 (−1.090) | −0.000 (−1.290) | −0.008 (−0.360) | 21.720* | 1.440 | −0.677 | – | – | 0.584 | 123 |
| RE[p] | 0.087* (4.270) | 0.792* (12.660) | −0.000 (−0.050) | −0.000 (−0.290) | −0.023* (−3.710) | −0.000* (−2.000) | −0.010 (−0.700) | – | – | – | 1.850 | 4.690 | 0.809 | 123 |
| OLS | 0.085* (4.340) | 0.798* (12.690) | −0.000 (−0.050) | −0.000 (−0.200) | −0.022* (−3.750) | −0.000* (−1.990) | −0.012 (−0.830) | 35.590* | – | – | – | – | 0.630 | 123 |
| Manufacture of tobacco products | | | | | | | | | | | | | | |
| FE[o] | 0.592* (2.170) | 0.531* (4.850) | −0.000 (−1.190) | −0.001** (−1.880) | −0.053 (−0.440) | −0.000 (−0.210) | −0.047* (−3.000) | 5.230* | 2.950* | −0.964 | – | – | 0.487 | 52 |
| RE[p] | 0.230* (3.140) | 0.502* (4.960) | −0.000 (−0.290) | −0.000** (−1.720) | −0.060 (−0.750) | −0.000 (−0.130) | −0.026* (−2.160) | – | – | – | 3.830* | 5.270 | 0.451 | 52 |
| OLS | – | – | – | – | – | – | – | – | – | – | – | – | – | – |

*Note*: [a]Constant; [b]Verdoorn coefficient; [c]Wages and Salaries coefficient; [d]Number of persons employed per enterprise coefficient; [e]Share of employment in manufacturing total coefficient; [f]Investment per person employed coefficient; [g]Share of R&D employment in the number of persons employed (%) coefficient; [h]Test F for fixed effects model and test Wald for random effects; [i]Test F for fixed effects or OLS (Ho is OLS); [j]Correlation between errors and regressors in fixed effects; [k]Test F for random effects or OLS (Ho is OLS); [l]Hausman test (Ho is GLS); [m]R square; [n]Number of observations; [o]Fixed effects model; [p]Random effects model

*Statistically significant at 5 %; **Statistically significant at 10 %

The decreasing order of increasing returns to scale, considering the Verdoorn coefficient, for the several forms of manufacturing, within the manufacture of food products, is the following: Production, processing, preserving of meat and meat products (0.959), manufacture of dairy products (0.833), manufacture of prepared animal feeds (0.771), manufacture of vegetable and animal oils and fats (0.711), manufacture of grain mill products, starches, and starch products (0.685), processing and preserving of fruit and vegetables (0.618), manufacture of other food products (0.660), and processing and preserving of fish and fish products (0.499). In these industries many times the fixed and random effects are rejected and when they are not rejected the fixed effects are more acceptable. The new variables either do not have statistical significance or do have, but the coefficient values are close to zero or many times negative.

The manufacture of tobacco products has the lower Verdoorn coefficient, but in the data analysis presented the greatest average in labor productivity growth rate. This signifies that the growth rate of this variable is not picked by the Verdoorn law and does not come from increasing returns to scale, but instead comes from other variables not considered in the study, as can be confirmed by the value of the constant coefficient and by the $R^2$ values being around 0.451.

In general, relative to the new variables, the variable wages and salaries do not show any case for statistic significance. The variables, number of people employed per enterprise, investment per person employed, and the share of R&D employment in the number of people, present values or insignificant statistics, or close to zero, or in some cases negatives. The total share of employment in manufacturing reflects strong negative effects upon the processing and preserving of fruit and vegetable sectors (−0.421), in the manufacture of grain mill products, starches, and starch products (−0.285), and in the manufacture of prepared animal feeds (−0.749). This signifies that in these sectors the total share of employment in manufacturing is not a consequence of the enterprise number or dimension, but rather a consequence of the dependency of the labor resources, with lower increasing returns.

**Conclusions**

The Verdoorn relationship has been studied by many authors for different periods of time, for several countries and regions, and for different sectors. Sometimes with the original relationship and at other times with extensions considering the Keynesian theories or other theories, as for example, the New Economic Geography (this theory along with the Keynesian theory defends the existence of increasing returns to scale as the base of circular and cumulative processes).

In this study, from the data analysis and from the results obtained with the several methods of econometric estimations, it was possible to conclude that in reality, in the differing countries that actually are members of the European Union, the economy is strongly diverse. The differences in the labor

(continued)

productivity growth rate between the 27 countries are significant, with countries such as France and Luxembourg with negative average productivity growth rates and countries such as Italy and Slovakia with the greatest growth rates.

The same happens with the different forms of manufacturing considered, namely those related with the manufacture of food products, beverages, and tobacco. The manufacture of tobacco products presents the greatest average labor productivity growth rate. Curiously this sector is that which possesses the lower Verdoorn coefficient. This needs further research in the future despite the explanation presented. The processing and preserving of fish and fish products showed the lower average productivity growth rate and the lower Verdoorn coefficient, sign of a weak increase in return for this sector.

The new variables, with exception to the total share of employment in manufacturing (which presents strong negative effects in some industries), have a residual effect and in some cases, also, negative. This means that the manufacturing sector is not enough, in the existing European Union countries, developed to catch opportunities that come from the spillover effects, externalities, endogeneity of the factors, and learning by doing effects. Consequently, these variables have a negative effect, when they were expected to have a positive effect.

In general, all the manufacturing sectors considered have significant increasing returns to scale, taking into account the Verdoorn coefficient. But these results could be better if the effects represented in the new variables were potentiated. In this line, it is important to promote strategies to make this possible.

## References

Alexiadis, S., & Tsagdis, D. (2006). Reassessing the validity of Verdoorn's law under conditions of spatial dependence: A case study of the Greek regions. *Journal of Post Keynesian Economics, 29*(1), 149–170.

Alexiadis, S., & Tsagdis, D. (2010). Is cumulative growth in manufacturing productivity slowing down in the EU12 regions? *Cambridge Journal of Economics, 34*(6), 1001–1017.

Angeriz, A., McCombie, J., & Roberts, M. (2008). New estimates of returns to scale and spatial spillovers for EU Regional manufacturing, 1986—2002. *International Regional Science Review, 31*(1), 62–87.

Angeriz, A., McCombie, J. S. L., & Roberts, M. (2009). Increasing returns and the growth of industries in the EU regions: Paradoxes and conundrums. *Spatial Economic Analysis, 4*(2), 127–148.

Dall'Erba, S., Percoco, M., & Piras, G. (2008). The European regional growth process revisited. *Spatial Economic Analysis, 3*(1), 7–25.

Drakopoulos, S. A., & Theodossiou, I. (1991). Kaldorian approach to Greek economic growth. *Applied Economics, 23*(10), 1683–1689.

Erixon, L. (2005). Combining Keynes and Schumpeter. Ingvar Svennilson's contribution to the Swedish growth school and modern economics. *Journal of Evolutionary Economics, 15*, 187–210.

Eurostat. (2013). *Several statistics*. http://epp.eurostat.ec.europa.eu/portal/page/portal/eurostat/home/

Fase, M. M. G., & Van Den Heuvel, P. J. (1988). Productivity and growth: Verdoorn's law revisited. *Economics Letters, 28*(2), 135–139.

Fase, M. M. G., & Winder, C. C. A. (1999). Baumol's law and Verdoorn's regularity. *De Economist, 147*(3), 277–291.

Harris, R. I. D., & Liu, A. (1999). Verdoorn's law and increasing returns to scale: Country estimates based on the cointegration approach. *Applied Economics Letters, 6*, 29–33.

Juarez, S., & Leobardo, I. (2011). Economic stagnation in Mexico, manufactures and increasing returns: A Kaldorian approach. *Investigacion Economica, 70*(277), 87.

Kaldor, N. (1966). *Causes of the slow rate of economic growth in the United Kingdom*. London: Cambridge University Press.

Kaldor, N. (1967). *Strategic factors in economic development*. Ithaca, NY: Cornell University.

Kaldor, N. (1970). The case for regional policies. *Scottish Journal of Political Economy, XVII*(3).

Kaldor, N. (1975). Economic growth and the Verdoorn Law – A comment on Mr. Rowthorn's article. *Economic Journal, 85*, 891–896.

Kaldor, N. (1981). The role of increasing returns, technical progress and cumulative causation in the theory of international trade and economic growth. *Économie Appliquée*, (4).

Katrakilidis, K., Tsaliki, P. V., & Tsiakis, T. (2013). The Greek economy in a Kaldorian developmental framework. *Acta Oeconomica, 63*(1), 61–75.

Kosfeld, R., & Dreger, C. (2006). Thresholds for employment and unemployment: A spatial analysis of German regional labour markets, 1992–2000. *Papers in Regional Science, 85*(4), 523–542.

Leon-Ledesma, M. A. (1999). Verdoorn's law and increasing returns: An empirical analysis of the Spanish regions. *Applied Economics Letters, 6*, 373–376.

León-Ledesma, M. A. (2002). Accumulation, innovation and catching-up: An extended cumulative growth model. *Cambridge Journal of Economics, 26*(2), 201–216.

Mamgain, V. (1999). Are the Kaldor-Verdoorn laws applicable in the newly industrializing countries? *Review of Development Economics, 3*(3), 295–309.

McCausland, W. D., & Theodossiou, I. (2012). Is manufacturing still the engine of growth? *Journal of Post Keynesian Economics, 35*(1), 79–92.

McCombie, J. S. L., & Roberts, M. (2007). Returns to scale and regional growth: The static-dynamic Verdoorn law paradox revisited. *Journal of Regional Science, 47*(2), 179–208.

Necmi, S. (1999). Kaldor's growth analysis revisited. *Applied Economics, 31*, 653–660.

Pieper, U. (2003). Sectoral regularities of productivity growth in developing countries—a Kaldorian interpretation. *Cambridge Journal of Economics, 27*(6), 831–850.

Pons-Novell, J., & Viladecans-Marsal, E. (1999). Kaldor's laws and spatial dependence: Evidence for the European regions. *Regional Studies, 33*(5), 443–451.

Ryzhenkov, A. V. (2009). A Goodwinian model with direct and roundabout returns to scale (an application to Italy). *Metroeconomica, 60*(3), 343–399.

Verdoorn, P. J. (1949). Fattori che Regolano lo Sviluppo della Produtivita del Lavoro. *L'Industria*, 45–53.

Wells, H., & Thirlwall, A. P. (2003). Testing Kaldor's growth laws across the countries of Africa. *African Development Review, 15*(2–3), 89–105.

# Chapter 5
# The Economic, Social, and Environmental Determinants for the Agricultural Output in Some European Union Countries

Vítor João Pereira Domingues Martinho

## 1 Introduction

Nowadays, the reality in the agricultural sector among the several countries of the European Union is very different. Presently the European Union constitutes of 28 different countries ranging from Eastern to Western Europe, with significantly diverse histories and traditions.

For example, the ten countries which became members of the European Union in 2004, the frequently named countries of central and oriental Europe, had, in large part, a history marked by an economic and political strategy which differed greatly from those verified in other European countries.

Other countries in Western Europe, such as Portugal for example, until 1974, had a history influenced by other economic and political orientations that the society referred to many times as nondemocratic regimes.

The orientations followed in Eastern Europe, as well in the west, had several effects upon different economic sectors, namely in the agricultural sector. These strategies, frequently with policies, known as those of the "proud and alone," were conducive to situations of low technical development, low competition, and drastic consequences for farming factors of production, such as the exhaustion of soils.

The agricultural policies of the European Union, namely those from the Common Agricultural Policy (CAP), often do not take into account these diverse realities in European countries. Some countries when they adhered to the European Union had many problems, as referred to before, with the dynamics and development of the agricultural sectors, and needed a CAP that helped with the improvement of the performance of their farming contexts. In contrast, these countries adopted a CAP that in general since 1992 was aimed to reduce production and extending, partly due to some problems related with the excess of production,

V.J.P.D. Martinho (✉)
Agricultural School, Polytechnic Institute of Viseu, 3500 Viseu, Portugal
e-mail: vdmartinho@esav.ipv.pt



V.J.P.D. Martinho (ed.), *The Agricultural Economics of the 21st Century*,
DOI 10.1007/978-3-319-09471-7_5

namely from the former countries of the European Economic Community (the first name for the European Union).

In this way, it seems important to develop this study, which to our knowledge is the first, by aiming to analyze with time series econometric techniques the determinants (economic, social, and environmental) of the agricultural output for some countries in the European Union. The countries selected are those which have the greatest dimension and those which suffered financial problems, such as Portugal, Ireland, and Greece. The intention is to analyze the influence of these determinants and the differences between the several countries of Europe using data from the World Bank (2014).

## 2 Background Literature

There are many factors in the European countries selected that influence the dynamics of agricultural economics. But, the preoccupation with, as referred to below, sustainability, the environment, renewable energies, the preservation of rural areas and growing populations is in the order of the day.

Agricultural production in Portugal is dependent upon many factors, such as the biological condition of several resources and, consequently, from pest and disease management. In these cases it is necessary to evaluate the costs and the benefits of such treatments (Gatto et al. 2009).

Some projects which were developed in Portuguese rural areas, such as hydroelectric power plants, need some amount of care, namely because of their impact upon the socioeconomic performance, agricultural sector, and resources in the environment (Almeida et al. 2005).

There is a tendency for certain regions of Spain, depending on several factors, such as, among others, the climate and the soil conditions, to become specialized in specific agricultural production. Southern Spain specializes, among other outputs, in olive production. Areal and Riesgo (2014) conducted a study, through a survey, to understand the future perspectives of these production practices in those regions and concluded that there are many factors that can determine this continuity, namely those related with social, economic, environmental, and spatial contexts. Spain has a good position, within the international context, in olive production, but, also, in the wine sector, in many indicators (Castillo and García 2013). The availability of water is one of the most important factors for the production in agriculture in some regions of Spain (Maestre-Valero et al. 2013). Multifunctionality and sustainability in the Spanish agricultural sector are fundamental areas, where forestry can play an important role (Hoyos et al. 2012). The use of pesticides and fertilizers needs some adjusted approaches in order to avoid problems with the pollution of water and soil (Peña-Haro et al. 2010).

Forestry is a crucial activity in France for the preservation of the environment, namely through carbon appropriation, but this contribution depends upon some factors, namely those related to public policies (Caurla et al. 2013). For French agricultural activities to be compatible with the environment, we must take into account the preservation of water and soil quality (Darradi et al. 2012).

Northern Italy has the largest area of apple production in Europe and fruit is the most important source of exports for the region. The triumph of this situation results, namely, from the education and the professional training in these issues (Via et al. 2013).

The search for agricultural practices that reduce the utilization of chemical products, such as fertilizers and herbicides, in German agriculture is a usual concern for farmers and, in general, for the population (Steinmann et al. 2012). Water contamination, namely with nitrogen, is a consequence of some agricultural production patterns (Hirt et al. 2012). The energy intensity in farming production is another concern, namely because of the decrease in the availability of resources (Kraatz 2012).

The nitrate concentration in the soil and water from agricultural activities are a problem in the UK that concerns namely public institutions (Wang et al. 2013). Today in the UK it is difficult to find a pattern of sustainability that conciliates several economic sectors, namely for agriculture with more developed industry (Krausmann et al. 2008).

The financial support afforded to Greece from the European Union for organic farming has had a dual effect upon the agro-biodiversity, because this agricultural practice preserves biodiversity, but can reduce it if farmers only perform these activities with subsidies (Nastis et al. 2013). Sheep farming is an important practice in Greece, namely, in the mountainous regions (Tzouramani et al. 2011). Rural tourism may be an important alternative source of revenue for farmers who depend on many factors such as the income from tourism, such as the information obtained before the trip and the origin of the information (Skuras et al. 2006).

Biomass crops appear in Ireland as an alternative to conventional agricultural production (Clancy et al. 2012).

## 3 Data Analysis

In the following figures the data described is relative to the variables considered as representative of the economic, social, and environmental determinants of the agricultural economics, namely that of agricultural output (represented by the value added).

Figure 5.1 is relative to the percentage of agricultural land (comparatively to the total area of each country) and shows that, from 1961 until 2011, Ireland, the UK, and Greece were the European countries with more relative land for farming. In contrast, Portugal has the lowest relative area for agriculture. Since the beginning of the 1990s there was some decrease in the percentage of agricultural land in Ireland and some years later there came some perturbations for Greece.

From 1990 to 2011, Fig. 5.2, Portugal had the largest area occupied with forest (about 35 %) and Ireland and the UK had the lowest areas (about 10 %).

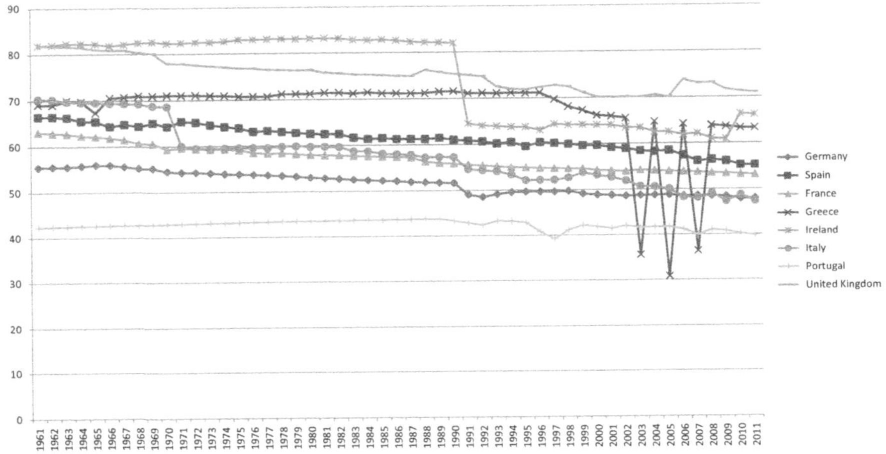


**Fig. 5.1** Agricultural land (% of land area) between European countries

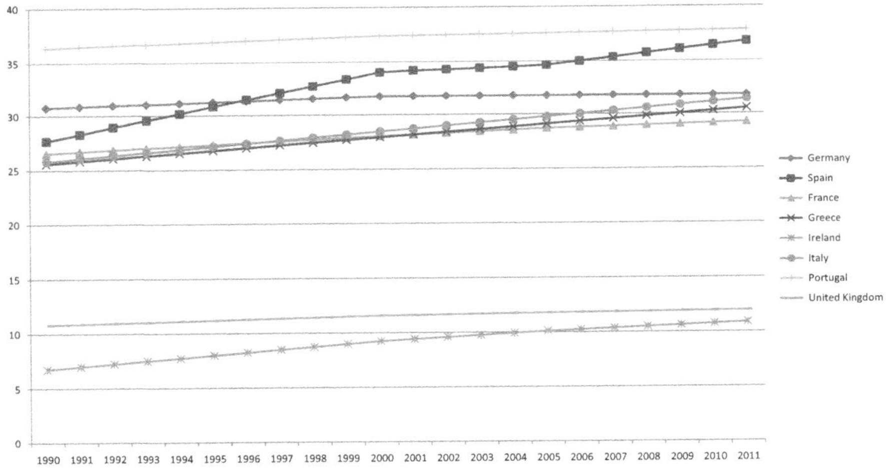


**Fig. 5.2** Forest area (% of land area) between European countries

France presented the best productivity in agriculture, from 1980 until 2010, and Portugal showed the worst agricultural productivity level (Fig. 5.3). The database considered lacked information relative to this variable for Greece, Ireland, and the UK. This data for Portuguese farming productivity proved to be interesting information that requires more careful analysis in future studies.

In general the European countries consumed energy predominantly from fossil fuel sources, with percentages of more than 80 % (Fig. 5.4). On the other hand, France is a good example having decreased its fossil fuel energy consumption,

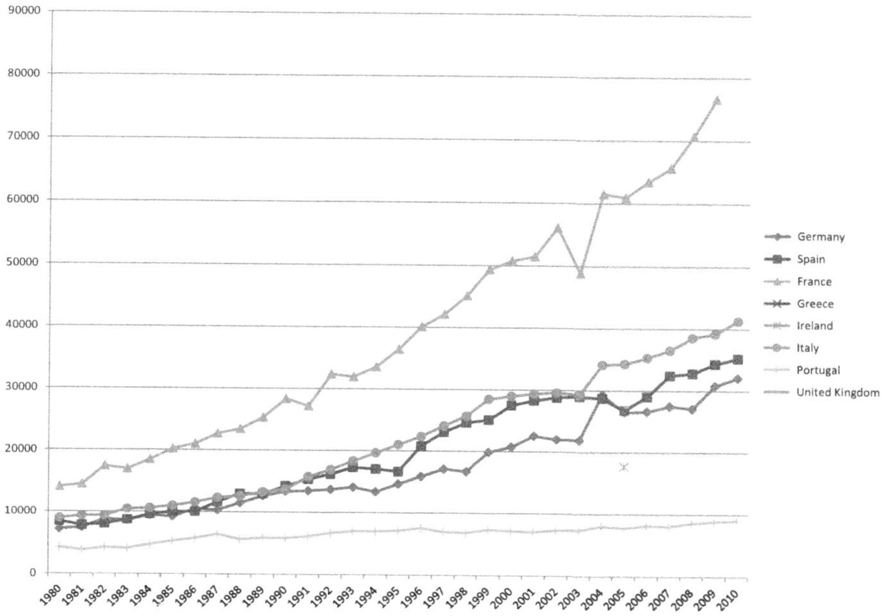


**Fig. 5.3** Agriculture value added per worker (constant 2005 US$) between European countries

**Fig. 5.4** Fossil fuel energy consumption (% of total) between European countries

since the beginning of the 1980s and by 2011 only 50 % of the energy consumed had been sourced from fossil fuel resources.

Portugal, from 1961 until 2009, had the lowest $CO_2$ emissions, comparatively to other European countries considered (Fig. 5.5). Indeed, France with the reduction of fossil fuel energy consumption, since the 1980s could have obtained the lowest levels of $CO_2$ emissions, which is a curious example.

The percentage of methane emission by agriculture in each country (Fig. 5.6), from 1990 to 2010, was superior in Ireland (about 80 %) and inferior in Portugal (more or less 30 % in the total of the economy).

Similar findings are possible to obtain from the Fig. 5.7 for the percentage of nitrous oxide emissions by agriculture in each country. These findings for Portugal are possibly in agreement with the lowest levels of productivity in farming for this country. However, as referred to before these observations need to be analyzed with other information and with some attention in future studies.

Portugal (about 40 %) and Greece (about 30 %) are the countries with more population in urban agglomerations (Fig. 5.8) and Germany (about 10 %), Italy (about 15 %), and France (about 20 %) are the countries with less population in large agglomerated urban areas.

Greece and Portugal are the countries that have more freshwater withdrawals for the agricultural sector (Fig. 5.9). On the other hand, the utilization of freshwater for farming is residual in Germany (less than 10 %).

The eight countries of the European Union considered followed a pattern more or less similar to that of inflation for consumer prices, from 1961 until 2012 (Fig. 5.10). The 1970s, the 1980s, and part of the 1990s were years with signs of strong inflation (maybe hyperinflation). Some countries such as France showed one of the lowest inflation rates for this period and Portugal and Greece had some problems with this economic variable, namely in the 1980s and part of the 1990s.

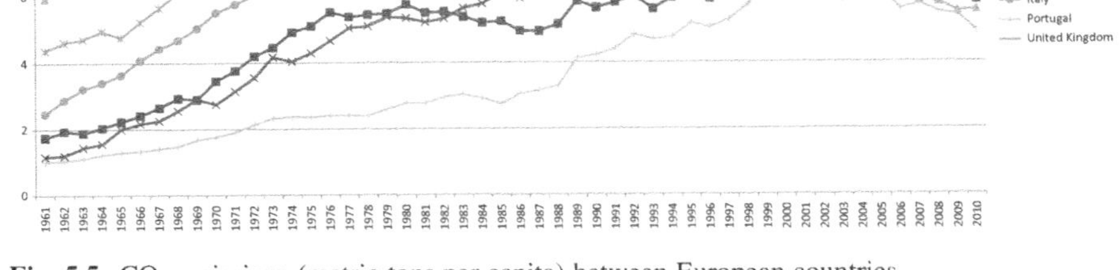


**Fig. 5.5** $CO_2$ emissions (metric tons per capita) between European countries

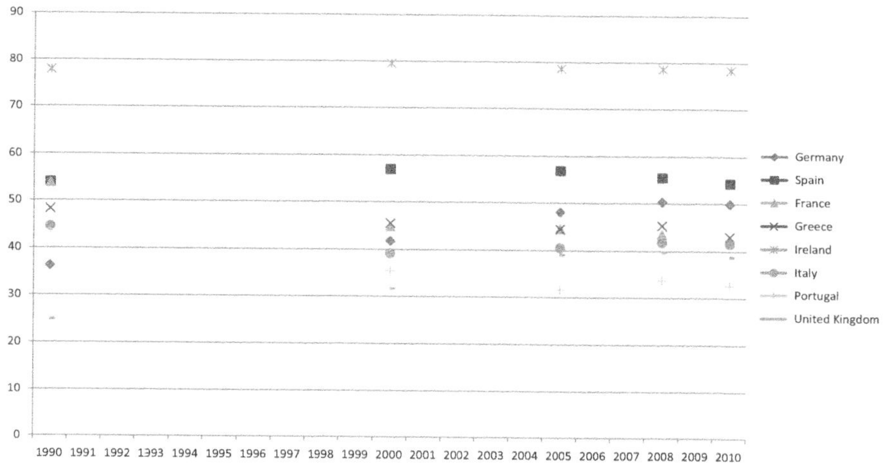


**Fig. 5.6** Agricultural methane emissions (% of total) between European countries

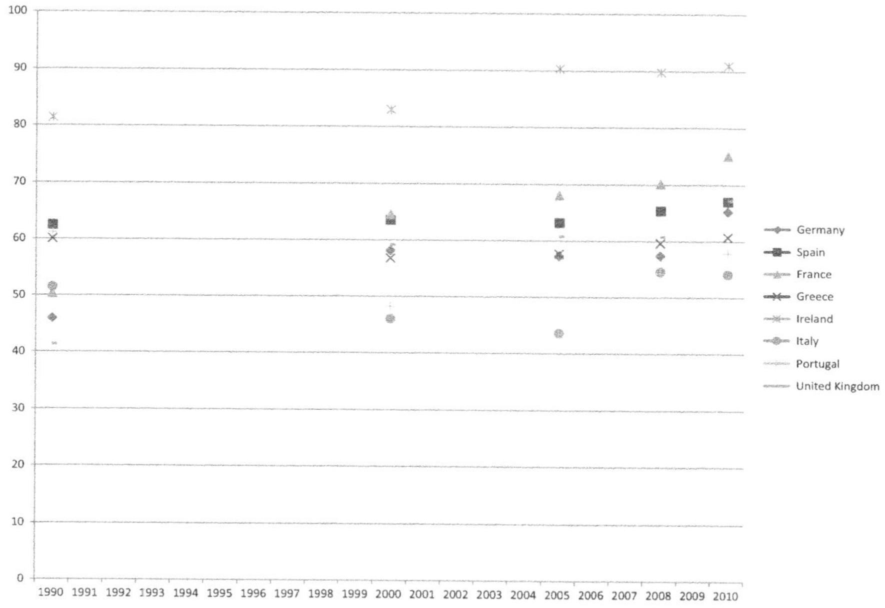


**Fig. 5.7** Agricultural nitrous oxide emissions (% of total) between European countries

More or less the same can be said about the lending interest rate (Fig. 5.11). Indeed, between the 1970s and the 1990s these rates were high and Portugal and Greece were the European countries having the most problems with this variable.

Italy and Greece were the countries with more central government debts, from 1995 to 2011 (about 120 % of the GDP), but after 2008 many countries saw their

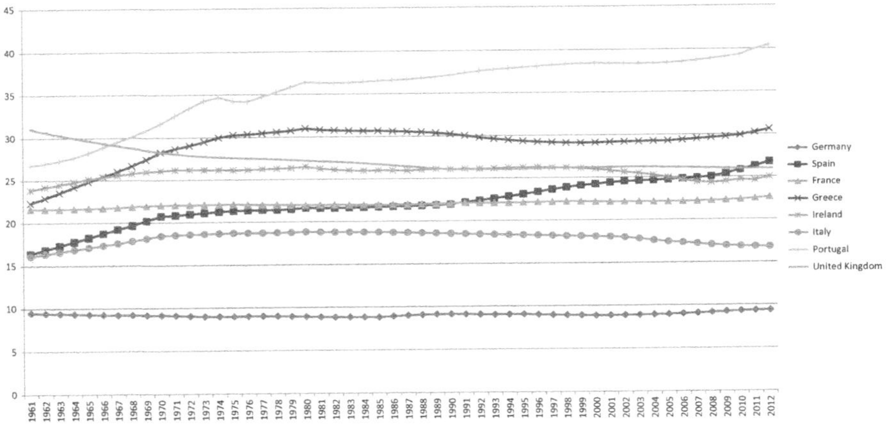


**Fig. 5.8** Population in urban agglomerations of more than one million (% of total population) between European countries

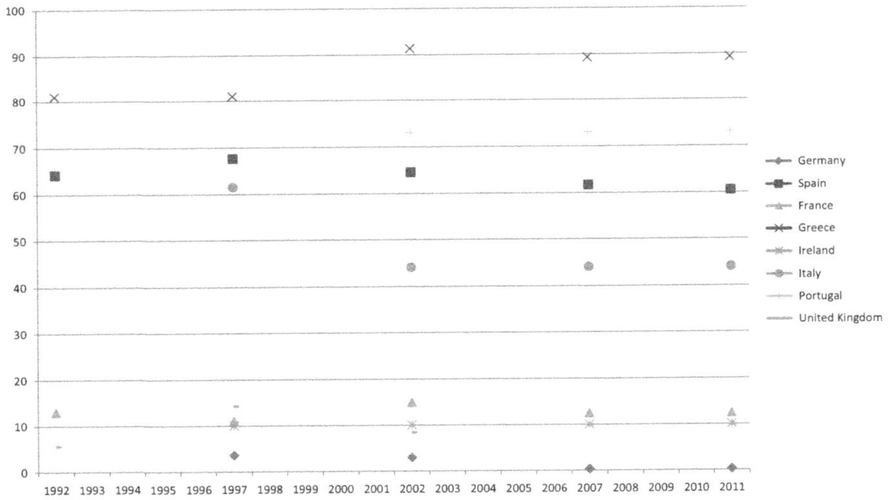


**Fig. 5.9** Annual freshwater withdrawals, agriculture (% of total freshwater withdrawal) between European countries

central debts increase, namely Portugal, Ireland, the UK, and France (Fig. 5.12). The financial crisis of the USA in 2008 had negative effects upon European countries.

The number of motor vehicles per 1,000 persons is greater in Italy and recently in Greece and lower in Ireland and the UK (Fig. 5.13). This is interrelated with some social attitudes, such as the preference for use of other means of transport to travel.

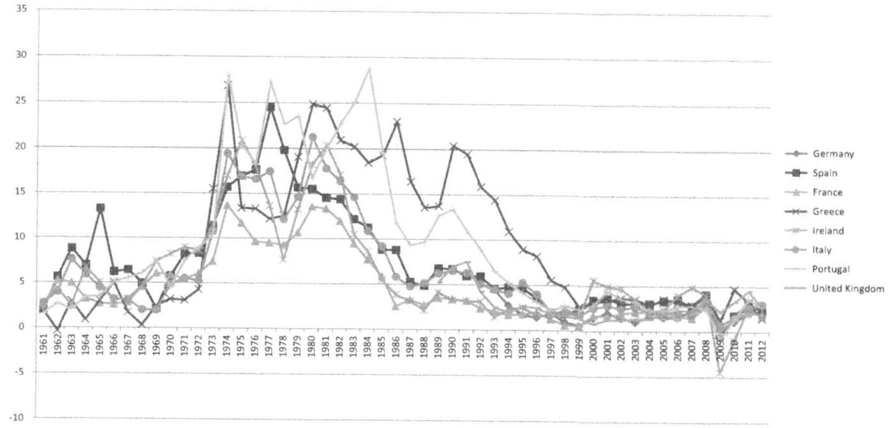


**Fig. 5.10** Inflation, consumer prices (annual %) between European countries

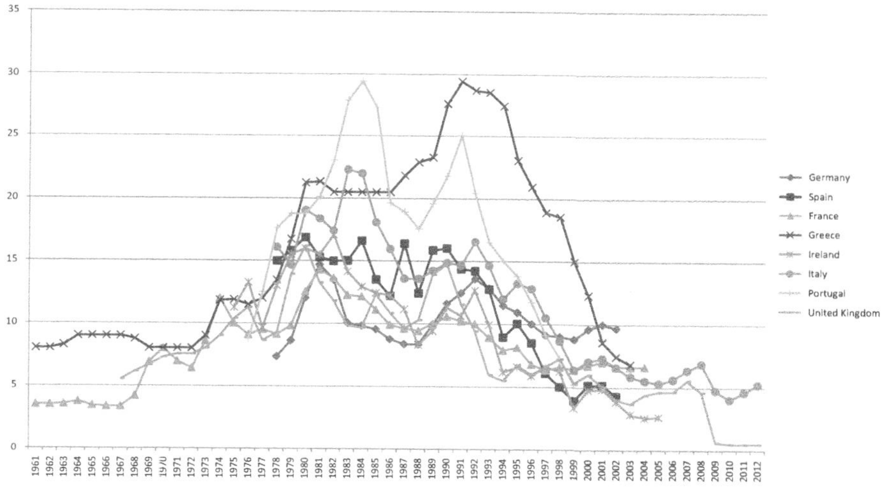


**Fig. 5.11** Lending interest rate (%) between European countries

Ireland is the country with the best performance in the percentage of export goods and services relative to its GDP (Fig. 5.14). Germany recently had a good performance, also, in exports, but the dynamics in Ireland are greater.

The evolution of the gross capital formation in percentage of the GDP followed a pattern more or less similar in the several countries considered and was about 20 % at the beginning of the 1960s and decreased slightly in 2011 (Fig. 5.15).

Portugal (about 30 %) and Ireland (about 15 %) were the countries with more percentage of the value added from agriculture into the total GDP at the beginning

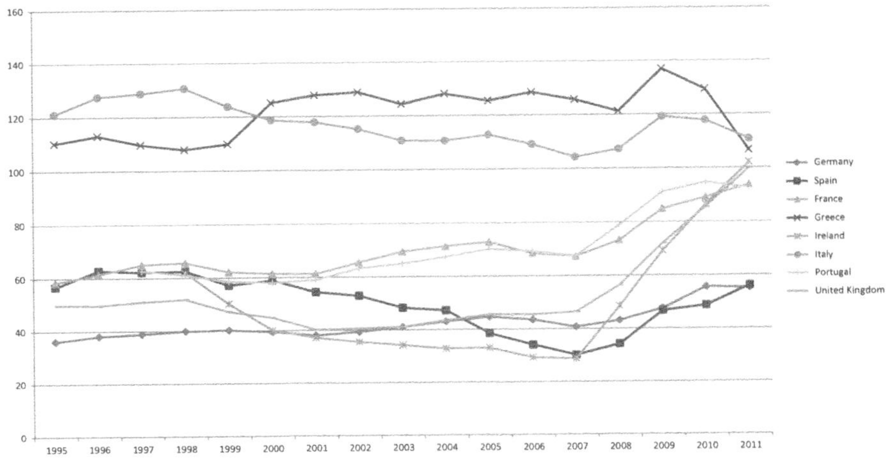


**Fig. 5.12** Central government debt, total (% of GDP) between European countries

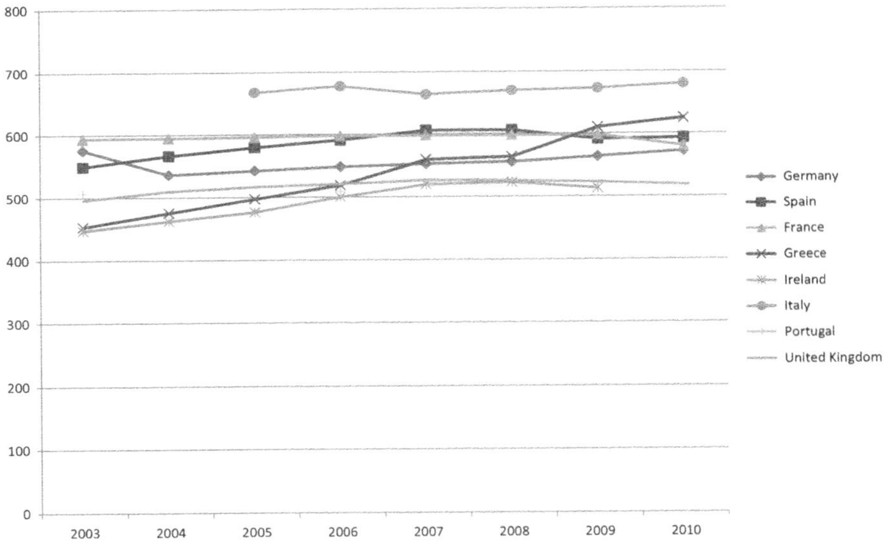


**Fig. 5.13** Motor vehicles (per 1,000 people) between European countries

of the 1970s (Fig. 5.16), but this weight decreased significantly and in 2010 all countries considered had a similar weight of about 2.5 %.

The weight in GDP from the industry was greater in Germany at the beginning of the 1970s and in 2010 it was Ireland which presented the best performance

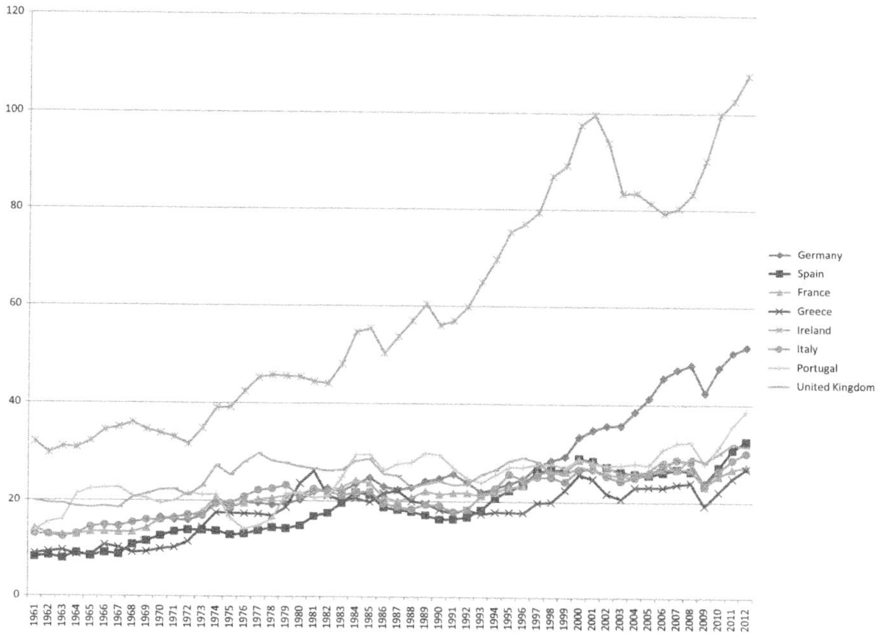


**Fig. 5.14** Exports of goods and services (% of GDP) between European countries

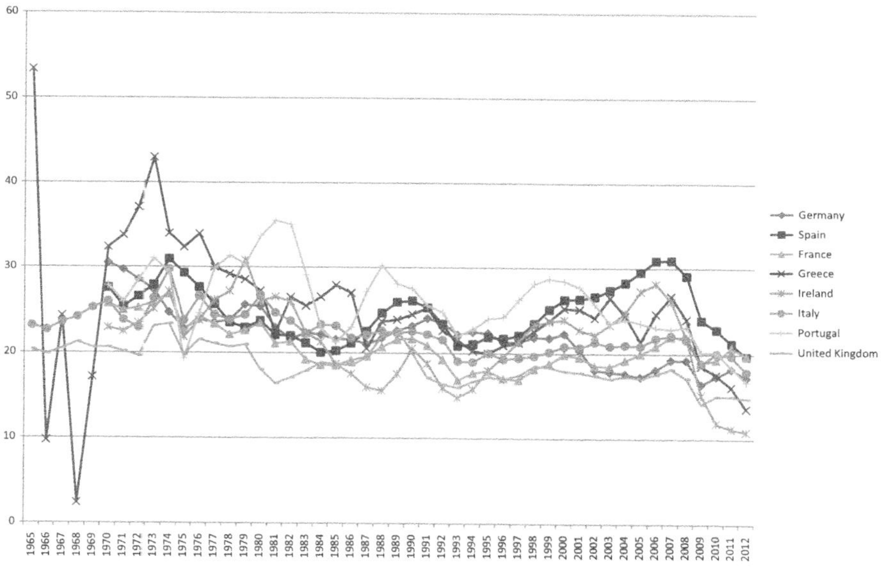


**Fig. 5.15** Gross capital formation (% of GDP) between European countries

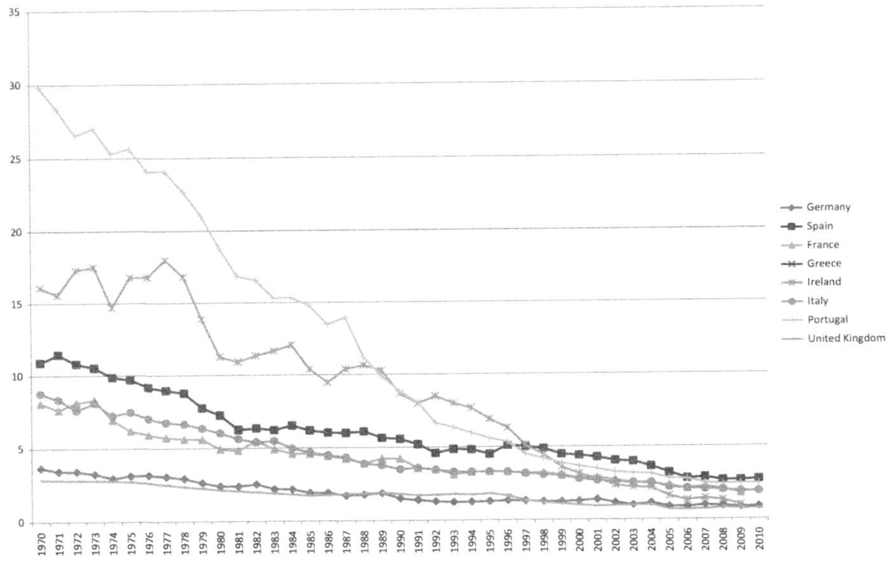


**Fig. 5.16** Agriculture, value added (% of GDP) between European countries

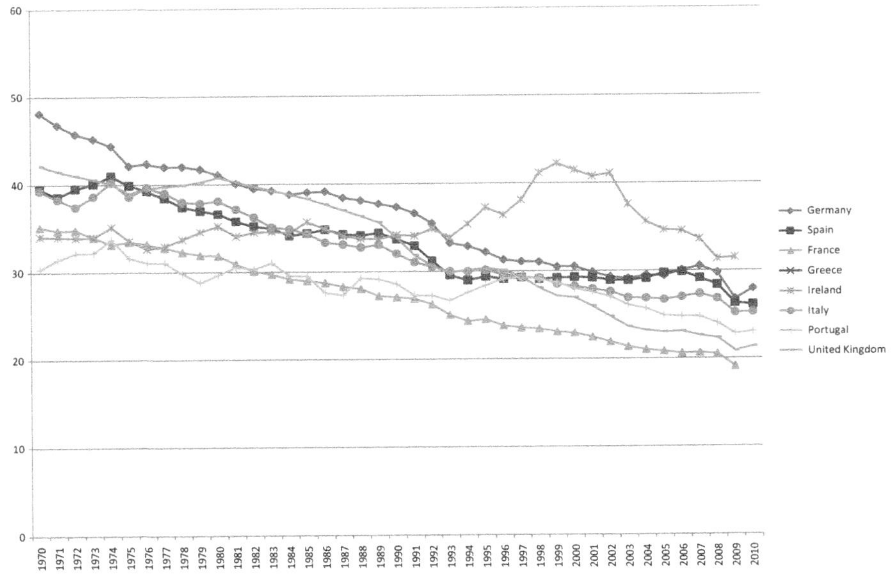


**Fig. 5.17** Industry, value added (% of GDP) between European countries

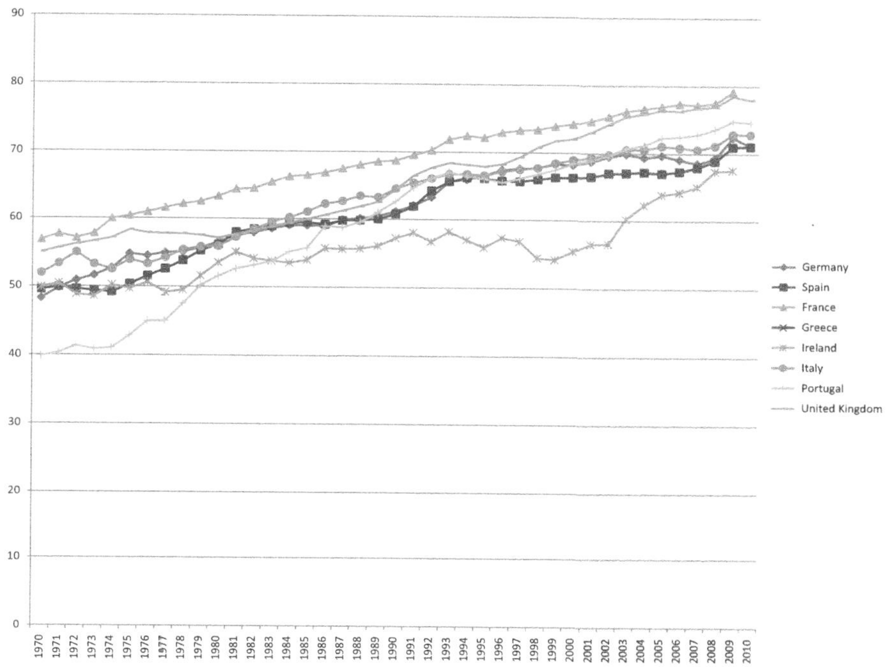


**Fig. 5.18** Services, etc., value added (% of GDP) between European countries

(Fig. 5.17), but Germany has also maintained a good level of dynamics over recent years. France is the country with lowest weight of the industry in GDP.

In terms of the importance of services in the total GDP, Ireland is the country with the lowest relevance and France the country with more weight (Fig. 5.18). The weight of services in the GDP of each European country increased from 1970 until 2010 in all countries considered, particularly in Portugal where the importance of services increased from about 40 % to about 75 % in the period referred to.

In general (Fig. 5.19), the GDP had negative growth, for the countries considered, in 1975, in 1993, and strongly in 2009. In 1975 and 2008 there were countries with growth rates of −5 %. In 2011, Greece had growth rates for GDP inferior to −5 %. In 2010 and 2011, Germany was the country with the highest growth rates of almost 5 % in 2010.

In recent years (Fig. 5.20) Ireland, Germany, and France were the countries with a greater GPD per capita. On the other hand, the lowest income per capita was verified in Portugal and Greece. This statistical information helps to understand some social and economic contexts verified by some European countries in the south.

Portugal had some literacy problems in the beginning of the 1980s (Fig. 5.21); this variable has improved significantly in recent years, from about 80 % in 1981 to about 95 % in 2011.

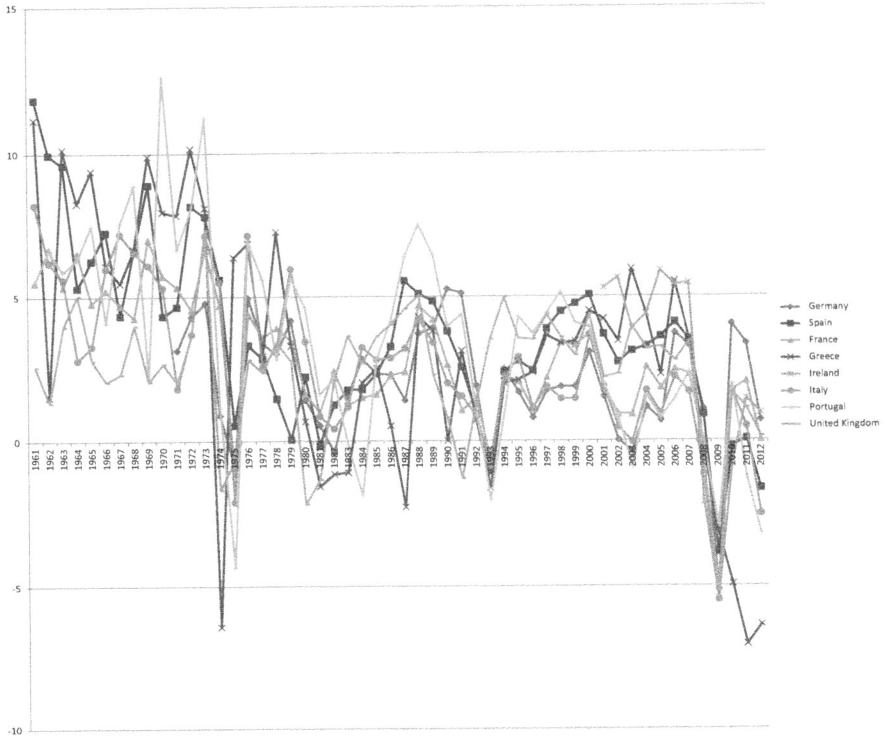


**Fig. 5.19** GDP growth (annual %) between European countries

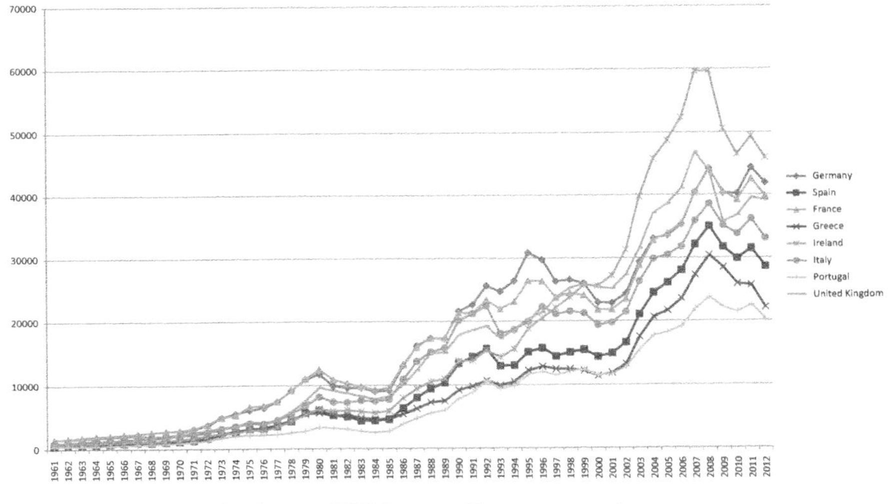


**Fig. 5.20** GDP per capita (current US$) between European countries

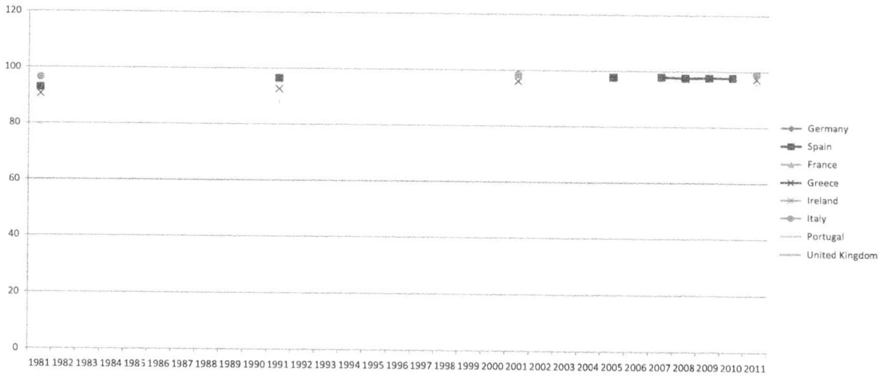


**Fig. 5.21** Literacy rate, adult total (% of people ages 15 and above) between European countries

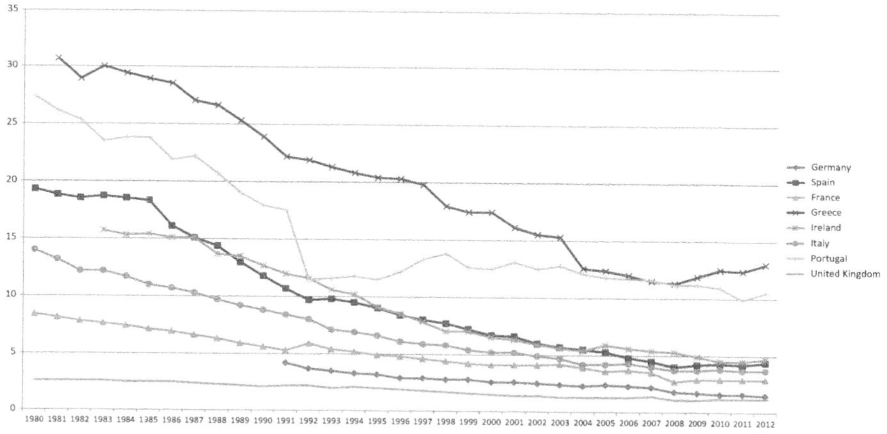


**Fig. 5.22** Employment in agriculture (% of total employment) between European countries

Employment in agriculture decreased in almost every country (Fig. 5.22) from 1980 to 2012, but Portugal and Greece are the two countries with more relative employment in farming (about 15–20 % in 2012) whereas Germany and the UK were those with less people employed by the agricultural sector (about 1–2 % in 2012).

Over the last 30 years the unemployment rate has always been high in Spain, with rates of about 25 % in 1994. These rates improved significantly after 2000, but the international financial crisis in 2008 increased the level of unemployment in Spain and in other European countries (Fig. 5.23).

Between 1961 and 2012 Portugal was the country with a higher percentage of population in rural areas, from about 65 % to about 40 % (Fig. 5.24). The UK (about 20 % during this period) and France are those with less rural population.

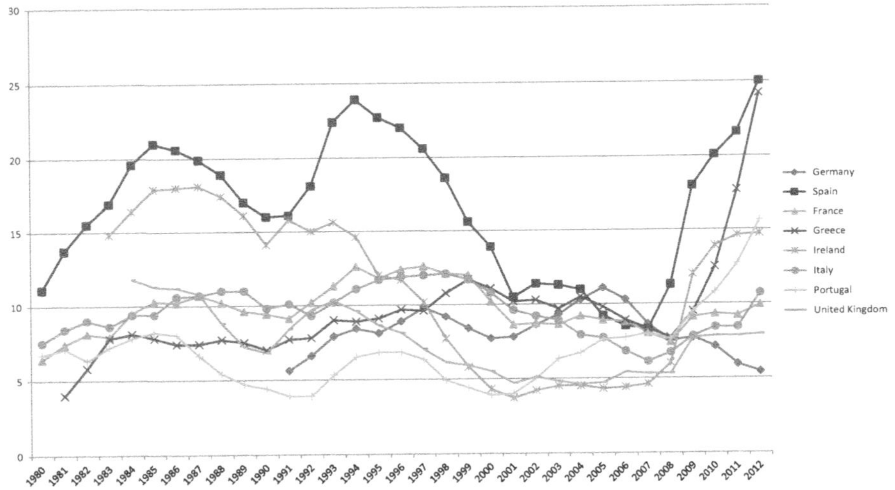


**Fig. 5.23** Unemployment, total (% of total labor force) between European countries

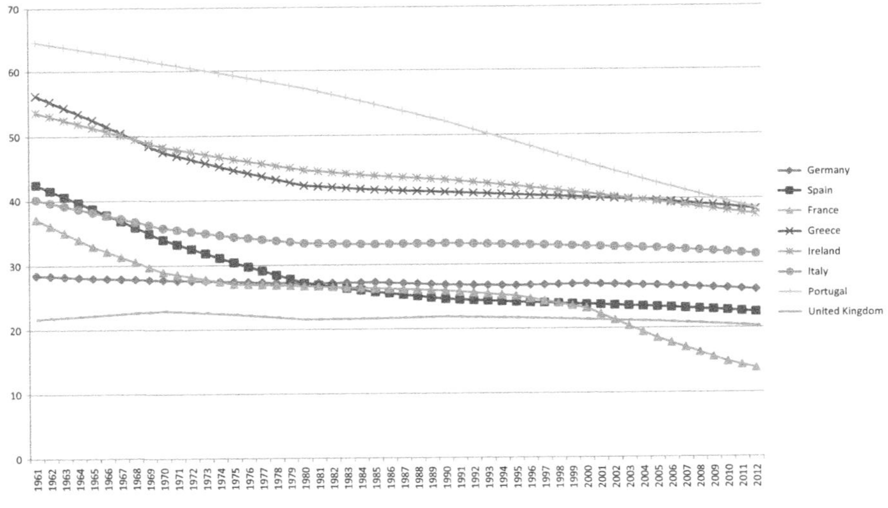


**Fig. 5.24** Rural population (% of total population) between European countries

# 4 Results

In the tables presented in this section results were obtained using time series econometric techniques for each one of the European countries considered, considering the Cobb and Douglas (1928) function of production. Table 5.1 shows the results found with the original Cobb–Douglas model, where the output is a function of productivity, employment, and capital (in our models capital is represented by

**Table 5.1** Results obtained with time series econometric techniques, based on the original Cobb–Douglas (1928) model (linear model obtained with logarithms), for the agricultural output in the period 1990–2011 (there are not results for Greece, due to a lack of data)

| | Germany | Spain | France | Ireland | Italy | Portugal | UK |
|---|---|---|---|---|---|---|---|
| Model | Prais–Winsten | Prais–Winsten | Prais–Winsten | Prais–Winsten | Prais–Winsten | Prais–Winsten | ARCH family regression (Robust) |
| Constant | | −8.804* (−6.010) [0.000] | 4.235** (1.910) [0.073] | −2.535* (−3.660) [0.002] | | 12.837** (2.070) [0.053] | −0.575* (−10.320) [0.000] |
| Agriculture value added per worker (constant 2005 US$) | | 0.758* (6.050) [0.000] | −0.360** (−2.060) [0.055] | | | −1.360* (−2.180) [0.042] | |
| Employment in agriculture (% of total employment) | 0.559* (2.140) [0.047] | 1.325* (12.050) [0.000] | 0.461** (1.800) [0.090] | 1.842* (5.490) [0.000] | 0.673** (1.890) [0.074] | | 1.513* (15.930) [0.000] |
| Augmented Dickey–Fuller test for unit root | −4.969* [0.000] | −2.984* [0.0364] | −2.890* [0.046] | −4.310* [0.000] | −3.247* [0.017] | −3.191* [0.020] | −3.202* [0.019] |
| EG-ADF test for co-integration | −2.081 [0.252] | −2.457 [0.126] | −1.877 [0.342] | −1.395 [0.584] | −2.353 [0.155] | −1.546 [0.510] | −2.149 [0.225] |
| Portmanteau test for white noise for autocorrelation | 36.191* [0.000] | 45.980* [0.000] | 34.061* [0.000] | 49.163* [0.000] | 51.964* [0.000] | 47.998* [0.000] | 52.960* [0.000] |
| Durbin's alternative test for autocorrelation | 3.794** [0.051] | 2.088 [0.148] | 2.858** [0.090] | 21.332* [0.000] | 8.361* [0.003] | 7.712* [0.005] | 1.128 [0.288] |
| Breusch–Godfrey LM test for autocorrelation | 3.833** [0.050] | 2.297 [0.129] | 3.031** [0.081] | 11.130* [0.000] | 6.923* [0.008] | 6.554* [0.010] | 1.239 [0.265] |
| Breusch–Pagan/Cook–Weisberg test for heteroskedasticity | 0.320 [0.572] | 2.200 [0.138] | 0.150 [0.697] | 0.190 [0.663] | 0.210 [0.643] | 0.040 [0.850] | 3.180** [0.074] |
| Ramsey RESET test using powers of the fitted values | 2.310 [0.120] | 3.510* [0.041] | 3.310** [0.051] | 8.630* [0.001] | 6.580* [0.004] | 2.050 [0.150] | 2.660** [0.083] |

(continued)

**Table 5.1** (continued)

| | Germany | Spain | France | Ireland | Italy | Portugal | UK |
|---|---|---|---|---|---|---|---|
| Model | Prais–Winsten | Prais–Winsten | Prais–Winsten | Prais–Winsten | Prais–Winsten | Prais–Winsten | ARCH family regression (Robust) |
| LM test for autoregressive conditional heteroskedasticity (ARCH) | 0.868 [0.351] | 0.040 [0.840] | 0.436 [0.508] | 1.630 [0.201] | 0.155 [0.693] | 0.566 [0.451] | 9.841* [0.001] |

*Note*: *Statistically significant at 5 %; **Statistically significant at 10 %

**Table 5.2** Results obtained with time series econometric techniques, considering the Cobb–Douglas (1928) model extended with economic, social, and environmental variables (linear model obtained with logarithms), for the agricultural output in the period 1990–2011 (there are not results for Greece, due to a lack of data)

| | Spain | France | Ireland | Italy | UK |
|---|---|---|---|---|---|
| Model | Prais–Winsten | Prais–Winsten | Prais–Winsten (Robust) | Prais–Winsten | Prais–Winsten (Robust) |
| Constant | −28.013* (−3.380) [0.004] | 6.129* (3.080) [0.007] | −11.334* (−3.900) [0.001] | −18.159* (−2.570) [0.020] | 6.061* (3.530) [0.002] |
| Agriculture value added per worker (constant 2005 US$) | 0.813* (7.060) [0.000] | −0.744* (−4.020) [0.001] | | | |
| Employment in agriculture (% of total employment) | 0.926* (4.740) [0.000] | | 2.929* (8.590) [0.000] | 0.813* (2.500) [0.023] | 0.747* (3.280) [0.004] |
| Additional variable[a] | 6.134* (2.350) [0.031] | 0.826* (3.580) [0.003] | 1.540* (2.960) [0.009] | 3.374* (2.670) [0.016] | −0.617* (−3.850) [0.001] |
| Breusch–Pagan/Cook–Weisberg test for heteroskedasticity | 0.010 [0.931] | 1.360 [0.244] | 3.000** [0.083] | 0.240 [0.621] | 4.180* [0.040] |
| Ramsey RESET test using powers of the fitted values | 2.190 [0.135] | 0.160 [0.919] | 2.060 [0.151] | 3.860* [0.033] | 2.110 [0.141] |
| LM test for autoregressive conditional heteroskedasticity (ARCH) | 0.065 [0.798] | 0.717 [0.397] | 1.411 [0.234] | 0.800 [0.371] | 0.097 [0.755] |

*Note*: *Statistically significant at 5 %; **Statistically significant at 10 %
[a]Rural population (% of total population) for Spain, Exports of goods and services (% of GDP) for France and Ireland, Fossil fuel energy consumption (% of total) for Italy, and GDP per capita (current US$) for the UK

the percentage of the gross capital formation and did not present statistical significance). In Table 5.2 the results presented for the models (countries) where the Ramsey RESET test using powers of the fitted values reveal a lack of independent variables. In this case several economic, social, and environmental variables analyzed in the previous section were tested, taking into account the availability of statistical information considered, in all estimations, only the period from 1990 to 2011. All the econometric estimations were made with Stata (2014) software.

Observing Table 5.1 it is possible to verify that there are no problems with the unit root and with the co-integration. There are some problems, however, with the autocorrelation and because of this the Prais–Winsten was used as an estimation method. On the other hand there are some complications with the heteroskedasticity and with the autoregressive conditional heteroskedasticity, for the model of the UK, and in this way the robust ARCH family regression was considered for the estimation. The Ramsey RESET test using powers of the fitted values reveal that there is a lack of independent variables in the models of Spain, France, Ireland, Italy, and the

UK. The results in this table reveal that agricultural employment has a positive effect on the agricultural output in almost every country (for Portugal this variable does not have statistical significance). The productivity of the labor force has a positive effect in Spain and a negative influence in France and Portugal.

In Table 5.2 the results suggest that the agricultural output is, also, influenced by the rural population (% of total population) in Spain, by the exports of goods and services (% of GDP) in France and Ireland, fossil fuel energy consumption (% of total) in Italy, and GDP per capita (current US$) in the UK.

The problems related with the lack of independent variables remain for Italy. Maybe, in future studies it will be possible to test other variables, not considered in this study.

**Conclusions**

A previous review of literature revealed that there are many determinants for agricultural output with diverse sources, namely, economic, social, environmental, and biological. Considering the importance of farming for the economic performance of countries, this original study is an important contribution towards the understanding of agricultural economic determinants in some of the European Union countries, namely those with greater dimension and those that had financial help from International Institutions, such as Portugal, Ireland, and Greece.

The data analysis reveals that the economic problems of countries such as Portugal and Greece have lasted for some time. For example, Portugal has suffered some difficulties in agricultural productivity, through the excess in farming employment, compared to other European countries, and in the number of people in urban agglomerations compared to rural areas. On the other hand, Portugal has more forest area and less pollutant emissions, namely from the agricultural sector. Both, Portugal and Greece, suffered problems derived from inflation and interest rates for lending.

Sometimes, it is difficult to understand how these differing countries can have the same economic rules and similar common policies, without other instruments of control. Maybe, it will be possible to find somewhere in time, a common steady state, after several mechanisms for catching up, but until now this continues to be difficult to discover how.

The econometric results show that the original Cobb–Douglas model, namely in agricultural productivity and employment, explains the near totality of the evolution for farming output in the several countries considered. Only the models associated with Spain, France, Ireland, Italy, and the UK needed to be complemented with some economic, social, and environmental variables.

There are yet some questions that need more specific analysis, which may prove to be an interesting opportunity for future research, namely in trying to

(continued)

better understand the agricultural economic dynamics in some countries at a microeconomic level.

Either way, this is one original approach to the agricultural economic performance in the European Union that aims to be a contribution for researchers and professionals of the sector, helping them to make informed choices and well-based decisions, namely at a macro level, but, also, at a micro level.

## References


Almeida, A. T., Moura, P. S., Marques, A. S., & Almeida, J. L. (2005). Multi-impact evaluation of new medium and large hydropower plants in Portugal centre region. *Renewable and Sustainable Energy Reviews, 9*, 149–167.

Areal, F. J., & Riesgo, L. (2014). Farmers' views on the future of olive farming in Andalusia, Spain. *Land Use Policy, 36*, 543–553.

Castillo, J. S., & García, M. C. (2013). Analysis of international competitive positioning of quality wine from Spain. *Ciencia e investigación agraria, 40*(3), 491–501.

Caurla, S., Delacote, P., Lecocq, F., Barthès, J., & Barkaoui, A. (2013). Combining an intersectoral carbon tax with sectoral mitigation policies: Impacts on the French forest sector. *Journal of Forest Economics, 19*, 450–461.

Clancy, D., Breen, J. P., Thorne, F., & Wallace, M. (2012). A stochastic analysis of the decision to produce biomass crops in Ireland. *Biomass and Bioenergy, 46*, 353–365.

Cobb, C. W., & Douglas, P. H. (1928). A theory of production. *American Economic Review, 18* (Suppl), 139–165.

Darradi, Y., Saur, E., Laplana, R., Lescot, J.-M., Kuentz, V., & Meyer, B. C. (2012). Optimizing the environmental performance of agricultural activities: A case study in La Boulouze watershed. *Ecological Indicators, 22*, 27–37.

Gatto, P., Zocca, A., Battisti, A., Barrento, M. J., Branco, M., & Paiva, M. R. (2009). Economic assessment of managing processionary moth in pine forests: A case-study in Portugal. *Journal of Environmental Management, 90*, 683–691.

Hirt, U., Kreins, P., Kuhn, U., Mahnkopf, J., Venohr, M., & Wendland, F. (2012). Management options to reduce future nitrogen emissions into rivers: A case study of the Weser river basin, Germany. *Agricultural Water Management, 115*, 118–131.

Hoyos, D., Mariel, P., Pascual, U., & Etxano, I. (2012). Valuing a Natura 2000 network site to inform land use options using a discrete choice experiment: An illustration from the Basque Country. *Journal of Forest Economics, 18*, 329–344.

Kraatz, S. (2012). Energy intensity in livestock operations – Modeling of dairy farming systems in Germany. *Agricultural Systems, 110*, 90–106.

Krausmann, F., Schandl, H., & Sieferle, R. P. (2008). Socio-ecological regime transitions in Austria and the United Kingdom. *Ecological Economics, 65*, 187–201.

Maestre-Valero, J. F., Martínez-Granados, D., Martínez-Alvarez, V., & Calatrava, J. (2013). Socio-economic impact of evaporation losses from reservoirs under past, current and future water availability scenarios in the semi-arid Segura Basin. *Water Resources Management, 27*, 1411–1426.

Nastis, S. A., Michailidis, A., & Mattas, K. (2013). Crop biodiversity repercussions of subsidized organic farming. *Land Use Policy, 32*, 23–26.

Peña-Haro, S., Llopis-Albert, C., Pulido-Velazquez, M., & Pulido-Velazquez, D. (2010). Fertilizer standards for controlling groundwater nitrate pollution from agriculture: El Salobral-Los Llanos case study, Spain. *Journal of Hydrology, 392*, 174–187.

Skuras, D., Petrou, A., & Clark, G. (2006). Demand for rural tourism: The effects of quality and information. *Agricultural Economics, 35*, 183–192.
Stata. (2014). *Statistics/Data analysis*. StataCorp, LP.
Steinmann, H. H., Dickeduisberg, M., & Theuvsen, L. (2012). Uses and benefits of glyphosate in German arable farming. *Crop Protection, 42*, 164–169.
Tzouramani, I., Sintori, A., Liontakis, A., Karanikolas, P., & Alexopoulos, G. (2011). An assessment of the economic performance of organic dairy sheep farming in Greece. *Livestock Science, 141*, 136–142.
Via, J. D., Mantinger, H., & Baric, S. (2013). Die Entwicklung des Obstbaus in Südtirol: I. Die landwirtschaftliche Aus- und Weiterbildung. *Erwerbs-Obstbau, 55*, 109–119.
Wang, L., Butcher, A. S., Stuart, M. E., Gooddy, D. C., & Bloomfield, J. P. (2013). The nitrate time bomb: A numerical way to investigate nitrate storage and lag time in the unsaturated zone. *Environmental Geochemistry and Health, 35*, 667–681.
World Bank. (2014). *Several statistics*. Washington, DC: World Bank.

# Chapter 6
# The Performance of the Agricultural Economics in BRICS Countries

Vítor João Pereira Domingues Martinho

## 1 Introduction

The agricultural sector has a primordial importance in the BRICS economies, because they are populous countries with a great need for food production to supply the markets with great dimension and with consumers, who now possess an ever increasing purchasing power. Indeed, some of these countries have growth rates that many of the older developed countries have not seen for a considerable time. These contexts, of course, to avoid problems in the markets, namely the food markets, need a dynamic farming sector to guarantee the national food provision.

Some of these countries have had both a political and economic history, namely Russia and China with the communist regimes, where agriculture was seen as fundamental to ensure the feeding of the population. On the other hand, Brazil had some economic problems, namely with inflation, where it was crucial to improve the performance of the farming sector.

In any case, it seems important to evaluate the dynamics for agriculture in these countries over the last five decades and the interrelation of this economic sector with the other sectors and with other indicators, to understand the evolution of the agricultural sector and its position within the whole economy.

Agriculture is, also, today confronted by many problems, namely those related to the pollution of the soil and water, due to, for example, nitrogen emissions and others pollutants, sometimes derived from organic production and other times from the use of fertilizers and other chemical factors for production. Brazil bears the Amazonian problem, with deforestation and the, sometimes, ill adjusted use of soils.

Climate change is another challenge for many productions across many regions of the world along with these BRICS countries too. As an example, there are many

---

V.J.P.D. Martinho (✉)
Agricultural School, Polytechnic Institute of Viseu, 3500 Viseu, Portugal
e-mail: vdmartinho@esav.ipv.pt



V.J.P.D. Martinho (ed.), *The Agricultural Economics of the 21st Century*,
DOI 10.1007/978-3-319-09471-7_6

regions, specifically in the southern hemisphere that suffer from lack of water and high temperatures.

The competition for land between agriculture for food, agriculture for biofuel production, and urban areas is a reality that can compromise the future of the regularity of supply within food markets.

In recent years there have been many technological advances in several areas and this applies to farming too. Today with precision agriculture it is possible to reduce the environmental impact and reduce the cost of production with reduced investments. On the other hand, alternative ways of food production, such as organic farming and others, can help in environmental preservation. But the tradeoff among the economic perspective of agriculture and other associated questions (social, environmental, and cultural) will continue over time.

## 2 Literature Review

Agriculture plays an important role in emerging economics, namely in the BRICS, considering that the countries need to have a developed farming sector in order to have a dynamic economy (Brosig et al. 2013).

There is a rising concern to develop an agriculture which is compatible with the environment and with the preservation of the biodiversity in Brazil (Souza et al. 2012).

The utilization and production of biofuel increased significantly over recent years, namely using corn grain in the USA and sugarcane juice in Brazil. There are other resources for producing biofuels; however, their economic viability depends upon several factors (Sainz 2009).

The distance to markets and the investments in farms are some of the main factors that can affect the value of the land in the Brazilian Amazon (Sills and Caviglia-Harris 2008). The occupation of the Brazilian Amazon is heterogeneous and depends, again, upon the distance to markets and environmental conditions (Aguiar et al. 2007).

In Brazil subsistence farmers have low technological skills, low education, practice a diverse agriculture, and have an inappropriate transgenic technology. So, the impact of the farming of transgenic products is diverse and depends on many factors, as do the characteristics of the farmers (Hall et al. 2008).

The reforms in Brazilian agricultural policies have improved the performance of the farming sector and converted this sector into one of the most dynamic in the economy (Helfand and Rezende 2004).

The environment, climate changes, and sustainability are, also, motives for concern in Russian agriculture (Smith et al. 2007; Beurs et al. 2009).

After the end of the Soviet Union in 1991, the agricultural land in Russia was privatized and can now be bought or sold. However, there are yet some barriers which prevent these land markets to become more dynamic, namely being the transaction costs and the lack of information about them (Lerman and Shagaida 2007).

The use of renewable energies in the Indian agricultural sector was a step towards sustainable farming production (Radulovic 2005).

Organic farming in India has increased in popularity, considering its contribution towards ecological, economic, and social sustainability (Purushothaman et al. 2013).

In the twentieth century the agricultural policy in China from the second War until the 1970s was based upon fixed prices with conditions for some farms to increase their grain. After the 1970s the agricultural policies improved the food markets and rural economic growth. In the twenty-first century the policy reforms positioned the sector in the market place, with the Chinese government supporting the production of grain at a low price, promoting the industry in detriment to agriculture. These policies maintain many famers within the sector at an income below that obtained in urban regions (Hurt 2010).

The most important determinant of grain output growth for farmers is the input growth, followed by productivity growth. Within the input growth is the intermediate input growth the most important variable after the planted area, the investment, and labor input. Between the elements of productivity, the greatest importance comes from technical progress, grain financial support, climate conditions, scale effects, and technical efficiency, respectively (Yong-fu et al. 2013).

Genetically modified agricultural production (Morse et al. 2006), the increased presence of supermarkets (D'Haese and Huylenbroeck 2005), the climate (Moeletsi et al. 2013), and water management (Hassan and Thurlow 2011) are questions that are raised in rural areas and in the agricultural sector in South Africa.

## 3 Data Description

The following figures show the evolution of the agricultural value added and other related variables, from the diverse areas of society, from 1961 until 2012, for the BRICS countries (World Bank 2014).

The statistical information reveals that indeed the reality of these countries is very different on several different levels, which means that the challenges facing each one will be singular and the strategies for the future on all levels, and namely for the agricultural sector, must and will be specific and adjusted to their personal needs.

The percentage of agricultural land across the different countries, from 1961 to 2011, was greater in South Africa and India and lower in Russia (Fig. 6.1). Brazil also lacked a great weight of land in the farming sector (about 30 %). The deforestation in the Brazilian Amazon for construction and to obtain land for agriculture has alerted some Brazilian fields in society.

On the other hand, in the period 1990–2011, Brazil had the higher proportion of area with forest (about 60 % in recent years), and South Africa the lowest, as well as

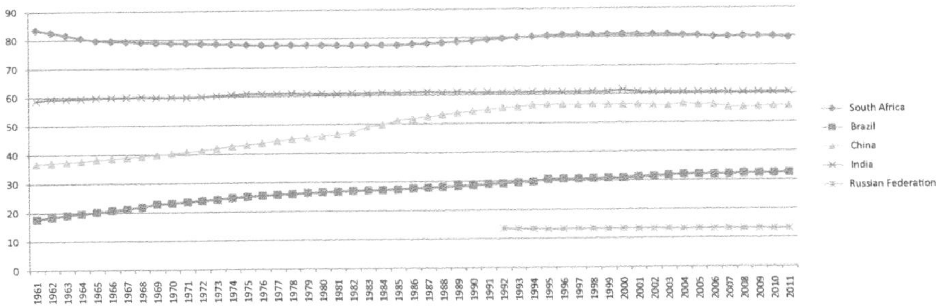


**Fig. 6.1** Agricultural land (% of land area) among BRICS countries

the Russian Federation (Fig. 6.2). India and China had about 20 % of their land occupied with forests.

Agricultural productivity was higher in Russia and South Africa, 1980–2012, and much lower in China and India, less than US$ per worker at constant prices of 2005 (Fig. 6.3). This requires some micro and careful analysis, because this low agricultural productivity, in monetary units, could be because of the low farming production per worker or due to low food prices, at producer level, verified in these countries.

From 1971 to 2011, Russia, South Africa, and recently China had a significant percentage of fossil fuel energy consumption, about 90 % (Fig. 6.4). India increased its fuel fossil consumption and Brazil has about 50 %. The alternative energies in Brazil have great importance, namely those from biofuel.

The $CO_2$ emissions per capita (1961–2010) are, more or less, in harmony with the fossil fuel energy consumption bias (Fig. 6.5), with an exception for India which despite great fossil fuel utilization has the lower $CO_2$ emission per capita. This is another question that needs specific attention in future studies. An explanation may be the proportion of fossil fuel consumption against the number of people.

The percentage of methane emissions by agriculture is more significant in Brazil and India (Fig. 6.6) and less relevant in the Russian Federation. This is related to the type of agricultural production and the techniques used for production.

The situation for nitrous oxide emissions in agriculture is more or less the same as to that referred to before for the agricultural methane emissions (Fig. 6.7). But in this case, appears, also, with significant percentages in China.

From 1961 to 2012, Brazil and South Africa appeared as the countries with more population concentrated in big cities (Fig. 6.8). India has the lowest percentage and China since the beginning of the 1990s increased its agglomeration of population into big urban centers.

The utilization of freshwater by agriculture has more expression in India (Fig. 6.9) and less in the Russian Federation (about 90 and 20 %, respectively). The other countries, over recent years, had percentages of about 60 %.

Brazil and Russia had problems at the beginning of the 1990s with the inflation of consumer prices (Fig. 6.10), but recently the BRICS countries have had their price fluctuation controlled at lower levels, but with some problems as in some

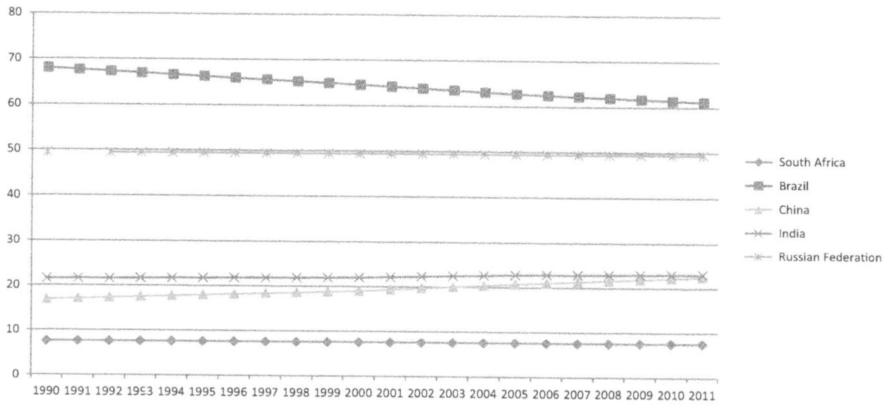


**Fig. 6.2** Forest area (% of land area) among BRICS countries

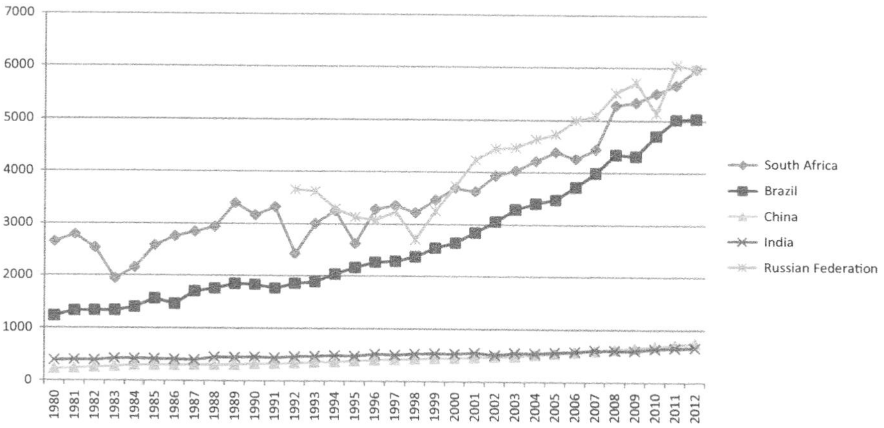


**Fig. 6.3** Agriculture value added per worker (constant 2005 US$) among BRICS countries

cases with inflation of about 10 %, as was the case for India in 2012. China is the country that shows a tendency to have less inflation (about 2.5 % in 2012).

The Russian Federation had some complications, also, in the 1990s with lending interest rates (Fig. 6.11), but has improved its performance over recent years. Brazil sustained some difficulties with these rates, bearing values of 40 % in 2012.

The central government debt may be a problem in India and Brazil, considering that these two countries had a central debt of about 50 % in 2011 (Fig. 6.12). On the other hand, there lacked statistical information in the database for other countries, namely China and South Africa for recent years, which prevents any conclusions about these countries for this variable.

The number of motor vehicles per 1,000 people was greater, from 2003 to 2010, respectively in Russia, Brazil, South Africa, China, and India (Fig. 6.13). This helps

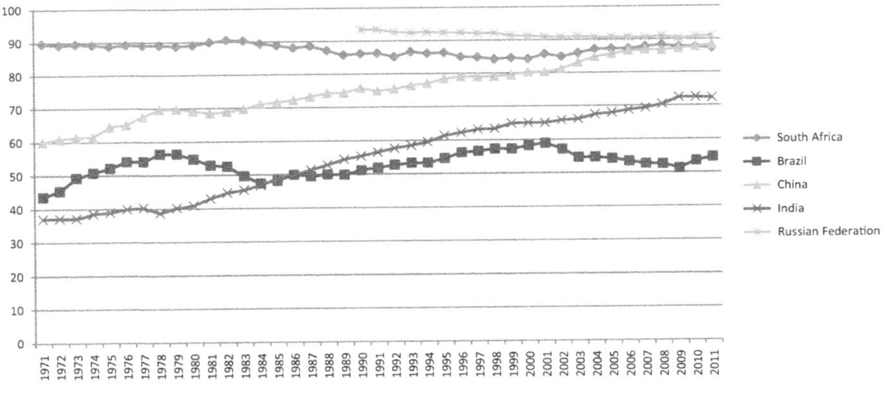


**Fig. 6.4** Fossil fuel energy consumption (% of total) among BRICS countries

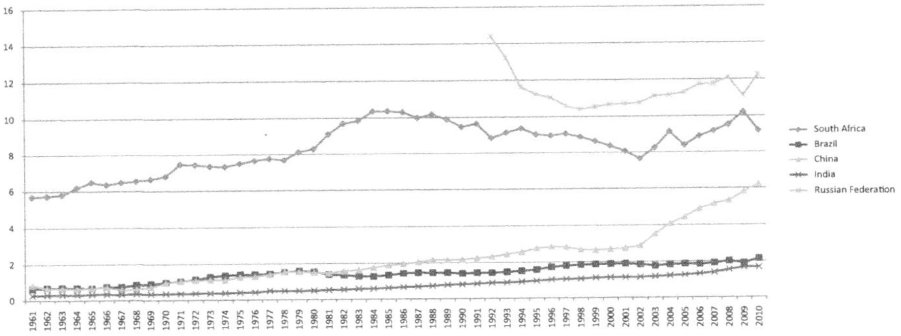


**Fig. 6.5** $CO_2$ emissions (metric tons per capita) among BRICS countries

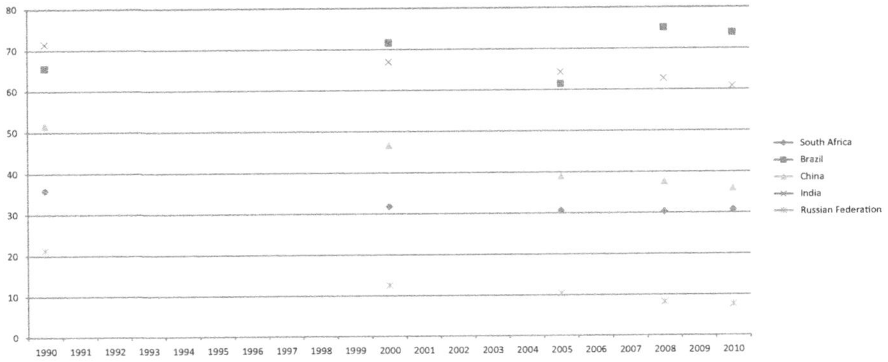


**Fig. 6.6** Agricultural methane emissions (% of total) among BRICS countries

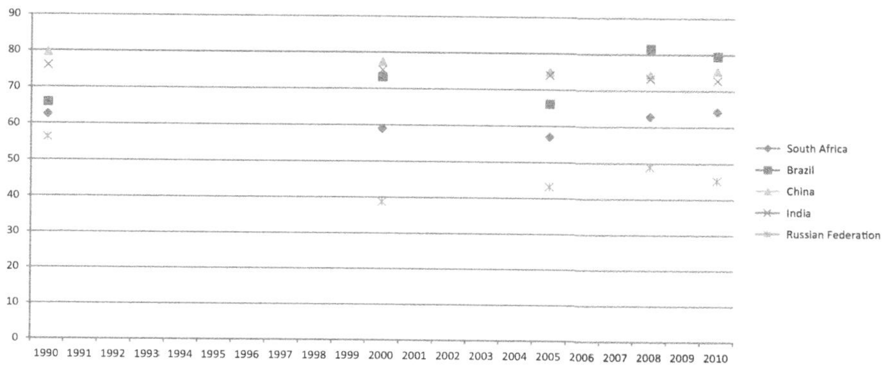


**Fig. 6.7** Agricultural nitrous oxide emissions (% of total) among BRICS countries

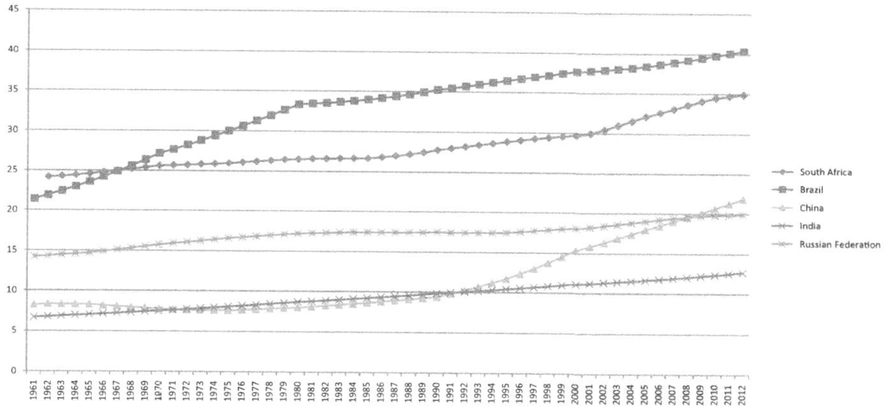


**Fig. 6.8** Population in urban agglomerations of more than one million (% of total population) among BRICS countries

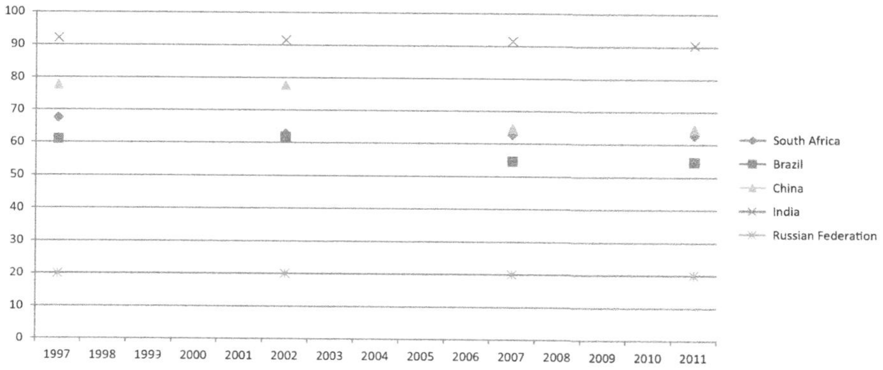


**Fig. 6.9** Annual freshwater withdrawals, agriculture (% of total freshwater withdrawal) among BRICS countries

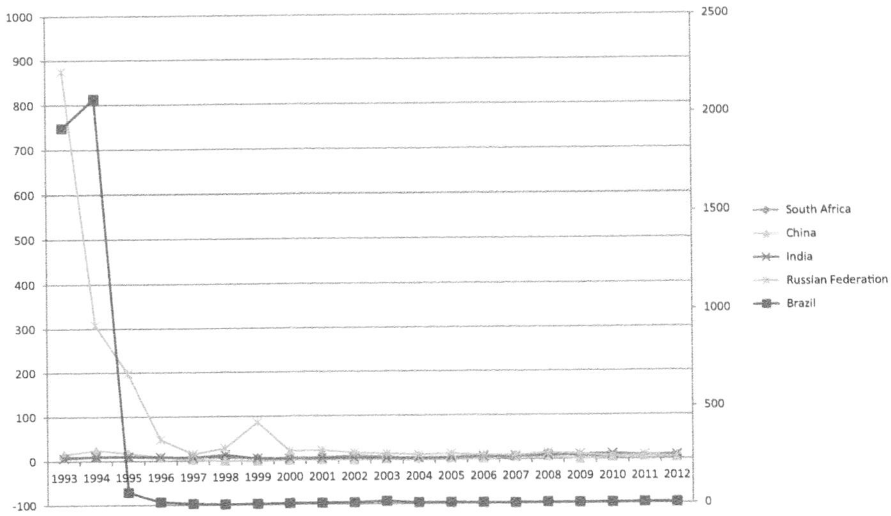


**Fig. 6.10** Inflation, consumer prices (annual %) among BRICS countries

us to understand the previous explanations for $CO_2$ emissions and the use of alternative energies in Brazil.

India and Brazil, namely the latter, have had the worst performance in terms of goods and services export (Fig. 6.14). China, for example, was the country that better improved its performance in terms of competition within the international market.

The weight of investment, measured by the gross capital formation in percentage of the GDP, was greater in China and India, a worrying sign with the modernization of the country and the economy (Fig. 6.15). The lowest investments, namely in recent years, were verified to be in Brazil and South Africa.

The value added by agriculture as a percentage of the GDP has decreased in all the BRICS countries, from 1961 until 2012, namely in India and China (Fig. 6.16). However, these two countries maintain the highest levels of value added proportion in the agricultural sector, namely India. South Africa has the lowest weight of value added in the farming sector, despite having the greatest land percentage in agriculture and a good performance in agricultural productivity.

India, between 1961 and 2012, had the lowest contribution from industry towards the GDP (Fig. 6.17), as well as Brazil and South Africa, from the beginning of the 1990s (about 30 % in 2012). The best performance was verified in China and in the Russian Federation.

The contribution of services to the GDP is higher in Brazil and South Africa (about 70 % in 2012) and lower in China (Fig. 6.18). If it is considered that industry is the engine of the economy, as argued by some economic theories (Keynesians, New Economic Geography, etc.), then China and Russia have some advantage in the field of international competition.

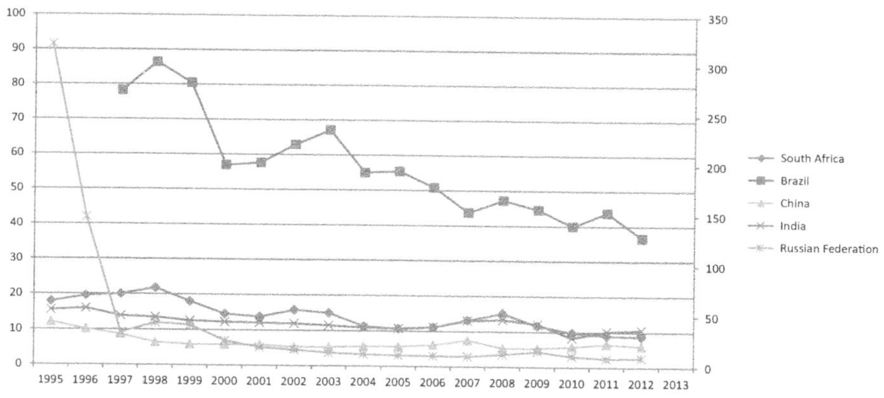


**Fig. 6.11** Lending interest rate (%) among BRICS countries

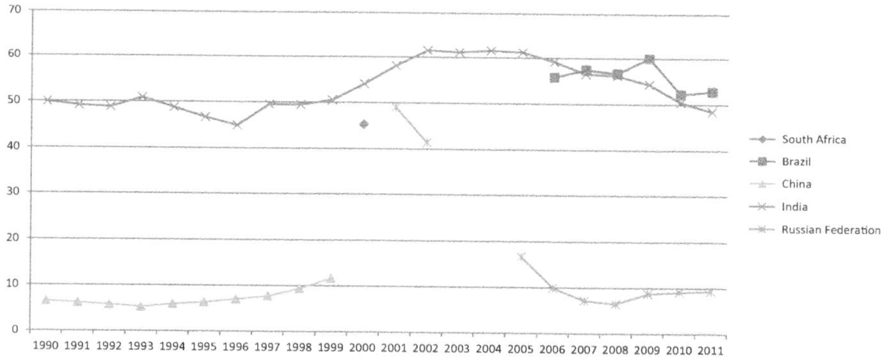


**Fig. 6.12** Central government debt, total (% of GDP) among BRICS countries

It is since the 1980s that China and, to a certain point, India have had the best performance in terms of GDP annual growth (Fig. 6.19). However, China, for example, had annual growth rates of about −27 and −6 % at the beginning of the 1960s.

The GDP per capita (at current prices) increased (1961–2012) for every BRICS country, but has grown more over recent years, respectively, in Russia, Brazil, China, and South Africa and yet lower in India (Fig. 6.20). In 2012 the GDP per capita in the Russian Federation was about US$14,000 and in India less than US $2,000. This is a significant difference in terms of welfare for the population among the two countries.

Russia presents the best rates of literacy (Fig. 6.21), about 100 % in recent years. The other countries have improved this variable in recent years, but India is the country with the lowest literacy rate of about 60 % over the last few years.

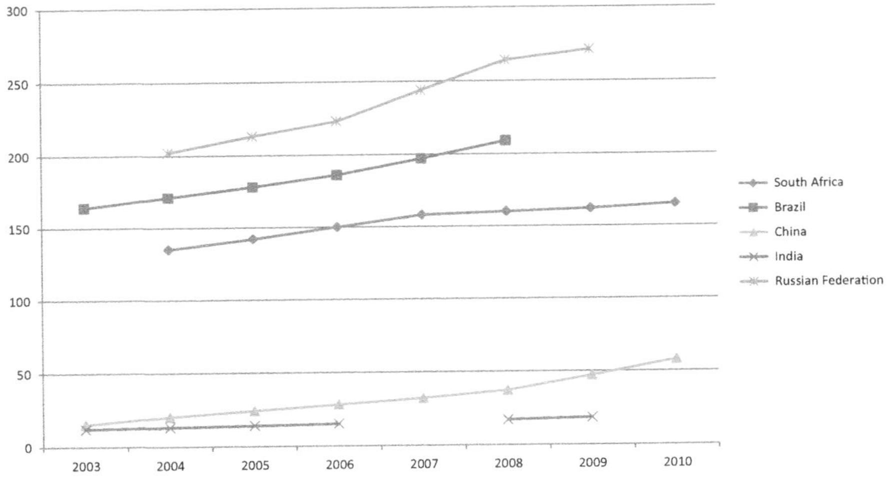


Fig. 6.13 Motor vehicles (per 1,000 people) among BRICS countries

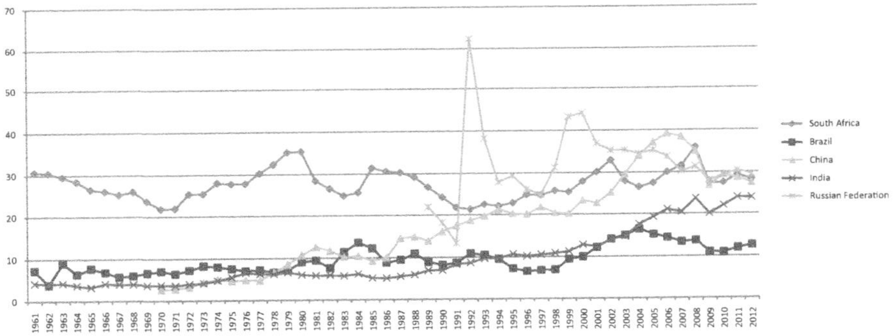


Fig. 6.14 Exports of goods and services (% of GDP) among BRICS countries

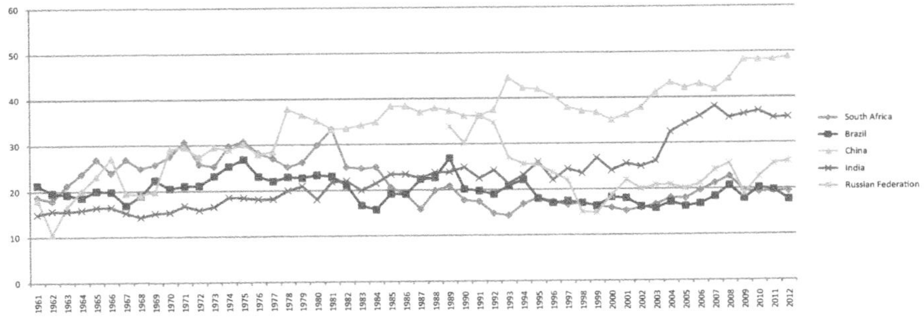


Fig. 6.15 Gross capital formation (% of GDP) among BRICS countries

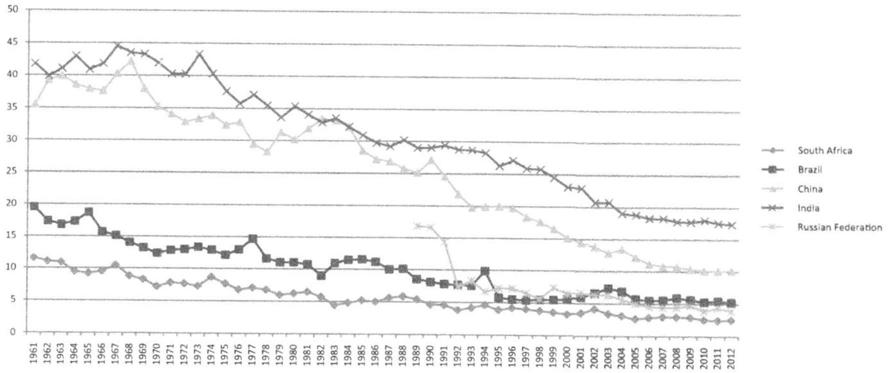


Fig. 6.16 Agriculture, value added (% of GDP) among BRICS countries

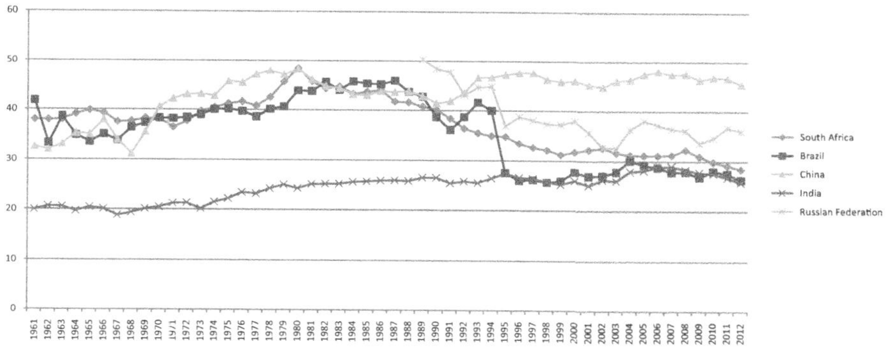


Fig. 6.17 Industry, value added (% of GDP) among BRICS countries

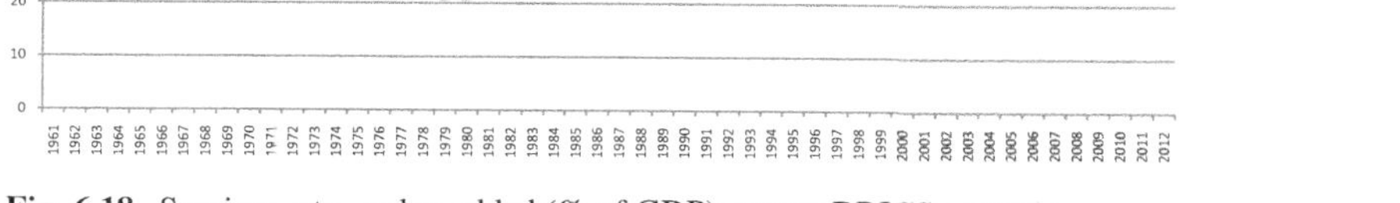


Fig. 6.18 Services, etc., value added (% of GDP) among BRICS countries

India is the country with complications, in terms of malnutrition prevalent in children under 5 years of age, with percentages of about 50 % (Fig. 6.22). The database used has no statistical information relating to this variable for Russia.

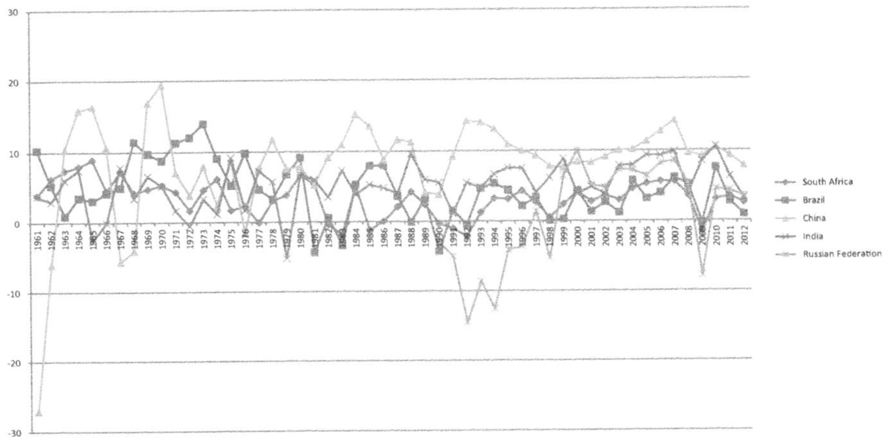


**Fig. 6.19** GDP growth (annual %) among BRICS countries

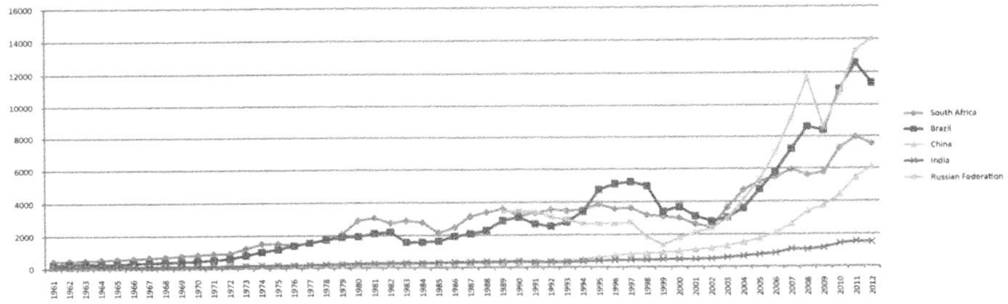


**Fig. 6.20** GDP per capita (current US$) among BRICS countries

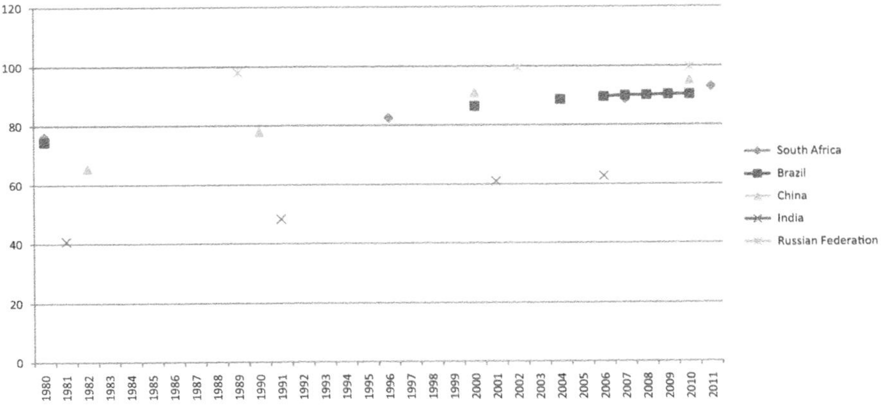


**Fig. 6.21** Literacy rate, adult total (% of people ages 15 and above) among BRICS countries

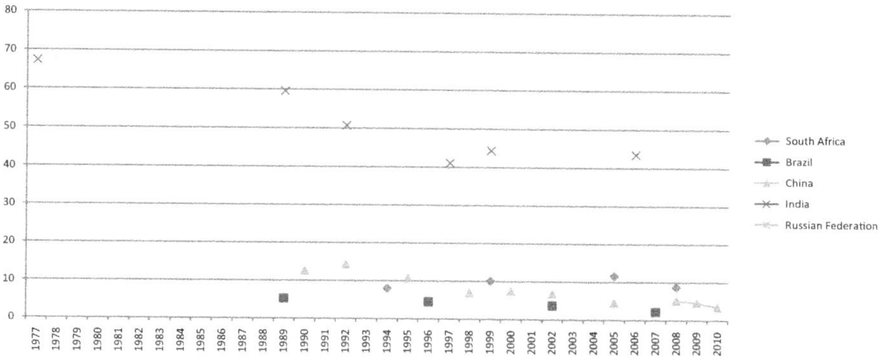


**Fig. 6.22** Malnutrition prevalence, weight for age (% of children under 5) among BRICS countries

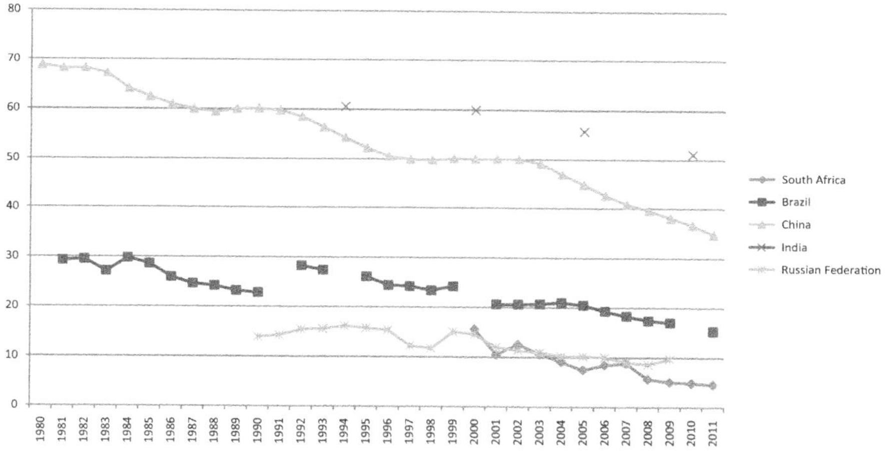


**Fig. 6.23** Employment in agriculture (% of total employment) among BRICS countries

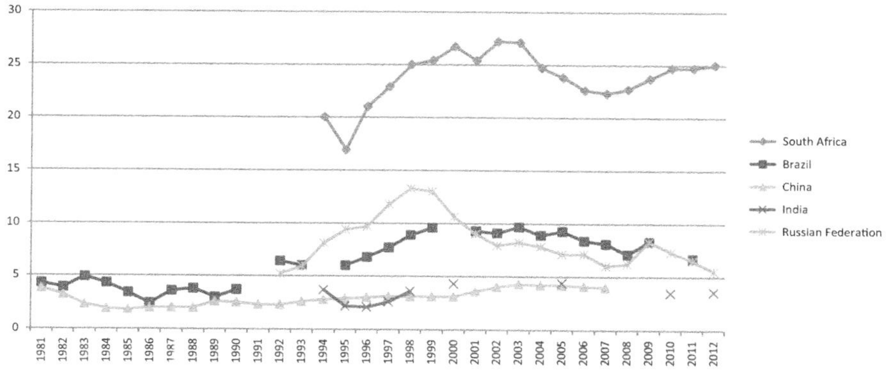


**Fig. 6.24** Unemployment, total (% of total labor force) among BRICS countries

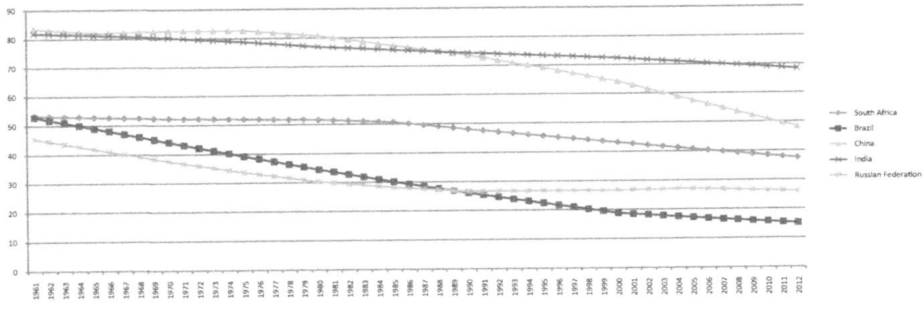


**Fig. 6.25** Rural population (% of total population) among BRICS countries

The percentage of employment in agriculture is lower in South Africa and the Russian Federation and higher in India (about 50 % in recent years) and China (Fig. 6.23). This is more or less in accordance with other previous accounts made before for other variables.

The unemployment rate may aggravate economic performance, namely for South Africa which presents values for this variable of about 25 % since 1998 (Fig. 6.24). India and China are the countries with a lower level of unemployment. The case of India may be explained by the weight of agriculture in the economy.

The rural population (Fig. 6.25), in 2012, was about 70 % in India, 50 % China, 40 % South Africa, 25 % Russia, and 15 % Brazil.

## 4 Results

The following Tables 6.1 and 6.2 show the results obtained for each BRICS country, using statistical information from 1961 until 2012, taking the function of production as a base (Cobb and Douglas 1928), where the dependent variable is the agricultural output (represented by the Agricultural value added in percentage of the GDP) and the independent variables are those which were previously analyzed. All the estimations were made with the Stata (2014) software and through the time series econometric techniques.

The results in Table 6.1 are relative to the estimations made before and the results in Table 6.2 were obtained in regressions made after to try and solve the problems identified by the "Ramsey RESET test using powers of the fitted values" related with the lack of variables in the model of some BRICS countries, namely South Africa, Brazil, China, and India.

In Table 6.1 the statistical tests "Augmented Dickey-Fuller test for unit root" and "EG-ADF test for co-integration" reveal no complications with the unit roots and with the co-integration of the variables in the models. The autocorrelation tests, namely "Portmanteau test for white noise for autocorrelation," "Durbin's alternative test for autocorrelation," and "Breusch–Godfrey LM test for autocorrelation" reveal some problems with this statistical infraction and therefore the "Prais–

**Table 6.1** Results obtained with time series econometric techniques, based on the function of production model (linear model obtained with logarithms), for the agricultural output in the period 1961–2012

| | South Africa | Brazil | China | India | Russia |
|---|---|---|---|---|---|
| Model | Prais–Winsten | ARCH family regression | Prais–Winsten (Robus) | Prais–Winsten | Prais–Winsten |
| Constant | 0.542* (3.130) [0.011] | 10.309* (3.080) [0.002] | −3.203* (−4.990) [0.000] | 5.552* (4.790) [0.000] | |
| Agriculture value added per worker (constant 2005 US$) | | −0.797* (−3.490) [0.000] | | −0.0376* (−2.020) [0.052] | |
| Employment in agriculture (% of total employment) | 0.272* (3.350) [0.007] | | 1.550* (9.690) [0.000] | | 0.829* (4.660) [0.000] |
| Augmented Dickey–Fuller test for unit root | −7.092* [0.000] | −6.115* [0.000] | −5.456* [0.000] | −5.765* [0.000] | −3.077* [0.028] |
| EG-ADF test for cointegration | −2.033 [0.272] | −2.489 [0.118] | −2.063 [0.259] | −1.973 [0.298] | −2.320 [0.165] |
| Portmanteau test for white noise for autocorrelation | 296.018* [0.000] | 308.999* [0.000] | 322.740* [0.000] | 320.681* [0.000] | 30.878* [0.000] |
| Durbin's alternative test for autocorrelation | 0.843 [0.358] | 20.264* [0.000] | 9.810* [0.001] | 6.336* [0.011] | 0.600 [0.438] |
| Breusch–Godfrey LM test for autocorrelation | 1.144 [0.284] | 12.646* [0.000] | 8.302* [0.004] | 5.754* [0.016] | 0.739 [0.389] |
| Breusch–Pagan/Cook–Weisberg test for heteroskedasticity | 1.730 [0.188] | 0.000 [0.984] | 6.350* [0.011] | 0.010 [0.929] | 0.040 [0.843] |
| Ramsey RESET test using powers of the fitted values | 18.570* [0.001] | 5.100* [0.008] | 10.490* [0.000] | 3.940* [0.018] | 2.470 [0.111] |
| LM test for autoregressive conditional heteroskedasticity (ARCH) | 0.551 [0.458] | 4.386* [0.036] | 1.194 [0.274] | 0.092 [0.761] | 0.527 [0.467] |

*Note*: *Statistically significant at 5 %

Winsten" time series estimation method was used. The "Breusch–Pagan/Cook–Weisberg test for heteroskedasticity" test revealed problems with the heteroskedasticity in China and so the "Prais–Winsten robust" was considered to solve this statistical infraction. The "LM test for autoregressive conditional heteroskedasticity (ARCH)" test presents difficulties in Brazil and taking this information into account the "ARCH family regression" estimation method was considered. Relative to the values of the coefficients, it is possible to conclude that the proportion of employment in agriculture has had a positive effect in the agricultural output in South Africa, China, and in the Russian Federation. The more important influence comes from the China with a contribution from employment in the output of 1.550,

**Table 6.2** Results obtained with time series econometric techniques, considering the function of production model extended with other variables (linear model obtained with logarithms), for the agricultural output in the period 1961–2012

| | South Africa | Brazil | China | India |
|---|---|---|---|---|
| Model | Prais–Winsten (Robust) | Prais–Winsten | Prais–Winsten (Robust) | Prais–Winsten |
| Constant | | 12.559* (6.850) [0.000] | | 9.333* (13.970) [0.000] |
| Agriculture value added per worker (constant 2005 US$) | | −1.108* (−8.240) [0.000] | | −0.720* (−4.900) [0.000] |
| Employment in agriculture (% of total employment) | | −1.022* (−3.690) [0.001] | 1.228* (2.350) [0.026] | |
| Additional variable[a] | 0.467* (3.020) [0.014] | 0.520* (6.380) [0.000] | −0.780* (−4.180) [0.000] | −0.504* (−4.630) [0.000] |
| Breusch–Pagan/Cook–Weisberg test for heteroskedasticity | 4.190* [0.040] | 0.300 [0.586] | 7.590* [0.005] | 0.000 [0.960] |
| Ramsey RESET test using powers of the fitted values | 0.240 [0.864] | 8.800* [0.000] | 36.620* [0.000] | 2.760** [0.061] |
| LM test for autoregressive conditional heteroskedasticity (ARCH) | 0.211 [0.645] | 0.128 [0.720] | 2.677 [0.101] | 0.771 [0.380] |

*Note*: *Statistically significant at 5 %; **Statistically significant at 10 %
[a]Lending interest rate (%) for South Africa, Exports of goods and services (% of GDP) for Brazil, Services, etc., value added (% of GDP) for China, and Gross capital formation (% of GDP) for India

followed by Russia with 0.829. On the other hand, agricultural productivity presents a negative in Brazil and India, of −0.797 and −0.376, respectively.

For the results in Table 6.2 the models were extended with the lending interest rate (%) for South Africa, export of goods and services (% of GDP) for Brazil, services, etc., value added (% of GDP) for China, and gross capital formation (% of GDP) for India.

The problems of having a lack of variables in the models were solved for South Africa and, to a certain degree for India, but not for Brazil and China with the variables considered in this study. This may be an interesting issue for future research. The lending interest rate (%) for South Africa and the export of goods and services (% of GDP) for Brazil have a positive impact on the agricultural output, in contrast with services, etc., value added (% of GDP) for China, and gross capital formation (% of GDP) for India.

**Conclusions**

The contexts for these five BRICS countries are in reality very different, not only in terms of economics but also in terms of dimensions.

Some of the preoccupations within the Brazilian agricultural sector are related to environmental problems, the utilization of farms to produce sugarcane for biofuel and with the Amazonian occupation. However, recent farming policies have improved the performance of this sector and made it into one of the most dynamic economic sectors.

In the Russian Federation some of the main concerns relate to the environmental impact of agriculture, climate change, and land privatization after the end of the Soviet Union.

Some central questions in Indian farming practices are about the renewable energies and with the agricultural practices which are compatible with the environment, namely those related to organic farming.

The priorities in China are directed namely towards industry, rather than for agriculture. However, the production of grain continues to be one of the most important and strategic productions in China.

In South Africa, namely due to the location of this country, the challenges are related to climate change and water management.

On the other hand, the data description made before revealed that, namely India, has many economic and social fragilities and, in some cases, so too does Brazil. This shows some difficulties for the future, in terms of competition across the international markets. For example, India still maintains some economic and social problems; specifically in terms of literacy rates and malnutrition prevalent in children under 5 years of age, and Brazil suffers lending rates of about 40 %. At the agricultural level, China and India have a lower level of farming productivity whereas South Africa and Russia possess the best performances. However, the evolution context of the farming contribution to GDP and for employment is, more or less, the inverse.

The results obtained with the estimations confirm the inverse relationship between agricultural productivity and the contribution of agriculture to GDP and the positive interrelationship between the weight/level of employment in agriculture and the proportion of the agricultural output for the national income of each BRICS country.

## References

Aguiar, A. P. D., Câmara, G., & Escada, M. I. S. (2007). Spatial statistical analysis of land-use determinants in the Brazilian Amazonia: Exploring intra-regional heterogeneity. *Ecological Modelling, 209*, 169–188.

Beurs, K. M., Wright, C. K., & Henebry, G. M. (2009). Dual scale trend analysis for evaluating climatic and anthropogenic effects on the vegetated land surface in Russia and Kazakhstan. *Environmental Research Letters, 4*(045012), 11pp.

Brosig, S., Teuber, R., Levkovych, I., Thiele, R., & Glauben, T. (2013). Introduction to the special feature: Will the BRIC decade continue? The role of rural areas and agriculture. *Journal of Agricultural Economics, 64*(1), 145–150.

Cobb, C. W., & Douglas, P. H. (1928). A theory of production. *American Economic Review, 18* (Suppl), 139–165.

D'Haese, M., & Huylenbroeck, G. V. (2005). The rise of supermarkets and changing expenditure patterns of poor rural households case study in the Transkei area, South Africa. *Food Policy, 30*, 97–113.

Hall, J., Matos, S., & Langford, C. H. (2008). Social exclusion and transgenic technology: The case of Brazilian agriculture. *Journal of Business Ethics, 77*, 45–63.

Hassan, R., & Thurlow, J. (2011). Macro–micro feedback links of water management in South Africa: CGE analyses of selected policy regimes. *Agricultural Economics, 42*, 235–247.

Helfand, S. M., & Rezende, G. C. (2004). The impact of sector-specific and economy-wide policy reforms on the agricultural sector in Brazil: 1980–98. *Contemporary Economic Policy, 22*(2), 194–212.

Hurt, R. D. (2010). American and Chinese Agricultural Policy since 1949: An overview. *Procedia Social and Behavioral Sciences, 41*, 6692–6701.

Lerman, Z., & Shagaida, N. (2007). Land policies and agricultural land markets in Russia. *Land Use Policy, 24*, 14–23.

Moeletsi, M. E., Moopisa, S. G., Walker, S., & Tsubo, M. (2013). Development of an agroclimatological risk tool for dryland maize production in the Free State Province of South Africa. *Computers and Electronics in Agriculture, 95*, 108–121.

Morse, S., Bennett, R., & Ismael, Y. (2006). Environmental impact of genetically modified cotton in South Africa. *Agriculture, Ecosystems and Environment, 117*, 277–289.

Purushothaman, S., Patil, S., & Francis, I. (2013). Assessing the impact of policy-driven agricultural practices in Karnataka, India. *Sustainability Science, 8*, 173–185.

Radulovic, V. (2005). Are new institutional economics enough? Promoting photovoltaics in India's agricultural sector. *Energy Policy, 33*, 1883–1899.

Sainz, M. B. (2009). Commercial cellulosic ethanol: The role of plant-expressed enzymes. *In Vitro Cellular and Developmental Biology—Plant, 45*, 314–329.

Sills, E. O., & Caviglia-Harris, J. L. (2008). Evolution of the Amazonian frontier: Land values in Rondônia, Brazil. *Land Use Policy, 26*, 55–67.

Smith, P., Smith, J. U., Franko, U., Kuka, K., Romanenkov, V. A., Shevtsova, L. K., et al. (2007). Changes in mineral soil organic carbon stocks in the croplands of European Russia and the Ukraine, 1990–2070; comparison of three models and implications for climate mitigation. *Regional Environmental Change, 7*, 105–119.

Souza, H. N., Graaff, J., & Pulleman, M. M. (2012). Strategies and economics of farming systems with coffee in the Atlantic Rainforest Biome. *Agroforestry Systems, 84*, 227–242.

Stata. (2014). *Statistics/Data analysis*. StataCorp, LP.

World Bank (2014). Several statistics. Washington, DC: World Bank.

Yong-fu, C., Zhi-gang, W., Tie-hui, Z., Lei, Y., Guo-ying, M., & Hsiao-ping, C. (2013). Agricultural policy, climate factors and grain output: Evidence from household survey data in rural China. *Journal of Integrative Agriculture, 12*(1), 169–183.

# Chapter 7
# Evaluation of Sustainable Economic Growth in Portuguese Agriculture and Other Sectors

Vítor João Pereira Domingues Martinho

## 1 Introduction

The tradeoff between economic growth and sustainability will be the big challenge in the future, considering the levels of economic growth needed and the increasing signs of sustainability problems, in different contexts (environmental, social, etc.) verified in many regions of the world.

In this way, all the good research studies in these subjects are well intended to shine some light on these problematic questions and to try and find some solutions for the conciliation between the earth's limits and human presence.

This study intends to be innovative in these fields, because it utilizes a Keynesian model based on the second law of Kaldor (1966, 1967) extended with new variables to capture the different levels of sustainability. There was no evidence found in theoretical literature for any study about the relationship between sustainability and economic growth using the relationship involving productivity growth as a function of the output growth (second law of Kaldor). In another way, performing this analysis for Portugal can be seen as another pertinent contribution, as there are very few studies concerning these aspects for Portuguese regions.

Indeed, Portugal has improved its performance, in a sustainable way, in many social, demographic, and educational indicators over recent years. This is proved by the data used, in this study, for the variables relating to population density, life expectancy, number of doctors in medicine, human resources in science and technology, and the infant mortality rate. The question here is to try to analyze if the evolution of these indicators is compatible with economic growth, from a sustainable perspective.

Nowadays, this is an important topic to discuss, what with the current debate in Portugal about sustainability and the pertinence, in terms of economic growth and

V.J.P.D. Martinho (✉)
Agricultural School, Polytechnic Institute of Viseu, 3500 Viseu, Portugal
e-mail: vdmartinho@esav.ipv.pt



V.J.P.D. Martinho (ed.), *The Agricultural Economics of the 21st Century*,
DOI 10.1007/978-3-319-09471-7_7

of the social public policies, considering the financial problems related with the Portuguese public budget.

In reality, there are many problems with the national public debt and the national economic growth, but without adjusted policies more problems may arise, namely those related to social, environmental, and demographic sustainability. The uneven development, in Portugal, between the north and south, between inland regions and on the shoreline, has been occurring over many years, but with unadjusted policies these asymmetries can increase.

## 2 Literature Background

Economic growth with sustainability in different areas of society, namely environmental, social, economic, demographic, and educational, is, indeed, the greatest challenge for world economies both nowadays and for the future. In this way, many authors such as Munasinghe (1995), Smulders (1995), Young (1999), Santagata (2002), Chukwu (2005), Garnaut (2005), Desrochers (2006), Greyson (2007), Fleisher et al. (2009), Kumagai (2009), Min et al. (2009), and Asheim and Mitra (2010), among others referred to below, have all discussed and demonstrated a strong concern for the issues related to this problem, which is a good sign, considering the pertinence of these questions for the future evolution of societies in several perspectives.

Certainly, the evolution of an economy is a complex process with several aspects and is a result of many interactions, such as those related to the aims of economic agents in obtaining great profits, conciliated with improvements in productivity of the factors and favorable public policies, the government's controls for climate change, taxes, wage pressures, competition, physical capital, consumers' preferences and capacity to consume, social conditions, and the availability of a workforce (Weber et al. 2005). The productivity of the factors is dependent upon the qualifications for human factors and on the level of scientific and technological development. Watanabe et al. (2005) also concluded about the importance of research, innovation, and technological development and diversification in some patterns of sustainable economic growth. The investment in scientific fields and in human resources may be determinant for economies to obtain competitive advantages, in the current world with high levels of globalization, in accordance with social and environmental sustainability, creating more jobs, improving efficiency, and preserving natural resources. From a similar perspective, Clarke and Islam (2005) analyzed the relationship between economic growth and welfare, considering social, economic, environmental, and political variables as well as some related to income, education, health, roads, the levels of urbanization, consumption, and others. They concluded that in some developing economies, without adjusted public policies, at some levels of economic growth, the countries achieve diminishing or negative welfare returns. In these cases the cost of economic growth can sometimes surpass the benefits. The relationship between welfare (measured by the domestic product), economic growth, and sustainable development was also a concern of

Dasgupta and Mitra (1999). About 2 years before, Islam et al. (2003) found similar conclusions, similar to those of Clarke and Islam (2005), considering variables linked to consumption, environmental quality, investment, technical progress, employment, workforce, social indicators, levels of waste, renewable resources, etc. The availability of scarce resources will be the big problem for future generations and may be the main determinant for the compatibility of sustainability with economic growth over the next few decades (Scholl and Semmler 2002).

Economic growth with financial and economic sustainability and stability is an issue in focus today for many countries facing their current domestic problems, including western and developed economies. For example, the discussion about the dimension of public debt is very much the order of the day in these economies, mostly because of the image of stability which is necessary to project to their creditors rather than the real implications of these debts in the economic evolution of these countries. Indeed Greiner (2013), with an endogenous growth model, found that the public debt does not influence the economic growth, in the long run, and does not change employment, but rather only affects economic stability. Sustainable economic growth in poor countries is another concern. Hunt (2011) defends an economic growth in these countries focused more upon the creation of institutions that promoted economic independence and competition rather than some form of investment. Economic sovereignty can be determinant, namely that related to the control of firms, specifically those with a high level of technology, export-oriented, and with great influence upon the domestic economy. This can be the main explanation for the recent differing behavior of the Swedish and Irish economies (Andreosso-O'Callaghan and Lenihan 2011). National policies should be able to promote some national industrial independence in order to mitigate the international impact upon the economy in times of crisis. The industrial sector and other sectors of tradable goods play a crucial role in the expansion of exports with direct implications for economic growth and for balanced job creation (N'Zué 2003).

In terms of economic growth and environmental sustainability, Chang and Carballo (2011) analyzed the relationship between energy use, carbon emissions, and economic growth in countries of Latin America and the Caribbean, with a co-integration model considering a vector error correction modeling, a vector autoregression, and Granger causality. The results show that it is difficult to implement strategies to promote more efficient energy consumption without affecting economic growth. The compromise between economic growth and the environment is often difficult to achieve in many countries. The discussions about the relationship between the environment and economic growth have occurred for decades (Cole 1999). In literature from the 1960s to the 1980s, few have clarified the questions related to the interactions between economic growth and the environment. Some authors defended that economic growth with sufficient technological progress will preserve the natural environment and others had the opinion that unlimited growth was not possible. In the 1990s the econometric estimations do not find, again, a unique explanation for these relationships, due to the varying effects of, for example, pollutants. Even the environmental Kuznets curve, that predicts some regularity between economic growth and the reduction of problems within the environment, merits many criticisms from Stern et al (1996). This author found that this regularity only occurs when based upon many unreal suppositions, namely that there is no influence upon environmental quality in production and no influence upon international trade. Zuo and Ai (2011) also studied the relationship between economic growth, sustainability, and energy consumption, with an endogenous growth model. They concluded that it is important to improve technologies of extraction and use of energy and to decrease dependence on nonrenewable energies. Indeed, countries such as China, for example, had to consider for their great levels of economic growth implementing policies of reducing the intensity of energy consumption and the consequent carbon emissions, namely due to the use of fossil fuels. Technical efficiency and technological progress were the source, after the Chinese economic reform in the 1970s, for improvements in productivity and of the consequent high and continuous levels of economic growth in China (Wu 2000). Certainly, if China benefited from a first stage form of some process of catching-up, it was after their successful economic growth, which in turn brought about innovation and returns from the investments made in new technologies. The efficiency and the necessity for adjusted policies in consumption and production of energy in developing countries was also analyzed by Keong (2005). The improvements in the evolution of economies and societies imply increased needs for energy by firms and by families and this can be solved by increasing energy production, but also with improvements in consumption behavior. Energy is crucial for economic evolution, but this progress must use clean energy, in an efficient way and competitively and by upgrading in productivity (Hefner 1995). It is also important to find strategies which distribute the income obtained in a perspective of sustainable and balanced development compatible with the environment (Li and Oberheitmann 2009). The relationship between economic growth and environmental sustainability was, also, examined by Chi et al. (2009), using an endogenous economic growth model. However, economic growth and environmental sustainability may not be reconcilable, considering the current demands for economic growth in order to reduce national public debts (Alier 2009). Fundamentally the questions related to environmental sustainability are about the efficiency of the exploitation, utilization, and resulting daily waste for natural resources from the daily activity of the various economic agents (families, enterprises, etc.). One of these crucial, yet limited, natural resources is drinkable water. Hallowes et al. (2008), for example, stressed the importance for efficient water use in South Africa, given its scarcity. It is predicted that in decades to come, water will be the major problem for sustainability in many countries including the more developed economies, facing high levels of pollution in soils, rivers, seas, and the atmosphere. The greenhouse effect derived from the high index of gaseous emissions has promoted climatic changes with great implications for the availability of water, namely in the world's southern regions. In order to solve the greenhouse problem, it is fundamental to think about better policies and regulations for the energy market (Ayres et al. 2007). There is a new concept of environmentally friendly economic growth which is referred to as "green growth." Green growth is based on the following principles (Janicke 2012): increasing resource productivity, refinanced investments for efficiency returns, innovation in conserving resources, improvements in the green markets, and prevention of damages from economic growth. However, this author claims that the best solution would be for rich countries to reduce the domestic product increase and improve their eco-innovation.

From a demographic point of view, Bai et al. (2012) analyzed the relationship between population indicators and sustainable economic growth in several cities and provinces of China. They found that cities with greater wealth and with a higher population tend to obtain more income and, in turn, attract more population. On the other hand, they also found that there are circular and cumulative processes between the population demographic and economic growth. In this way if the Chinese authorities intend to have a sustainable economic growth, they must clearly define their adjusted public policies.

## 3 Model, Data, and Results

The model considered was the equation of the second law of Kaldor, where the productivity growth rate is dependent upon the output growth rate, extended with more new variables related with demographic, social, and educational aspects, namely the following: the population density, life expectancy, number of doctors in medicine, human resources in science and technology, and the infant mortality rate. The outputs considered in the variables of the original Kaldor second law equation were used in real prices, after having removed inflation with consumer index prices. This model was built for the different Portuguese sectors considered in this current study, namely the following: agriculture, forestry, and fishing; industry (except construction); manufacturing; construction; wholesale and retail trade, transport, accommodation, and food service activities, information technology and communication; financial and insurance activities, real estate activities, and professional, scientific, and technical activities, administrative and support services; public administration and defense; compulsory social security, education, human health, and social work activities, arts, entertainment, and recreation; repair of household goods; and other services. The original equation of the Kaldor second law captures endogeneity of the factors, economic dynamics, spillover effects, and increasing returns to scale.

The data used were those related with the variables referred to before and were obtained, for the period 1995–2010, from Eurostat (2013) for the seven Portuguese NUTs II. Indeed, Portugal has an unbalanced development between the several seven regions, where two are islands, and it will be interesting to analyze these dynamics in their relationship to economic growth and the indicators related to other components of society, whether trying to identify compatibility and sustainability or not.

The results were obtained with the Stata (2011) software, with panel data methods (namely fixed and random effects), and tested with many statistical tests which are presented in Table 7.1 (where the new variables are considered in levels) and in Table 7.2 (where the new variables are considered for growth rate). The idea

**Table 7.1** Estimation results of the Kaldor second law equation extended (new variables in levels), with panel data, for Portuguese economic sectors, over the period 1995–2010 and over the seven Portuguese NUTs II

| | Const.[a] | Coef.[b] | Coef.[c] | Coef.[d] | Coef.[e] | Coef.[f] | Coef.[g] | F/Wald (mod.)[h] | F (Fe_OLS)[i] | Corr (u_i)[j] | F (Re_OLS)[k] | Hausman[l] | $R^2$ [m] |
|---|---|---|---|---|---|---|---|---|---|---|---|---|---|
| All economy | | | | | | | | | | | | | |
| Fe[n] | −0.375** (−1.730) | 0.847* (16.290) | 6.640e-06 (0.040) | 0.004 (1.070) | 0.001** (1.920) | −8.150e-06 (−0.130) | 0.001 (0.800) | 49.180* | 6.390* | −0.747 | | 45.570* | 0.762 |
| Agriculture, forestry, and fishing | | | | | | | | | | | | | |
| OLS[o] | −0.0442 (−0.070) | 1.006* (8.940) | 0.000 (0.400) | 0.001 (0.150) | 0.000 (0.100) | −0.000 (−0.810) | −0.006 (−1.130) | | | | 0.000 | 11.700** | 0.438 |
| Industry (except construction) | | | | | | | | | | | | | |
| OLS[o] | −0.318 (−1.390) | 0.895* (18.710) | 0.000 (1.260) | 0.004 (1.460) | −0.000 (−0.150) | −0.000 (−0.980) | −0.002 (−0.720) | | | | 0.000 | 10.960** | 0.778 |
| Manufacturing | | | | | | | | | | | | | |
| OLS[o] | −0.403 (−1.490) | 0.871* (20.500) | 0.000 (0.870) | 0.005 (1.480) | 0.000 (0.340) | −0.000 (−1.290) | −.000 (−0.120) | | | | 0.000 | 12.020** | 0.810 |
| Construction | | | | | | | | | | | | | |
| OLS[o] | −0.112 (−0.250) | 0.413* (6.330) | 0.000 (0.750) | 0.002 (0.350) | −0.000 (−0.940) | 0.000 (0.850) | −0.005 (−1.210) | | | | 0.000 | 8.340 | 0.270 |
| Wholesale and retail trade; transport, accommodation, and food service activities; information and communication | | | | | | | | | | | | | |
| Fe[n] | −0.448 (−1.300) | 0.923* (13.340) | −0.000 (−0.090) | 0.004 (0.660) | 0.001** (1.880) | 0.000 (0.390) | 0.006* (2.590) | 33.390* | 2.300* | −0.777 | | 13.11* | 0.685 |
| Financial and insurance activities; real estate activities; professional, scientific, and technical activities; administrative and support service | | | | | | | | | | | | | |
| OLS[o] | −0.297 (−0.790) | 1.032* (21.240) | 0.000 (0.380) | 0.004 (0.700) | 0.000 (0.420) | −0.000 (−1.610) | 0.000 (0.060) | | | | 0.000 | 9.950** | 0.818 |

| | | | | | | | | | | | | | |
|---|---|---|---|---|---|---|---|---|---|---|---|---|---|
| Public administration and defense; compulsory social security, education, human health, and social work activities; arts, entertainment, and recreation; repair of household goods; and other services | | | | | | | | | | | | | |
| OLS[o] | −0.148 (−1.010) | 0.775* (14.450) | 5.490e-06 (0.300) | 0.002 (0.970) | 2.000e−06 (0.030) | −0.000 (−0.490) | −0.002 (−1.080) | | | | 0.000 | 6.890 | 0.700 |

*Note*: [a]Constant; [b]Kaldor second law coefficient; [c]Population density coefficient; [d]Life expectancy coefficient; [e]Medicine doctors coefficient; [f]Human resources in science and technology coefficient; [g]Infant mortality rate coefficient; [h]Test F for fixed effects model and test Wald for random effects; [i]Test F for fixed effects or OLS (Ho is OLS); [j]Correlation between errors and regressors in fixed effects; [k]Test F for random effects or OLS (Ho is OLS); [l]Hausman test (Ho is GLS); [m]R square; [n]Fixed effects (Fe); [o]Ordinary last square (OLS)

*Statically significant at 5 %; **Statically significant at 10 %

**Table 7.2** Estimation results of the Kaldor second law equation extended (new variables in growth rates) with panel data, for Portuguese economic sectors, over the period 1995–2010 and over the seven Portuguese NUTs II

| | Const.[a] | Coef.[b] | Coef.[c] | Coef.[d] | Coef.[e] | Coef.[f] | Coef.[g] | F/Wald (mod.)[h] | F (Fe_OLS)[i] | Corr (u_i)[j] | F (Re_OLS)[k] | Hausman[l] | $R^2$ [m] |
|---|---|---|---|---|---|---|---|---|---|---|---|---|---|
| All economy | | | | | | | | | | | | | |
| OLS[n] | −0.002<br>(−0.400) | 0.656*<br>(12.770) | −0.458*<br>(−2.570) | 0.176<br>(0.500) | 0.083<br>(0.690) | −0.000<br>(−0.020) | −0.000<br>(−0.020) | | | | 0.000 | 5.610 | 0.664 |
| Agriculture, forestry, and fishing | | | | | | | | | | | | | |
| OLS[n] | 0.004<br>(0.280) | 0.980*<br>(8.900) | −1.767*<br>(−2.830) | 1.017<br>(0.770) | 0.490<br>(1.120) | 0.040<br>(0.730) | −0.031<br>(−1.480) | | | | 0.000 | 3.810 | 0.485 |
| Industry (except construction) | | | | | | | | | | | | | |
| OLS[n] | 0.009<br>(1.580) | 0.835*<br>(17.810) | −0.133<br>(−0.530) | −0.010<br>(−0.020) | 0.181<br>(1.030) | 0.036<br>(1.630) | −0.007<br>(−0.870) | | 2.040** | | | 210.110* | 0.765 |
| Manufacturing | | | | | | | | | | | | | |
| OLS[n] | 0.008<br>(1.170) | 0.830*<br>(19.510) | −0.132<br>(−0.440) | 0.212<br>(0.350) | 0.156<br>(0.750) | 0.040<br>(1.510) | −0.002<br>(−0.190) | | 1.490 | | | 14.900* | 0.793 |
| Construction | | | | | | | | | | | | | |
| OLS[n] | −0.002<br>(−0.210) | 0.361*<br>(5.960) | −0.745<br>(−1.550) | 0.611<br>(0.620) | 0.068<br>(0.200) | 0.011<br>(0.250) | −0.001<br>(−0.040) | | | | 0.000 | 1.680 | 0.250 |
| Wholesale and retail trade, transport, accommodation, and food service activities, information and communication | | | | | | | | | | | | | |
| OLS[n] | −0.010<br>(−1.580) | 0.762*<br>(11.280) | −0.309<br>(−1.200) | −0.167<br>(−0.320) | 0.012<br>(0.070) | −0.025<br>(−1.110) | 0.010<br>(1.200) | | | | 0.000 | 1.470 | 0.603 |
| Financial and insurance activities, real estate activities, professional, scientific, and technical activities, administrative and support service | | | | | | | | | | | | | |
| OLS[n] | −0.041*<br>(−4.340) | 1.040*<br>(21.400) | 0.349<br>(0.870) | 0.943<br>(1.170) | 0.561<br>(2.050) | 0.008<br>(0.220) | 0.005<br>(0.380) | | | | 0.000 | 1.320 | 0.825 |

| | | | | | | | | | | | | | |
|---|---|---|---|---|---|---|---|---|---|---|---|---|---|
| Public administration and defense; compulsory social security; education; human health and social work activities; arts, entertainment, and recreation; repair of household goods; and other services | | | | | | | | | | | | | |
| OLS[n] | −0.008* (−2.100) | 0.657* (14.080) | 0.013 (0.090) | 0.132 (0.420) | 0.110 (1.040) | −0.024 (−1.800) | 0.013* (2.570) | | 1.140 | | | 24.060* | 0.704 |

*Note*: [a]Constant; [b]Kaldor second law coefficient; [c]Population density coefficient; [d]Life expectancy coefficient; [e]Medicine doctors coefficient; [f]Human resources in science and technology coefficient; [g]Infant mortality rate coefficient; [h]Test F for fixed effects model and test Wald for random effects; [i]Test F for fixed effects or OLS (Ho is OLS); [j]Correlation between errors and regressors in fixed effects; [k]Test F for random effects or OLS (Ho is OLS); [l]Hausman test (Ho is GLS); [m]R square; [n]Ordinary last square (OLS)

*Statistically significant at 5 %; **Statistically significant at 10 %

of considering these two models was to analyze the effects, in levels and in growth rate, of the social, demographic, and educational indicators in economic growth (represented by the productivity and its influence on the output).

By observing the two tables, it is possible to conclude that the indicators related to sustainability and represented by the new variables have had little influence upon the economic growth of the seven Portuguese NUTs II sectors, over the last two decades, even less when they are considered in levels.

But looking namely at Table 7.2, where the results are statistically more consistent, it can be observed that the Kaldor second law coefficient (expected to assume values between 0 and 1, considering that when this coefficient has a value next to 1 this signifies that the respective sector presents great increasing returns to scale and better economic growth) shows better values in agriculture, industry, manufacturing, and in sectors related with financial and insurance activities; real estate activities; professional, scientific, and technical activities; and administrative and support services. Construction presents the worse levels of economic growth dynamics and this is confirmed by the $R^2$.

Relative to the new variables (Table 7.2) the results show that the population density had a negative effect on the whole economic growth for the Portuguese economy (all aggregated economic sectors) and in agriculture, which in terms of sustainability may be an interesting conclusion that needs further investigation in future studies. This is because the New Economic Geography refers that the same effects represented in the original equation related to the second law of Kaldor appear where there is a larger population and concentration of enterprises (known as the centripetal forces). But, the New Economic Geography also considers the centrifugal forces which arrive from the agricultural sector and from effects of congestion on more populated areas. Maybe, this is the phenomena present here in these findings. In other words, for example, it is in industry and, principally, in manufacturing, which is considered by Kaldor to be the driving sector for economic growth, because in the capacity of producing tradable products and having scale dynamics, the evolution of economic growth is independent from the indicators used to represent sustainability at different levels. This is an alternative approach to analyzing the behavior of the demographic, social, and educational indicators in conciliation with economic growth over the last two decades within the seven Portuguese NUTs II and for the different economic sectors, namely agriculture, industry, construction, and several services.

**Conclusions**

Economic growth in economics literature is well explained by different ideologies, namely those related with the Classical theory, Keynesian theory, the Neo-classical theory, the theory of Endogenous Growth, and the recent New Economic Geography. Each one gives their perspective about the evolution for economic growth in different countries and regions, about the

(continued)

variables that must be considered and about regional convergence or divergence, and about constant returns to scale or increasing returns to scale. But few studies try to conciliate the models of these theories with the variables that represent sustainability at different levels (social, scientific, cultural, etc.).

In this study an attempt has been made to analyze the compatibility between economic growth, using the Kaldor second law equation, and some indicators for sustainability. The results show that, as expected by Kaldor, the sectors with more increasing returns to scale are industry and manufacturing, but also agriculture (maybe due to the modernization of the sector with more machinery and less labor force) and some services (namely financial and insurance services). On the other hand, the new variables have little influence upon economic growth for the various sectors of the Portuguese economy. Only population density presents a negative impact upon the economic performance of the whole economy and the agricultural sector.

These conclusions may be important indications for public institutions in defining public policies. This is because it is often claimed, for example, that some social policies can cause some damage towards economic growth. But the reality is that over the last two decades in Portugal there was no relation, considering these results, between the few social indicators considered here (interrelated with others) and economic growth.

In future studies it will be important to find further explanation for the conclusions presented here, namely, why economic growth in Portugal was, more or less, over the last 20 years independent from some indicators for sustainability. Indeed, some relation was expected between the several dimensions of society and the economic performance in Portugal.

## References

Alier, J. M. (2009). Socially sustainable economic de-growth. *Development and Change, 40*(6), 1099–1119.

Andreosso-O'Callaghan, B., & Lenihan, H. (2011). Responding to the crisis: Are policies aimed at a strong indigenous industrial base a necessary condition for sustainable economic growth? *Policy Studies, 32*(4), 325–345.

Asheim, G. B., & Mitra, T. (2010). Sustainability and discounted utilitarianism in models of economic growth. *Mathematical Social Sciences, 59*, 148–169.

Ayres, R. U., Turton, H., & Casten, T. (2007). Energy efficiency, sustainability and economic growth. *Energy, 32*, 634–648.

Bai, X., Chen, J., & Shi, P. (2012). Landscape urbanization and economic growth in China: Positive feedbacks and sustainability dilemmas. *Environmental Science and Technology, 46*, 132–139.

Chang, C. C., & Carballo, C. F. S. (2011). Energy conservation and sustainable economic growth: The case of Latin America and the Caribbean. *Energy Policy, 39*, 4215–4221.

Chi, C., Ma, T., & Chen, J. (2009). An endogenous economic growth model: Analyzing the sustainable development in China. *CSO, 2*, 494–498. 2009 International Joint Conference on Computational Sciences and Optimization.
Chukwu, E. N. (2005). Sustainable global economic growth. *Nonlinear Analysis, 63*, 785–798.
Clarke, M., & Islam, S. M. N. (2005). Analysis: Diminishing and negative welfare returns of economic growth: An index of sustainable economic welfare (ISEW) for Thailand. *Ecological Economics, 54*, 81–93.
Cole, M. A. (1999). Limits to growth, sustainable development and environmental Kuznets curves: An examination of the environmental impact of economic development. *Sustainable Development, 7*, 87–97.
Dasgupta, S., & Mitra, T. (1999). On the welfare significance of national product for economic growth and sustainable development. *The Japanese Economic Review, 50*(4), 422–442.
Desrochers, P. (2006). Reviews: A poverty of reason: Sustainable development and economic growth by Wilfred Beckerman, The Independent Institute, Oakland (CA), 2002, xiii þ 94 pp., paper US$17.95 (ISBN 0-945999-85-2). *The Canadian Geographer/Le Géographe canadien, 50*(2), 265–266.
Eurostat. (2013). *Several statistics*. Statistics of the European Union.
Fleisher, B. M., Liu, Z., & Prime, P. B. (2009). Introduction to the Symposium: Economic transition, regional growth, and sustainable development. *China Economic Review, 20*, 373.
Garnaut, R. (2005). The sustainability and some consequences of Chinese economic growth. *Australian Journal of International Affairs, 59*(4), 509–518.
Greiner, A. (2013). Sustainable public debt and economic growth under wage rigidity. *Metroeconomica, 64*(2), 272–292.
Greyson, J. (2007). An economic instrument for zero waste, economic growth and sustainability. *Journal of Cleaner Production, 15*, 1382–1390.
Hallowes, J. S., Pott, A. J., & Döckel, M. (2008). Managing water scarcity to encourage sustainable economic growth and social development in South Africa. *International Journal of Water Resources Development, 24*(3), 357–369.
Hefner, R. A., III. (1995). Toward sustainable economic growth: The age of energy gases. *International Journal of Hydrogen Energy, 20*(12), 945–948.
Hunt, S. D. (2011). Sustainable marketing, equity, and economic growth: A resource-advantage, economic freedom approach. *Journal of the Academy of Marketing Science, 39*, 7–20.
Islam, S. M. N., Munasinghe, M., & Clarke, M. (2003). Analysis: Making long-term economic growth more sustainable: Evaluating the costs and benefits. *Ecological Economics, 47*, 149–166.
Janicke, M. (2012). "Green growth": From a growing eco-industry to economic sustainability. *Energy Policy, 48*, 13–21.
Kaldor, N. (1966). *Causes of the slow rate of economic growth in the United Kingdom*. Cambridge: Cambridge University Press.
Kaldor, N. (1967). *Strategic factors in economic development*. Ithaca, NY: Cornell University.
Keong, C. Y. (2005). Energy demand, economic growth, and energy efficiency—The Bakun dam-induced sustainable energy policy revisited. *Energy Policy, 33*, 679–689.
Kumagai, S. (2009). Book reviews: Sustainable growth and economic development: A case study of Malaysia by Renuka Mahadevan, Cheltenham and Northampton, Mass.: Edward Elgar Publishing, 2007, xiii + 223 pp.. *The Developing Economies, 47*(2), 230–232.
Li, Y., & Oberheitmann, A. (2009). Challenges of rapid economic growth in China: Reconciling sustainable energy use, environmental stewardship and social development. *Energy Policy, 37*, 1412–1422.
Min, Z., Bang-jun, W., & Feng, J. (2009). Coalmining cities' economic growth mechanism and sustainable development analysis based on logistic dynamics model. The 6th International Conference on Mining Science & Technology. *Procedia Earth and Planetary Science, 1*, 1737–1743.

Munasinghe, M. (1995). Forum: Making economic growth more sustainable. *Ecological Economics, 15*, 121–124.
N'Zué, F. F. (2003). Le Rôle des Exportations dans le Processus de Croissance Economique de la Côte d'Ivoire: Ses Implications pour des Stratégies de Création d'Emplois Durables. *African Development Review, 15*(2–3), 199–217.
Santagata, W. (2002). Cultural districts, property rights and sustainable economic growth. *International Journal of Urban and Regional Research, 26*(1), 9–23.
Scholl, A., & Semmler, W. (2002). Sustainable economic growth and exhaustible resources: A model and estimation for the US. *Discrete Dynamics in Nature and Society, 7*(2), 79–92.
Smulders, S. (1995). Environmental policy and sustainable economic growth an endogenous growth perspective. *De Economist, 143*(2), 163–195.
Stata. (2011). *Statistics/Data analysis*. StataCorp, LP.
Stern, D. I., Common, M. S., & Barbier, E. B. (1996). Economic growth and environmental degradation: The environmental Kuznets curve and sustainable development. *World Development, 24*(7), 1151–1160.
Watanabe, C., Hur, J. Y., & Matsumoto, K. (2005). Technological diversification and firm's techno-economic structure: An assessment of Canon's sustainable growth trajectory. *Technological Forecasting & Social Change, 72*, 11–27.
Weber, M., Barth, V., & Hasselmann, K. (2005). Analysis: A multi-actor dynamic integrated assessment model (MADIAM) of induced technological change and sustainable economic growth. *Ecological Economics, 54*, 306–327.
Wu, Y. (2000). Is China's economic growth sustainable? A productivity analysis. *China Economic Review, 11*, 278–296.
Young, C. W. (1999). Book reviews: Environment, technology and economic growth: The challenge to sustainable development. By A. Tylecote and J. van de Straaten (eds), Edward Elgar Publishing, Cheltenham, 1997, ISBN: 1-85898-214-6, pp. 272, £49.95. *R&D Management, 29*(4), 423.
Zuo, H., & Ai, D. (2011). Environment, energy and sustainable economic growth. 2011 International Conference on Green Buildings and Sustainable Cities. *Procedia Engineering, 21*, 513–519.

# Chapter 8
# Analysis of the Relationship Between Agriculture, Economic Growth, and the Environment Through Keynesian Models

**Vítor João Pereira Domingues Martinho**

## 1 Introduction

There are many studies dealing with the relationship between economic growth and environmental aspects, namely using the environmental Kuznets curve and the endogenous growth theory, but few exist for Portugal and fewer or none using the Keynesian models, namely those which consider the Verdoorn law.

The environmental Kuznets curve theory is based upon the idea that there is an inverse relationship between the income per capita and environmental problems, because in more advanced stages of economic growth there is more preoccupation with the environment and, therefore, the countries are better equipped to protect the environment. So, in some instances economic growth can prove to be beneficial for living standards.

The endogenous economic growth theory appears to have some intentions towards improving upon the neoclassical theory of the absolute convergence for the same steady state. The idea of the endogenous theory is that economies converge but for different steady states, depending on certain conditions, namely that of human capital.

These concerns for economic growth and the environment have been increasing, specifically because of the need to produce more in order to create more employment and the consequent problems that can create namely for the environment. The whole economic system in developed and emergent countries is oriented towards promotion of consumption, through aggressive marketing strategies, and as a consequence to create more industries and more jobs. This orientation implies the use of more resources, which can compromise availability for following generations, and creates more waste for the environment, by increasing the so-called

V.J.P.D. Martinho (✉)
Agricultural School, Polytechnic Institute of Viseu, 3500 Viseu, Portugal
e-mail: vdmartinho@esav.ipv.pt



V.J.P.D. Martinho (ed.), *The Agricultural Economics of the 21st Century*,
DOI 10.1007/978-3-319-09471-7_8

ecological footprint. This is one of the greatest challenges for the future, namely for our governments, in order to promote a sustainable economic growth.

So, in this context this study functions as a healthy contribution towards international scientific research, by considering economic contexts (Portugal) seldom explored by the research community at the level of the relationship between economic growth and the environment and considering a background theory, which to our knowledge has never been used, in these issues, such as the Keynesian theory.

## 2 Literature Review

The relationship between the economic growth of countries and regions and the environment has been studied by many authors, specifically those for the environmental Kuznets curve, others with the endogenous theory, and others which utilize alternative approaches.

For example, for Korea, Baek and Kim (2013), using dynamic co-integration approaches, and considering the environmental Kuznets curve, found dependency of environmental performance from economic growth. These authors conclude, for the period from the 1970s to 2007, in a time series framework, that economic growth had a positive effect on the environment and that nuclear energy had a favorable influence on the environment, whereas the use of fossil fuels in both the production of electricity and energy consumption had a negative impact on the quality of the environment. They used variables as the dynamics of income measured by the GDP per capita, energy consumption (energy use per capita), electricity production (conventional thermal—for example, coal, natural gas, oil—and nuclear sources), and quality of the environment ($CO_2$ emissions).

Bartz and Kelly (2008) found similar conclusions for the USA. These authors performed tests with time series data based on the environmental Kuznets curve, from diverse periods, for the USA, considering five different pollutants, and found that the results whilst mixed were consistent with the predictions from Kuznets theory.

By also considering the environmental Kuznets curve, with panel data, from 1990 to 2003, for 90 developed and developing countries, Kleemann and Abdulai (2013) analyzed the relationship between economic growth, international trade, and quality of the environment. They considered variables related with environmental quality [consumption of chlorofluorocarbons in kilograms per capita, emissions of organic water pollutants in tons per day, energy use in tons of oil equivalent per capita, adjusted net savings in percentage of gross national income, international trade intensity (trade as a percentage of GDP, applied tariff rate, weighted mean of all products), the GDP, and population density]. The "adjusted net savings in percentage of gross national income" was considered to be a sustainability indicator. The results support that the relationship between economic growth, international trade, and environmental quality depends upon income levels and geographic location. For example, the trade liberalization seems to have had positive effects upon the sustainability of rich countries but unfavorable for poor locations. The interaction between economic growth, the environment, and international relations was also studied by Gollain (2011). The preoccupation with economic growth and the quality of the environment has existed for some decades now, but attention towards the relationship between international trade and living standards are relatively recent (Proops 2001; Ekins 2002).

Upon reviewing empirical literature, questions relating to economic growth and pollution, environment regulation and economic growth, and trade liberalization and environment were observed by Chua (1999), some years earlier. This author concluded that empirical literature does not support evidence that the economic growth causes more pollution; the environment regulations diminish economic growth and that international trade liberalization promotes more environmental problems. However, the author suggests that these conclusions may come from the omission of some factors, such as innovation, the international movement of technologies, and externalities from the quality of the environment.

Indeed the stage of development is important; Gao (2011), for example, analyzed the impacts of economic growth upon resources and the environment in a large Chinese province, taking into account the environmental Kuznets curve and time series data from 1994 to 2009, and the results still suggest some negative effects of the economic growth on environmental sustainability.

China is an example where the economic growth was not followed by improvements in the environment and living standards. China has politics, the environment, and resources as potential obstacles. In China inequality and movement of the abundant workforce to urban regions still occur (Elek 2009).

Energy consumption and pollution is a problem for economic growth and development in China. In this way, Yanqing and Mingsheng (2012) with panel data from 30 Chinese provinces, in the period 2001–2008, built a model to analyze the interactions between energy consumption, the environment, and economic growth. The conclusions reveal that in this period the economic performance in China still had negative impacts upon energy consumption and on environmental sustainability because of the high levels of pollution at different stages. In the model built variables such as the income per capita, pollution, energy consumption, average capital stock, average human capital, labor, and openness and population density were considered.

The positive effects of economic growth on the environment are mainly because of improvements in building standards and better choices on the demand side of developed and developing countries that became more efficient in their energy consumption (Krupa 2013).

From a political perspective, considering the environmental Kuznets curve, Eriksson and Persson (2003) developed a model to analyze the influence of democracy on the levels of pollution and found results which revealed that more democratic countries, in *ceteris paribus* conditions and with the same points of income, pollute less. Before, Newman (1992) focused on aspects related to natural resources and policymaking in developing countries, from a perspective of environment, economic growth, and income distribution.

A good sustainable development is the challenge for the future. In this way, Zuo and Ai (2011) analyzed the relationship between energy consumption, economic growth, and environmental sustainability, with an endogenous economic growth model.

From another perspective, with panel data econometric techniques, by considering 213 countries and for the period 1970–2008, Aşıcı (2013) analyzed the relationship between economic growth and environmental sustainability. This author used variables related with net forest depletion, mineral depletion, energy depletion, carbon dioxide damage, real pressure on nature (this is calculated by the natural disinvestment component of the Adjusted Net Savings data of the World Bank that is the sum of energy, mineral, net forest depletions, and carbon dioxide damage, all measured in US dollars), real gross national income, population density, education, openness, rule of law, and democracy. The conclusions suggest that there is a close relationship between economic growth and the lack of environmental sustainability, namely in middle-income countries, although the effects may change across the variables. For example, while the pressure on forests decreases with economic growth, carbon dioxide and mineral extraction damage increases.

The interactions between the environment, technology, economic growth, and sustainability were also analyzed by Arrow et al. (1995) and Young (1999).

The changes which occurred in society's evolution over the last century were determinant for the recent concerns related with economic growth and the environment. The transition from agricultural to industrial sectors can be an important determinant of the environmental quality (Cherniwchan 2012). This author considering the neoclassical models and the environmental Kuznets curve studied these contexts with panel data, in 157 countries from 1970 to 2000. The conclusions indicate that industrialization processes are the main determinants for the increase in sulfur emissions. The variables considered are associated with the sulfur emissions per capita, share of industrial production in GDP, saving rates, population growth rate, openness, lack of schooling, school years, and hard coal supply.

Analyzing the influence of the environmental quality in economic growth, in an inverse perspective, and taking into account the endogenous theory, Barman and Gupta (2010) built a model to analyze the relationship between economic growth, public expenditure, the effects of congestion, and the environmental quality and conclude that the environmental quality positively affects economic growth. Ewijk and Wijnbergen (1995) examined the interactions between pollution, abatement strategies, and economic growth, considering a model for the endogenous growth theory. They concluded that pollution had, indeed, a negative impact on productivity.

From a perspective of interaction among economic growth, environment, and health, Egger (2009) gave some interesting insights about the perverse effects of economic improvements upon the appearance of new diseases and environmental problems.

The questions related to the relationship between economic growth, employment, and environmental ethics and quality were debated by O'Riordan (2005), Urama (2005), and Davenport and Mohamed (2007).

Employment and human living standards are fundamental aspects to take into account in these discussions. From a sample of 179 countries, from 1970 to 2003, Costantini and Monni (2008) built a model combining the contributions from the Resource Curse Hypothesis and from the Environmental Kuznets Curve theories within the context of human development, by trying to analyze the interactions between economic growth, sustainability, and human living standards. The results support the idea that for a sustainable development, investments in human capital and in the quality of institutions are needed. These authors used variables related with the GDP per capita, initial GDP per capita, investments, foreign direct investment, openness, inflation, government effectiveness, rule of law, quality of institutions, life expectancy at birth, diffused resources, natural resources, human development, trade, industry value added, saving per capita, and $CO_2$ emissions.

Before, Culbertson (1989) discussed the questions associated with the domain of the economic growth perspectives over the environmental and population aspects, arguing for concerns in both these areas. In a similar way, Hueting (1985) analyzed the interactions between economic growth, employment, and environmental policies and demonstrated that environmental regulations can create jobs.

The influence of economic growth upon the environment is not equal for different social groups. In this line, for the period 1965–1993, in the Brazilian economy, with times series data, Torras (2001) studied the income per capita, taking into account the income shared by different social groups, resources used, and the relationship between these factors. The results are not conclusive about the economic growth in welfare earnings.

The importance of the spatial level in these analyses was given by Walker (1995). This author brought the discussion of the relationship between economic growth and the environment as a national, regional, and local scale priority.

For Portugal, using linear programming models, Henriques and Antunes (2012) examined the influence of recently implemented policies in Portugal, derived from the current crisis, on economic growth, social structure, and the environment. The results suggest that economic growth is most efficient, only when energy use in the economy is, also, efficient.

When we talk about economic growth, there are many theories described in economic literature related with these issues. One of these theories is the Keynesian approach about economic evolution and different spatial levels. Many studies, based on the Keynesian theory, analyze economic growth utilizing the Verdoorn law (1949). This law was later rediscovered by Kaldor (1966, 1967, 1970, 1975, 1981) and more recently tested by many other authors. The Verdoorn law defends a positive relationship between the growth rate of productivity and the growth rate of output, between 0 and 1. In this relation the growth rate productivity is endogenous and depends on the growth rate of the output, catching increasing returns to scale, endogeneity of the factors, spillover effects, and learning by doing aspects, all of which are questions defended before by other authors, but not in a systematic and

**Table 8.1** Literature review summarized

| Variables | Authors | Background theory/ relationships | Countries |
|---|---|---|---|
| Productivity, output, and investment | Kaldor (1966, 1967, 1970, 1975, 1981) | Keynesian theory | UK |
| Five different pollutants | Bartz and Kelly (2008) | Environmental Kuznets curve | USA |
| GDP per capita, initial GDP per capita, investments, foreign direct investment, openness, inflation, government effectiveness, rule of law, quality of institutions, life expectancy at birth, diffuse resources, natural resources, human development, trade, industry value added, saving per capita, and $CO_2$ emissions | Costantini and Monni (2008) | Resource curse hypothesis and from the environmental Kuznets curve | 179 countries |
| Sulfur emissions per capita, share of industrial production in GDP, saving rates, population growth rate, openness, no school, school years, and hard coal supply | Cherniwchan (2012) | Neoclassical models and the environmental Kuznets curve | 157 countries |
| Economic policies, social indicators, and environmental variables | Henriques and Antunes (2012) | Influence of the recent policies on the economic growth, on the social structure, and on the environment | Portugal |
| Income per capita, pollution, energy consumption, average capital stock, average human capital, labor, openness, and population density | Yanqing and Mingsheng (2012) | Interactions between the energy consumption, the environment, and the economic growth | China |
| Net forest depletion, mineral depletion, energy depletion, carbon dioxide damage, real pressure on nature (is calculated by the natural disinvestment component of the Adjusted Net Savings data of the World Bank that is the sum of energy, mineral, net forest depletions, and carbon dioxide damage, all measured in US dollars), real gross national income, population density, education, openness, rule of law, and democracy | Aşıcı (2013) | Relationship among the economic growth and the environmental sustainability | 213 countries |
| Dynamics of the income measured by the per capita GDP, the energy consumption (per capita | Baek and Kim (2013) | Environmental Kuznets curve | Korea |

(continued)

**Table 8.1** (continued)

| Variables | Authors | Background theory/ relationships | Countries |
|---|---|---|---|
| energy use), electricity production (conventional thermal—e.g., coal, natural gas, oil—and nuclear sources) and the environment quality ($CO_2$ emissions) | | | |
| Environmental quality (consumption of chlorofluorocarbons in kilograms per capita, emissions of organic water pollutants in tons per day, energy use in tons of oil equivalent per capita, adjusted net savings in percentage of gross national income), the international trade intensity (trade as a percentage of GDP, applied tariff rate, weighted mean of all products), the GDP, and the population density | Kleemann and Abdulai (2013) | Environmental Kuznets curve | 90 developed and developing countries |

interrelated way. For Kaldor the engine of economies is the industrial sector and it is in this sector where this law presents its best results. These conclusions from Kaldor were obtained for Great Britain with a Verdoorn coefficient around 0.5. These explanations developed by Kaldor had the implicit idea of circular and cumulative processes in the economies. In these processes the engine is the external demand (from exports) that lead to an increase in the output. This increase in the output promotes an increase in productivity (Verdoorn law) and this fact alone originates improvements in the salary of efficiency (salary weighted against productivity). The improvements in the salary of efficiency enable a reduction in prices and this increases demand, namely external demand, and subsequently we return to the beginning of the process and so on.

To better understand the following built model, the literature review is summarized in Table 8.1.

## 3 Data Analysis

The data was obtained from the Statistics of Portugal (INE 2013) and is relative to the Portuguese manufacturing sector disaggregated at the NUTs III level, over the period 2004–2011, and considers the following groups: food industries; manufacture of beverages; tobacco industry; manufacture of textiles; clothing industry; manufacture of leather and leather products; manufacture of wood and cork and articles thereof, except furniture, and manufacture of works of straw and plaiting materials; manufacture of pulp, paper, paperboard, and articles thereof; printing and

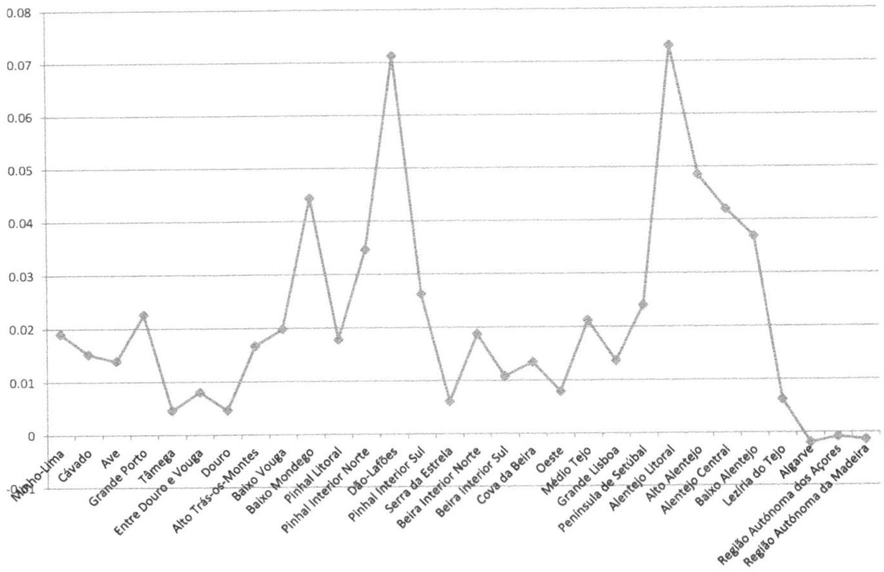


**Fig. 8.1** Labor productivity (Production value/number of persons employed) growth rate in averages (over the period 2004–2011 and across the different forms of the manufacturing sector considered) for the 30 NUTs III of Portugal

reproduction of recorded media; manufacture of coke, refined petroleum products, and fuel pellets; manufacture of chemicals and man-made fibers, except pharmaceuticals; manufacture of basic pharmaceutical products and pharmaceutical preparations; manufacture of rubber and plastic products; manufacture of other nonmetallic mineral products; manufacture of basic metals; fabricated metal products, except machinery and equipment; manufacture of computer, communications equipment, and electronic and optical products; manufacture of electrical equipment; manufacture of machinery and equipment, i.e., manufacture of motor vehicles, trailers, semi-trailers, and vehicle components; manufacture of other transport equipment; manufacture of furniture and mattresses; other manufacturing; and repair, maintenance, and installation of machinery and equipment.

The data is relative to the productivity (production value/number of persons employed), the output, the investment, and other environmental variables, following the Keynesian theory and the literature review carried out earlier and summarized in Table 8.1. The output was deflated with the index consumer prices available for the period considered and for the Portuguese NUTs II.

Figures 8.1 and 8.2 show the evolution of the productivity growth rate, in average, for the different Portuguese NUTs III and for the different manufacturing sectors considered, respectively.

Figure 8.1 shows that the Algarve, Açores, and Madeira presented a negative productivity growth rate, on average, over the period 2004–2011 and across the several manufacturing sectors. On the other hand, Baixo Mondego, Dão-Lafões,

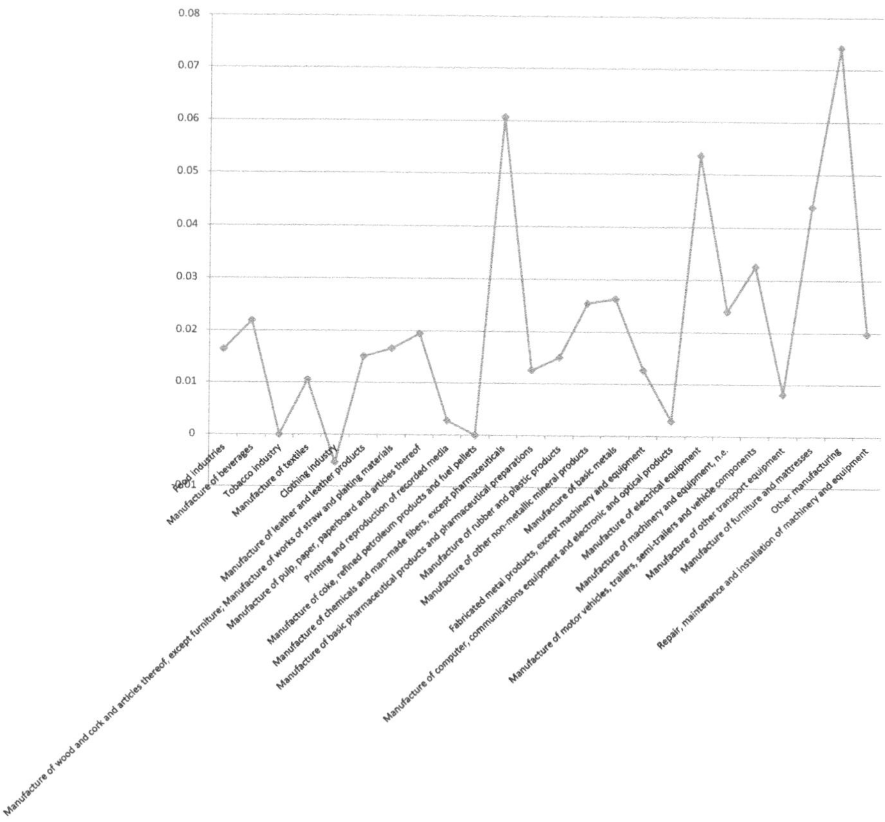


**Fig. 8.2** Labor productivity (Production value/number of persons employed) growth rate in averages (over the period 2004–2011 and across the 30 Portuguese NUTs III) for the different forms of the manufacturing sector considered

and Alentejo Litoral are the Portuguese NUTs III with the biggest productivity growth rate.

From Fig. 8.2 it is possible to verify that there is no data for the tobacco industry and for the manufacture of coke, refined petroleum products, and fuel pellets. The clothing industry shows a negative productivity growth rate over the period considered and across the different manufacturing sectors considered. The manufacture of chemicals and man-made fibers, except pharmaceuticals, manufacture of electrical equipment, and other manufacturing are the industries with a larger productivity growth rate in the Portuguese NUTs III.

## 4 The Model

The model was built based on the Verdoorn law, where the productivity growth rate is endogenous and dependent upon the output growth rate, plus the investment (Costantini and Monni 2008; Yanqing and Mingsheng 2012) and with some environmental variables in growth rate. The environmental variables considered are relative to the water quality (Kleemann and Abdulai 2013), expenditure on environment (Costantini and Monni 2008), proportion of municipal waste collected selectively (Costantini and Monni 2008; Cherniwchan 2012; Henriques and Antunes 2012; Yanqing and Mingsheng 2012; Aşıcı 2013), municipal waste collected (Yanqing and Mingsheng 2012), and sales of liquid and gaseous fuels as a proxy for gaseous emissions (Bartz and Kelly 2008; Costantini and Monni 2008; Cherniwchan 2012; Aşıcı 2013; Baek and Kim 2013; Kleemann and Abdulai 2013).

The model can be presented as following:

$$p_{it} = a_0 + a_1 q_{it} + a_2 i_{it} + a_3 wt_{it} + a_4 \mathrm{ee}_{it} + a_5 \mathrm{wss}_{it} + a_6 \mathrm{wsr}_{it} + a_7 \mathrm{sgl}_{it}$$

where all the variables are in growth rates, $p$ is the productivity, $q$ the output, $i$ the investment, wt the water quality, ee the expenditure on environment, wss the waste collected selectively, wsr the waste collected, and the sgl is the sales of liquid and gaseous fuels. The index $i$ and $t$ are, respectively, relative to the regions and time.

## 5 The Results

All the results obtained with the model presented before and with econometric estimations, considering panel data techniques and the Stata (2011) software, are presented in Table 8.2.

Some industries such as the tobacco industry and the manufacture of coke, refined petroleum products, and fuel pellets do not have sufficient available data to make statistically significant estimations, due to this their results are not shown in Table 8.2.

In all estimations the statistical tests reject the hypotheses of fixed or random effects and confirm that the OLS method is the most adjusted. This is more or less in line with the fact that the constant coefficient is not statistically significant for almost all the estimations, except in the clothing industry, printing and reproduction of recorded media, and manufacture of other nonmetallic mineral products. On the other hand, the majority of the $R^2$ are superior to 50 %.

All the Verdoorn coefficients are statistically significant, except for the manufacture of furniture and mattresses, and the majority are greater than 0.5. The greatest values for this coefficient are presented by the manufacture of machinery and equipment, i.e., (0.874), other manufacturing (0.886), and food industries (0.861), respectively. The lowest values are shown by the repair, maintenance,

**Table 8.2** Estimation results for the Verdoorn equation extended, with panel data, across the several forms of the manufacturing sector considered, over the period 2004–2011 and over the 30 Portuguese NUTs III

| | Const.[a] | Coef.[b] | Coef.[c] | Coef.[d] | Coef.[e] | Coef.[f] | Coef.[g] | Coef.[h] | F(Re_OLS)[l] | Hausman[m] | $R^2$ [n] |
|---|---|---|---|---|---|---|---|---|---|---|---|
| Food industries | | | | | | | | | | | |
| OLS | 0.007<br>(1.270) | 0.861*<br>(17.710) | −0.002<br>(−0.300) | 0.206<br>(0.860) | −0.003<br>(−0.140) | 0.011<br>(0.640) | −0.110<br>(−1.310) | −0.042<br>(−1.500) | 0.000 | 2.020 | 0.842 |
| Manufacture of beverages | | | | | | | | | | | |
| OLS | 0.043<br>(1.580) | 0.486*<br>(3.550) | 0.003*<br>(2.250) | −0.752<br>(−0.810) | 0.046<br>(0.470) | −0.060<br>(−0.077) | 0.235<br>(0.337) | 0.082<br>(0.195) | 0.000 | 0.940 | 0.382 |
| Manufacture of textiles | | | | | | | | | | | |
| OLS | 0.020<br>(1.180) | 0.711*<br>(9.190) | −0.008<br>(−1.480) | 2.327*<br>(4.340) | −0.009<br>(−0.170) | 0.155*<br>(2.940) | −0.192<br>(−0.960) | −0.055<br>(−0.480) | 0.000 | 9.590 | 0.764 |
| Clothing industry | | | | | | | | | | | |
| OLS | 0.052*<br>(2.520) | 0.537*<br>(6.990) | 0.000<br>(0.270) | −1.692*<br>(−2.220) | 0.043<br>(0.460) | 0.054<br>(1.070) | −0.043<br>(−0.180) | −0.002<br>(−0.020) | 0.000 | 1.250 | 0.518 |
| Manufacture of leather and leather products | | | | | | | | | | | |
| OLS | 0.071<br>(0.570) | 0.619**<br>(1.800) | −0.057<br>(−1.340) | −3.038<br>(−0.380) | −1.629*<br>(−3.380) | −0.013<br>(−0.030) | 3.343<br>(0.910) | 0.209<br>(0.490) | 0.000 | 9.030 | 0.245 |
| Manufacture of wood and cork and articles thereof, except furniture, and manufacture of works of straw and plaiting materials | | | | | | | | | | | |
| OLS | −0.009<br>(−0.390) | 0.378*<br>(4.190) | −0.003<br>(−0.800) | −0.712<br>(−0.800) | 0.049<br>(0.540) | 0.188*<br>(2.880) | −0.101<br>(−0.320) | −0.066<br>(−0.630) | 0.000 | 3.600 | 0.284 |
| Manufacture of pulp, paper, paperboard, and articles thereof | | | | | | | | | | | |
| OLS | 0.021<br>(1.140) | 0.770*<br>(11.660) | 0.000<br>(0.160) | 1.303<br>(0.920) | −0.023<br>(−0.320) | 0.018<br>(0.340) | −0.336<br>(−1.470) | −0.130<br>(−0.960) | 0.000 | 3.460 | 0.803 |
| Printing and reproduction of recorded media | | | | | | | | | | | |
| OLS | 0.030*<br>(2.070) | 0.442*<br>(5.020) | −0.001<br>(−0.680) | −0.508<br>(−0.890) | 0.031<br>(0.540) | −0.035<br>(−0.840) | −0.187<br>(−0.930) | −0.005<br>(−0.080) | 0.090 | 9.660 | 0.316 |
| Manufacture of chemicals and man-made fibers, except pharmaceuticals | | | | | | | | | | | |
| OLS | 0.018<br>(0.800) | 0.697*<br>(28.010) | −0.009<br>(−0.640) | −1.244<br>(−1.400) | 0.074<br>(0.730) | 0.006<br>(0.080) | 0.100<br>(0.320) | −0.055<br>(−0.540) | 0.000 | 4.510 | 0.960 |

(continued)

**Table 8.2** (continued)

| | Const.[a] | Coef.[b] | Coef.[c] | Coef.[d] | Coef.[e] | Coef.[f] | Coef.[g] | Coef.[h] | F(Re_OLS)[l] | Hausman[m] | $R^2$ [n] |
|---|---|---|---|---|---|---|---|---|---|---|---|
| Manufacture of rubber and plastic products | | | | | | | | | | | |
| OLS | 0.004 (0.320) | 0.726* (11.080) | 0.000 (0.280) | 0.595 (1.130) | −0.046 (−0.840) | 0.048 (1.360) | 0.119 (0.660) | −0.051 (−0.530) | 0.000 | 2.900 | 0.768 |
| Manufacture of other nonmetallic mineral products | | | | | | | | | | | |
| OLS | 0.048* (4.940) | 0.807* (37.220) | −0.002 (−0.770) | 0.820* (2.150) | 0.012 (0.320) | 0.036 (1.160) | −0.023 (−0.170) | 0.007 (0.150) | 0.000 | 1.530 | 0.965 |
| Manufacture of basic metals | | | | | | | | | | | |
| OLS | 0.042 (0.860) | 0.547* (5.190) | −0.010 (−0.660) | −1.861 (−0.610) | 0.043 (0.270) | −0.116 (−0.710) | 0.046 (0.090) | 0.082 (0.250) | 0.000 | 9.590 | 0.482 |
| Fabricated metal products, except machinery and equipment | | | | | | | | | | | |
| OLS | 0.007 (0.640) | 0.699* (12.000) | 0.008 (0.680) | −0.307 (−0.690) | 0.003 (0.060) | −0.023 (−0.690) | 0.031 (0.190) | 0.013 (0.250) | 0.000 | 2.000 | 0.7210 |
| Manufacture of computer, communications equipment, and electronic and optical products | | | | | | | | | | | |
| OLS | −0.075 (−1.280) | 0.223* (5.680) | −0.001 (−1.460) | 3.601 (1.180) | −0.064 (−0.370) | 0.318 (1.600) | −0.897 (−0.640) | −0.470 (−0.880) | 0.000 | 2.650 | 0.658 |
| Manufacture of electrical equipment | | | | | | | | | | | |
| OLS | 0.002 (0.090) | 0.426* (34.460) | −0.003 (−1.400) | 1.221 (0.660) | −0.105 (−0.970) | 0.082 (1.160) | 0.415 (1.260) | 0.086 (0.470) | 1.280 | 0.560 | 0.968 |
| Manufacture of machinery and equipment, n.e. | | | | | | | | | | | |
| OLS | 0.031 (1.610) | 0.874* (15.340) | 0.015* (2.010) | 0.451 (0.570) | −0.018 (−0.220) | −0.066 (−1.140) | 0.169 (0.610) | 0.179* (1.960) | 0.000 | 12.930 | 0.820 |
| Manufacture of motor vehicles, trailers, semi-trailers, and vehicle components | | | | | | | | | | | |
| OLS | 0.005 (0.120) | 0.500* (6.740) | −0.021 (−1.310) | 1.097 (0.910) | −0.155 (−1.120) | 0.189 (1.430) | −0.178 (−0.380) | −0.008 (−0.040) | 0.000 | 13.200 | 0.581 |
| Manufacture of furniture and mattresses | | | | | | | | | | | |
| OLS | 0.131 (0.850) | 0.436 (0.600) | 0.000 (0.070) | 2.952 (0.460) | −0.316 (−0.480) | 0.152 (0.310) | −1.686 (−0.720) | −0.119 (−0.150) | 0.000 | 7.090 | 0.028 |

| | | | | | | | | | | | |
|---|---|---|---|---|---|---|---|---|---|---|---|
| Other manufacturing | | | | | | | | | | | |
| OLS | 0.031 (0.990) | 0.886* (15.620) | −0.001 (−0.520) | −0.941 (−0.570) | −0.141 (−0.420) | −0.572* (−5.880) | −0.738* (−1.97) | −0.049 (−0.250) | 0.000 | 0.400 | 0.930 |
| Repair, maintenance, and installation of machinery and equipment | | | | | | | | | | | |
| OLS | 0.000 (0.010) | 0.043* (2.160) | 0.020** (1.830) | −0.455 (−0.320) | −0.112 (−0.770) | −0.109 (−1.020) | 0.765 (1.530) | −0.052 (−0.300) | 0.000 | 1.600 | 0.114 |

*Note*: [a]Constant; [b]Verdoorn coefficient; [c]Investment coefficient; [d]Water quality coefficient; [e]Expenditure on environment coefficient; [f]Waste collected selectively; [g]Waste collected; [h]Sales of liquid and gaseous fuels; [i]Test F for fixed effects model and test Wald for random effects; [j]Test F for fixed effects or OLS (Ho is OLS); [k]Correlation between errors and regressors in fixed effects; [l]Test F for random effects or OLS (Ho is OLS); [m]Hausman test (Ho is GLS); [n]R square

*Statistically significant at 5 %; **Statistically significant at 10 %

and installation of machinery and equipment industry (0.043), computer manufacture, communications equipment, electronic and optical products (0.223), and manufacture of wood and cork and articles thereof, except furniture, and manufacture of straw work and plaiting materials (0.378).

Relative to the other variables added to the Verdoorn relationship, the manufacture of beverages presents statistical significance for the investment, with a weak elasticity (0.003), the manufacture of textiles for water quality (2.327) and for the waste collected selectively (0.155), the clothing industry for water quality (−1.692), the manufacture of leather and leather products for the expenditure on environment (−1.629), the manufacture of wood and cork and articles thereof, except furniture, manufacture of straw work and plaiting materials for the waste collected selectively (0.188), the manufacture of other nonmetallic mineral products for water quality (0.820), the manufacture of machinery and equipment, i.e., for investment (0.015) and for the gaseous emissions proxy (0.179), other manufacturing for waste collected selectively (−0.572) and for waste collected (−0.738), and the repair, maintenance, and installation of machinery and equipment for investment (0.020). For other industries the other variables do not present statistical significance. In general, and considering the industries where the new variables added to the Verdoorn law have statistical significance, investment presents both weak and positive effects. Water quality shows strong effects, in some cases positive and in other cases negative. Expenditure on the environment only presents statistical significance for the manufacture of leather and leather products and curiously both strong and negative. Waste collected selectively shows positive and medium effects, with exception for other manufacturing where it is negative. The proxy for gaseous emissions only bears significance for the manufacture of machinery and equipment, and is positive.

From the results previously analyzed it seems that the original relationship of Verdoorn is enough to study the productivity growth rate of the manufacturing sector in the Portuguese NUTs III, namely considering the constant coefficient, the $R^2$ values, and the significance of the variables added to the Verdoorn equation. This is a sign that productivity growth and economic growth in Portugal, in the majority of cases, for the period considered, do not depend upon environmental conditions. On the other hand, the majority of the manufacturing sector present great increasing returns to scale, considering the Verdoorn coefficient values.

**Conclusions**

This study is an innovative approach for the analysis of the relationship between economic growth and the environment, namely because it considers the Keynesian theory for the Portuguese context as a base. The main objective of this study was principally to analyze the influence of environmental variables, in growth rates, in the productivity growth rate, through the Verdoorn law over the period 2004–2011, with data disaggregated in the 30 Portuguese

(continued)

NUTs III and in several groups of the manufacturing sector, considering the importance of these activities for the Keynesian theorists, namely for Kaldor.

There are many studies, for several countries, related with the analysis of the relationship across the economic growth and the environment, some considering the environmental Kuznets curve, others utilizing some models from the economic growth theory and others with alternative approaches. These studies namely consider variables related to economic growth (GDP, GDP per capita, and productivity), the investment, education, the institutions, human capital, pollution, the quality of life, sustainability, and gaseous emissions.

From previous data analysis it is possible to conclude that the evolution of the productivity growth rate among the Portuguese NUTs III is not uniform and there are some regions where this variable, on average over the period considered and over the several forms of manufacturing taken into account, presents negative values such as in the Algarve, Açores, and Madeira. This is an expected value considering the economic characteristics of these regions, with little importance for the manufacturing sector. The same happens for the productivity growth rate, on average, across the different groups of manufacturing considered, the clothing industry being the most concerning with negative values.

The results obtained via the estimations show that the original Verdoorn relationship is the most adjusted model and is enough to explain the evolution of productivity growth rate in Portugal over the period considered, taking into account the constant coefficient values and the $R^2$. On the other hand, the variables added to the Verdoon equation in this study, namely with the intention of considering environmental variables, in general, present statistical significance in very few cases, which means that economic growth in Portugal, for many cases, is not influenced by environmental conditions. Agriculture seems, also, to not be a problem for the increasing returns for the industries based in this sector (e.g., the food industry presents a value of 0.861 for the Verdoorn coefficient).

However, having said that, all the new variables considered showed statistical significance, although not for all the industries considered and, in some cases, not simultaneously.

In future research it will be important to analyze the influence of economic growth in Portugal within the environment and try to further investigate some results obtained for the new variables added to the Verdoorn relationship related with environmental aspects, namely in trying to understand why in some industries the productivity growth rate is influenced by some environmental variables and in other industries it is not.

## References


Arrow, K., Bolin, B., Costanza, R., Dasgupta, P., Folke, C., Holling, C. S., et al. (1995). Forum: Economic growth, carrying capacity, and the environment. *Ecological Economics, 15*, 91–95.

Aşıcı, A. A. (2013). Economic growth and its impact on environment: A panel data analysis. *Ecological Indicators, 24*, 324–333.

Baek, J., & Kim, H. S. (2013). Is economic growth good or bad for the environment? Empirical evidence from Korea. *Energy Economics, 36*, 744–749.

Barman, T. R., & Gupta, M. R. (2010). Public expenditure, environment, and economic growth. *Journal of Public Economic Theory, 12*(6), 1109–1134.

Bartz, S., & Kelly, D. L. (2008). Economic growth and the environment: Theory and facts. *Resource and Energy Economics, 30*, 115–149.

Cherniwchan, J. (2012). Economic growth, industrialization, and the environment. *Resource and Energy Economics, 34*, 442–467.

Chua, S. (1999). Economic growth, liberalization, and the environment: A review of the economic evidence. *Annual Review of Energy and the Environment, 24*, 391–430.

Costantini, V., & Monni, S. (2008). Analysis environment, human development and economic growth. *Ecological Economics, 64*, 867–880.

Culbertson, J. M. (1989). "Economic growth," population, and the environment. *Population and Environment: A Journal of Interdisciplinary Studies, 11*(2), 83–100.

Davenport, D. S., & Mohamed, R. (2007). Book Review: Hooked on a metaphor: Hooked on growth: Economic addictions and the environment. *The American Review of Public Administration, 37*, 117–119.

Egger, G. (2009). Health, "Illth," and economic growth: Medicine, environment, and economics at the crossroads. *American Journal of Preventive Medicine, 37*(1), 78–83.

Ekins, P. (2002). Book Review: Trade liberalisation, economic growth and the environment. By Cole (Matthew A.). (Aldershot and Lyme, NH: Edward Elgar, 2000. Pp. xi + 144. £45.00 hardback. ISBN 1 84064 176 2.). *The Economic Journal, 112*, 477, F146–F148.

Elek, A. (2009). China's dilemma: Economic growth, the environment and climate change - Edited by Ligang Song and Wing Tye Woo. *Asian-Pacific Economic Literature, 23*(1), 122–123.

Eriksson, C., & Persson, J. (2003). Economic growth, inequality, democratization, and the environment. *Environmental and Resource Economics, 25*, 1–16.

Ewijk, C. V., & Wijnbergen, S. V. (1995). Can abatement overcome the conflict between environment and economic growth? *De Economist, 143*(2), 197–216.

Gao, B. (2011). The impacts of economic growth on resources and environment in Henan Province. *Procedia Environmental Sciences, 11*, 810–816.

Gollain, F. (2011). Economic growth, the environment and international relations. The growth paradigm. *Environmental Politics, 20*(6), 948–949.

Henriques, C. O., & Antunes, C. H. (2012). Interactions of economic growth, energy consumption and the environment in the context of the crisis – A study with uncertain data. *Energy, 48*, 415–422.

Hueting, R. (1985). An economic scenario that gives top priority to saving the environment rather than encouraging production growth. *The Environmentalist, 5*(4), 253–262.

INE. (2013). *Several statistics available online*. Statistics of Portugal.

Kaldor, N. (1966). *Causes of the slow rate of economic growth in the United Kingdom*. Cambridge: Cambridge University Press.

Kaldor, N. (1967). *Strategic factors in economic development*. Ithaca, NY: Cornell University.

Kaldor, N. (1970). The case for regional policies. *Scottish Journal of Political Economy, XVII*(3).

Kaldor, N. (1975). Economic growth and the Verdoorn Law – A comment on Mr. Rowthorn's article. *Economic Journal, 85*, 891–896.

Kaldor, N. (1981). The role of increasing returns, technical progress and cumulative causation in the theory of international trade and economic growth. *Économie Appliquée*, (4).

Kleemann, L., & Abdulai, A. (2013). The impact of trade and economic growth on the environment: Revisiting the cross-country evidence. *Journal of International Development, 25*, 180–205.

Krupa, J. (2013). Re-examining the nexus of energy, economic growth, and the environment. *Energy Policy, 52*, 839–840.

O'Riordan, T. (2005). Book review: Economic growth versus the environment: The politics of wealth, health and air pollution, Judith A. Cherni (Ed.). Palgrave, Basingstoke, Hampshire, UK (2002), 264 pp., ISBN: 033392956X. *Ecological Economics, 52*(4), 544–545.

Newman, D. H. (1992). Book Review: Ascher, William and Robert Healy, Natural resource policymaking in developing countries: Environment, economic growth, and income distribution. Durham: Duke University Press, 1990.223 pp. *Policy Sciences, 25*, 351–354.

Proops, J. (2001). Book Review: Trade liberalisation, economic growth and the environment: By M.A. Cole, Edward Elgar, 2000. ISBN 1-84064-1762; xi + 144 pp., p. 160, £45. *Ecological Economics, 37*(3), 477–478.

Stata. (2011). *Computer software*. StataCorp, LP.

Torras, M. (2001). Welfare accounting and the environment: Reassessing Brazilian economic growth, 1965–1993. *Development and Change, 32*(2), 205–229.

Urama, K. C. (2005). Book Review: Hooked on growth: Economic addictions and the environment. *Ecological Economics, 55*(3), 445–448.

Verdoorn, P. J. (1949). Fattori che Regolano lo Sviluppo della Produtivita del Lavoro. *L'Industria*, 45–53.

Walker, B. (1995). Forum: National, regional and local scale priorities in the economic growth versus environment trade-off. *Ecological Economics, 15*, 145–147.

Yanqing, X., & Mingsheng, X. (2012). A 3E model on energy consumption, environment pollution and economic growth – An empirical research based on panel data. *Energy Procedia, 16*, 2011–2018.

Young, C. W. (1999). Book Reviews: Environment, technology and economic growth: The challenge to sustainable development. By A. Tylecote and J. van de Straaten (eds), Edward Elgar Publishing, Cheltenham, 1997, ISBN: 1-85898-214-6, pp. 272, £49.95. *R&D Management 29*(4), 423.

Zuo, H., & Ai, D. (2011). Environment, energy and sustainable economic growth. *Procedia Engineering, 21*, 513–519.

# Chapter 9
# Agricultural Economics in the Context of Portuguese Rural Development

Vítor João Pereira Domingues Martinho

## 1 Introduction

The discussion about rural development is often interminable because it possesses many problems, and it is therefore very difficult to find solutions to the questions related to the lack of population, lack of firms and economic activity, a lack of infrastructures, some of which are basic and others not so basic (but also important for current times, if the intention is to maintain populations), and a lack of good access. The most problematic from these contexts is that in some situations the catching-up may not be sufficient to prevent the circular and cumulative processes, well defined by the authors of the New Economic Geography and of the Keynesian theory, where richer areas have preliminary advantages and the poorer areas have initial disadvantages.

There are many studies about the dynamics in rural zones and about rural development, but few or none (according to our knowledge) about the cross-sectional econometric analysis of the influence of the other sectors related with the agricultural sector and of the structural characteristics of the farms in the output of agriculture. In this way, this research provides for an original analysis, because it examines in Portuguese municipalities, over the year 2009, through cross-sectional descriptions and estimations, the influence, in agriculture (agriculture, animal production, hunting, and related service activities) performance (output), of the output of some industries (food, textile, wood, cork, and related activities) and some services (accommodation, restaurants, and consulting services), more or less related with the farming sector. They were tested for their influence on the output of other activities related with agriculture such as the forestry, fishery, aquaculture, and other industry (paper industry) and services, but none presented a statistical

V.J.P.D. Martinho (✉)
Agricultural School, Polytechnic Institute of Viseu, 3500 Viseu, Portugal
e-mail: vdmartinho@esav.ipv.pt



V.J.P.D. Martinho (ed.), *The Agricultural Economics of the 21st Century*,
DOI 10.1007/978-3-319-09471-7_9

significance. It is still, however, an original study, because it investigates the implications of some structural characteristics of farms in terms of agricultural output, such as agricultural employment and the number of farms with multi-functional activities inside (mixed production with vegetal and animal activities, forestry, services provision, and production of renewable energies) and outside (with the income of the farmer household coming principally from external sources). Other variables were also tested, namely related to other activities developed inside the farms, but without statistical relevance.

This study aims to be an important contribution towards Portuguese rural development and comprehension of its dynamics, an instrument for private economic operators in these regions and as a support for national and European public institutions that design policies for Portuguese rural areas. It is important to find new mechanisms that promote economic activity in these regions, namely those that create employment.

## 2 Background Literature

Over the last two decades the discussion between European Union countries changed from agricultural growth to rural development. Agriculture, derived from several factors, began to be viewed as an activity that can and must be interrelated with other economic dynamics in the rural zones (Hildén et al. 2012). The reforms of the European Union's agricultural policies brought a determinant increment to the integrated rural progress perspective (Dwyer et al. 2007). Unwin (1997) defended these integrated possibilities as an interesting perspective for rural evolution in some social and economic environments. Sometimes, these new strategies collide with the existing agricultural practices and with the traditional covering of the landscape (Pinto-Correia 2000). However, agriculture continues to be the most important sector in rural areas, namely within European Union countries (Rizov 2006; Granvik et al. 2012). The territorial branding and the associated territorial marketing are seen as important tools for the integrated rural development that can have very important contributions in these rural processes (Mettepenningen et al. 2012). The territorial branding can be used to promote, in an interrelated way, the endogenous products (from agriculture, small industry, the landscape, etc.) of the zone covered.

Multifunctional agriculture appears as an alternative for traditional productivity farming. An activity is multifunctional for agriculture if it brings benefits to this sector, if it helps to build a new paradigm within the farming sector, and if the contributions facilitate the welfare of the whole population (Marsden and Sonnino 2008). Multifunctionality in agriculture means that despite the production function of this sector, it can contribute to the economic, social, and environmental dynamics through other activities (Renting et al. 2009). Heringa et al. (2013) identified the following four different forms of multifunctionality in agriculture: environment concerns, tourism, sustainable services, and sales in the farm direct to the consumer.

However not all potentialities of multifunctional agriculture are already explored, namely in peri-urban zones (Zasada 2011). In any case, the environmental concerns related with rural evolution, namely for a sustainable development, played a crucial role in the decisions for rural zones over the last few decades in many countries (Howells et al. 1998). Agricultural activity can contribute to the mitigation of gas emissions, namely in the sequestration of carbon (Branca et al. 2013). Curiously, the ten countries of central and oriental Europe when joining the European Union showed much interest, namely, in the European agricultural strategies related with multifunctionality (Râmniceanu and Ackrill 2007). The multifunctionality of the farming sector was, in addition, a question studied by Rossing et al. (2007), Zander et al. (2007), Groot et al. (2009), Refsgaard and Johnson (2010), Hassink et al. (2012), and Hassink et al. (2013). The intentional consumption of some multifunctional goods and services from agriculture is dependent upon attitudes and perceived attributes related with farms, the existing programs, the markets, and the world environment (Moon and Griffith 2011). The neoliberal perspective for recent negotiations in the context of World Trade Organizations can bring new discussions about the multifunctional character of agriculture, considering the intentions of becoming a farming sector-oriented market (Dibden et al. 2009). The tradeoffs between the multifunctional farming and the new tendencies in economic, social, and institutional organization were also analyzed by Labarthe (2009). Indeed, agricultural dynamics and rural development have so many specifics that adjusted strategies different to those implemented in other sectors are sometimes needed. The spatial level of the multifunctional characteristics of agriculture is another discussion, but it seems correct to think that the base is the farm and that later its effects are spread across both local and regional levels (Wilson 2009). The characteristics of the farm landscape were, also, considered as being a crucial factor in the contribution towards agricultural multifunctionality for the welfare of the society (Parra-López et al. 2008).

The analysis of the economic dynamics depends upon other dynamics such as those from social contexts. These social scenarios must be analyzed carefully in order to avoid obtaining biased conclusions (Shortall 2008). The sociologic approach, with participatory techniques, can provide an interesting contribution to the understanding and the intervention in rural development, namely that with a sustainable evolution (Magnani and Struffi 2009). The participation of local social and economic operators in the design of rural strategies was, also, argued by Fleury et al. (2008). These participatory approaches were also considered by Choisis et al. (2010) in the analysis of mixed crop and animal farms in southwestern of France.

There are many factors that can influence the economic activity in rural zones, but Bathrellos et al. (2013) identified factors related to geology, geomorphology, and social, economic, and natural causes, as some of the most important causes. Geology was, also, referred to by Bakri (2001) as having a determinant impact on agricultural economic growth and rural development. On the other hand, Firmino (1999) identified implications from natural influences and human activity. Yong-fu et al. (2013) found other determinants of agricultural activity such as intermediate consumption, investment, the workforce, the area used, technical progress and efficiency, climate, and subsidies. However, intermediate consumption appears to be the most determining factor for economic performance in agriculture.

The agricultural sector has many potentialities and can contribute, with adjusted policies, to a sustainable rural development, but for that the specificities of agriculture and of rural zones, where there are many tradeoffs between the multifunctional and the productivity perspective, must be taken into account.

## 3 The Empirical Model

The model considered in this study is based upon the Cobb and Douglas (1928) function of production, where the output depends on productivity, employment, and capital. To obtain the model used here, adjusted for the proposed objectives, the Cobb–Douglas model was linearized with the logarithms.

In this linear model the agricultural output is shown as functions of farming employment, the output of some industries (food, textile, and wood and cork) and some services (accommodation and restaurants and consulting services), more or less related to the farming sector, and is a function, too, of the number of mixed farms (crops and livestock production) and the number of farms with other sources of income, internal (forestry, services provision, and renewable energy production) and external.

The linear model can be represented as following:

$$\begin{aligned}\ln(\mathrm{AO}_i) = {} & a_0 + a_1 \ln(\mathrm{FIO}_i) + a_2 \ln(\mathrm{TIO}_i) + a_3 \ln(\mathrm{WIO}_i) + a_4 \ln(\mathrm{ACO}_i) \\ & + a_5 \ln(\mathrm{CSO}_i) + a_6 \ln(\mathrm{NFO}_i) + a_7 \ln(\mathrm{NSP}_i) + a_8 \ln(\mathrm{NER}_i) \\ & + a_9 \ln(\mathrm{NMI}_i) + a_{10} \ln(\mathrm{NOT}_i)\end{aligned}$$

where the index $i$ represents Portuguese municipalities and $a$ the coefficients of regression. The variables AO represent agricultural output, FIO food industry output, TIO textile industry output, WIO wood and cork industry output, ACO accommodation and restaurants output, CSO consulting services output, NFO number of farms with forestry, NSP number of farms with services provision, NER number of farms with renewable energy production, NMI number of mixed farms with crops and livestock, and NOR number of farms with sources of income mainly from outside.

Considering the heterogeneity of the variables considered and to avoid some statistical infractions, namely multi-colinearity, the model was disaggregated into different models for each case, considering the relationship between agricultural output and employment as a model base for every situation.

## 4 Data Description

All the statistical information was obtained via the Statistics of Portugal (INE 2014) and is relative to the variables described in the previous section.

The distribution of the values associated with each variable, across Portuguese municipalities, is shown in the following Figs. 9.1 (relative to the output of agriculture and other related sectors) and 9.2 (for the employment and the number of multifunctional farms).

From Fig. 9.1 it is possible to observe that the large part of economic activity, considered here to be more or less related to the farming sector, is concentrated within the Portuguese municipalities of the coastal north, center, and around Lisbon, with some exceptions for the coastal south (Alentejo) in the case of the agricultural output and for the textile industry that is concentrated mainly around the Oporto region. There are some exceptions, also, for the accommodation, restaurants, and consultant services in the municipalities of the extreme south of Portugal (Algarve).

Figure 9.2 shows that the number of farms with multifunctional activities does not follow the pattern referred to in Fig. 9.1. This context is expected considering that the alternative activities in the farms appear as a complement, plausibly in areas where agriculture has less productivity.

For example, the greater number of farms with forestry are situated in the municipalities of the interior of Portugal, namely in the central interior. The municipalities with a greater number of farms with services provision are located in the north (inland and coastal). Renewable energy production is verified, namely, in the regions near Lisbon and in the south interior.

Employment is greater in regions near Oporto, Lisbon, and in the coastal south (Alentejo). In this case, this pattern is more or less similar to that of the evolution of the agricultural output across the Portuguese municipalities.

The greatest number of farms with mixed production (crops and livestock) and with income coming from outside sources are situated in the interior north of Portugal, namely around the municipality of Bragança. These zones are indeed a part of Portugal with many difficulties, but with many dynamics.

Figures 9.3 and 9.4 are relative to the global spatial autocorrelation measured through Moran's I statistics. Moran's I can have values from $-1$ (perfect negative spatial autocorrelation) to 1 (perfect positive autocorrelation).

The negative global spatial autocorrelation means, for a variable, that the values in a municipality negatively influence the values of neighboring municipalities (the number of neighbors dependent on the distance or contiguity matrix considered), in the Portuguese context, for the case analyzed here, and vice versa.

These figures were obtained with GeoDa software (2014), considering a queen contiguity matrix for one (showing stronger global spatial autocorrelation) and five (almost without global spatial autocorrelation). When it is intended to analyze, for a certain variable, the relationships between closer spatial unities (municipalities, regions, countries, etc.) the considering of distance or contiguity matrix is crucial.

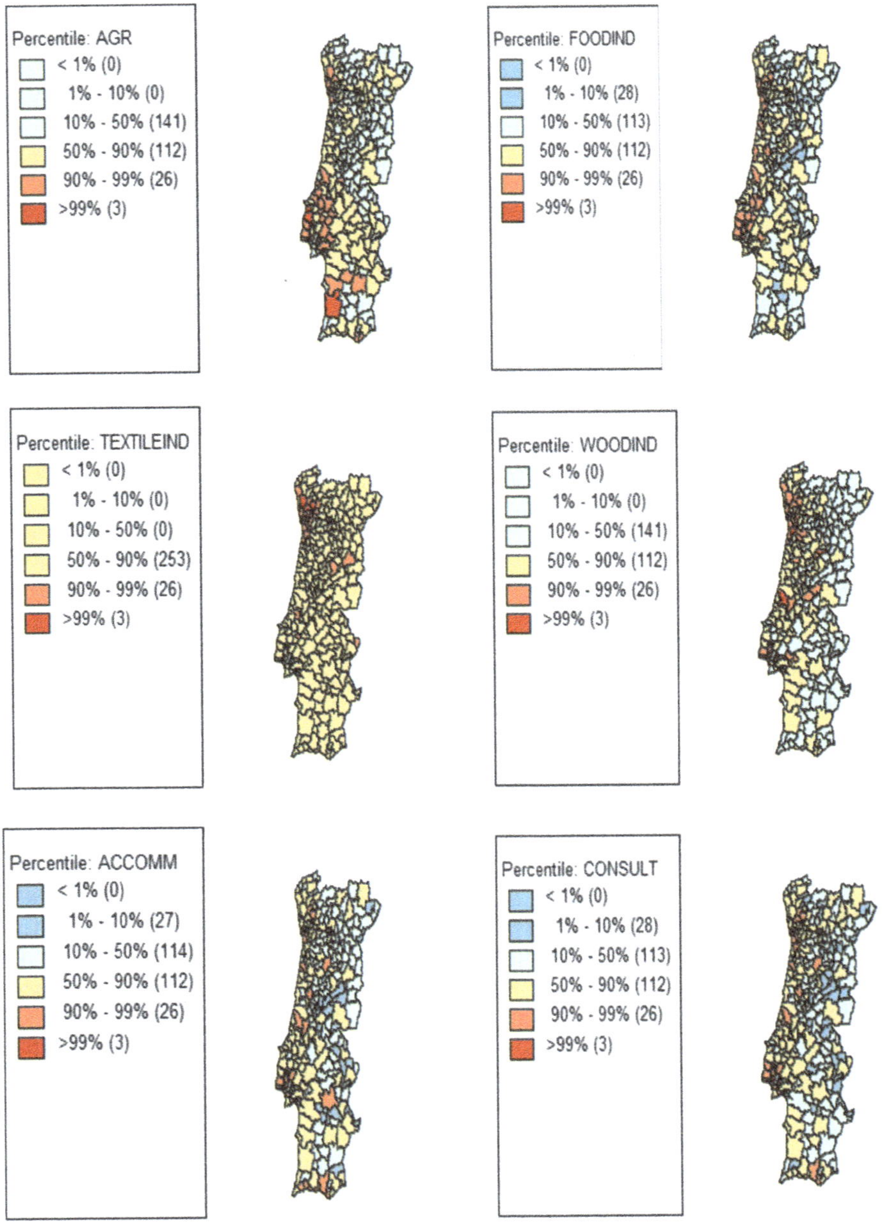


**Fig. 9.1** Distribution by Portuguese municipalities, over the year 2009, of the output of agriculture and others economic activities related with this sector. *Note*: AGR, agriculture; FOODIND, food industry; TEXTILEIND, textile industry; WOODIND, wood and cork industry; ACCOMM, accommodations and restaurants; CONSULT, consultant services

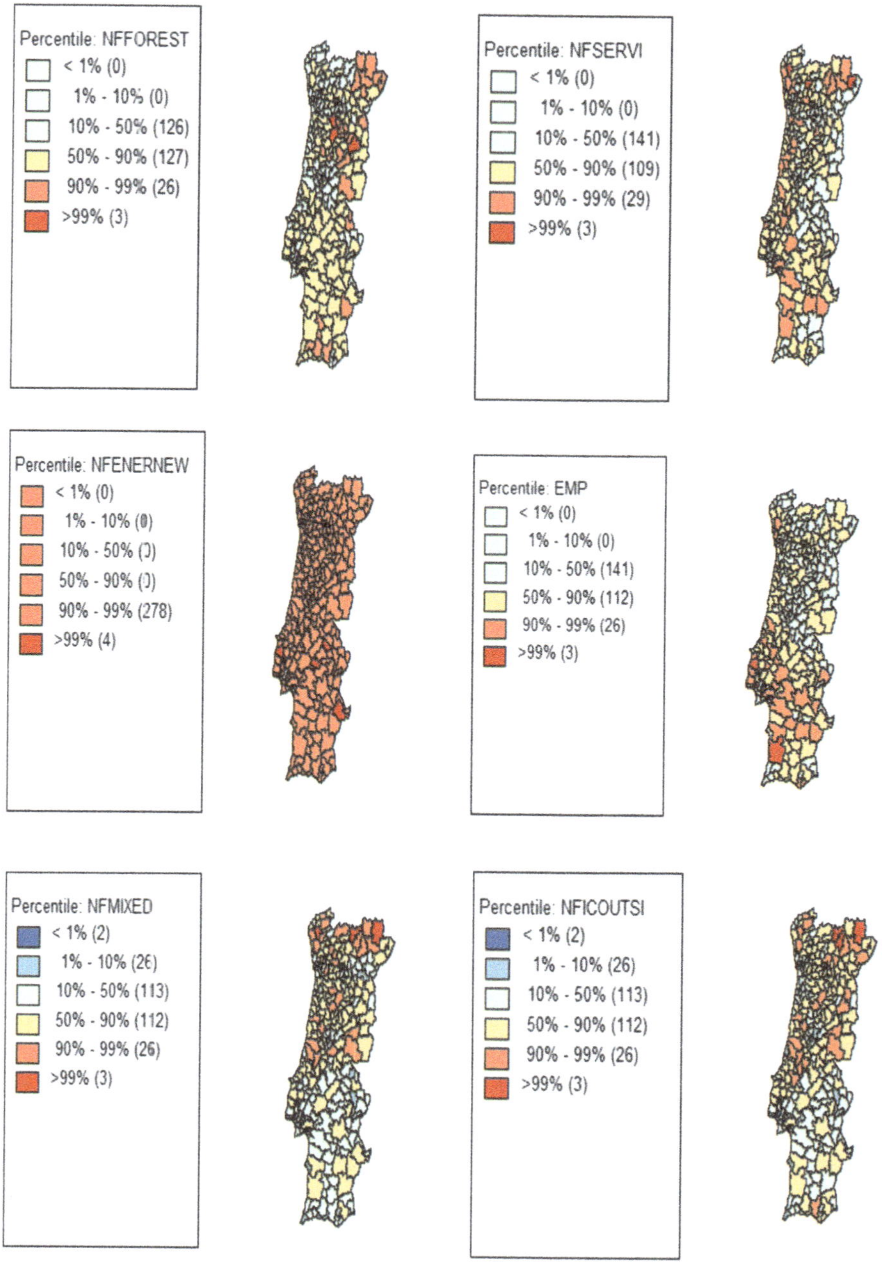


**Fig. 9.2** Distribution by Portuguese municipalities, over the year 2009, of the employment and the number of mixed farms and with other lucrative activities, from inside and outside. *Note*: NFFOREST, number of farms with forestry; NFSERVI, number of farms with service provision; NFENERNEW, farms of production of renewable energy; EMP, agricultural employment; NFMIXED, farms with mixed vegetal and animal production; NFICOUTSI, farms with income coming principally from outside

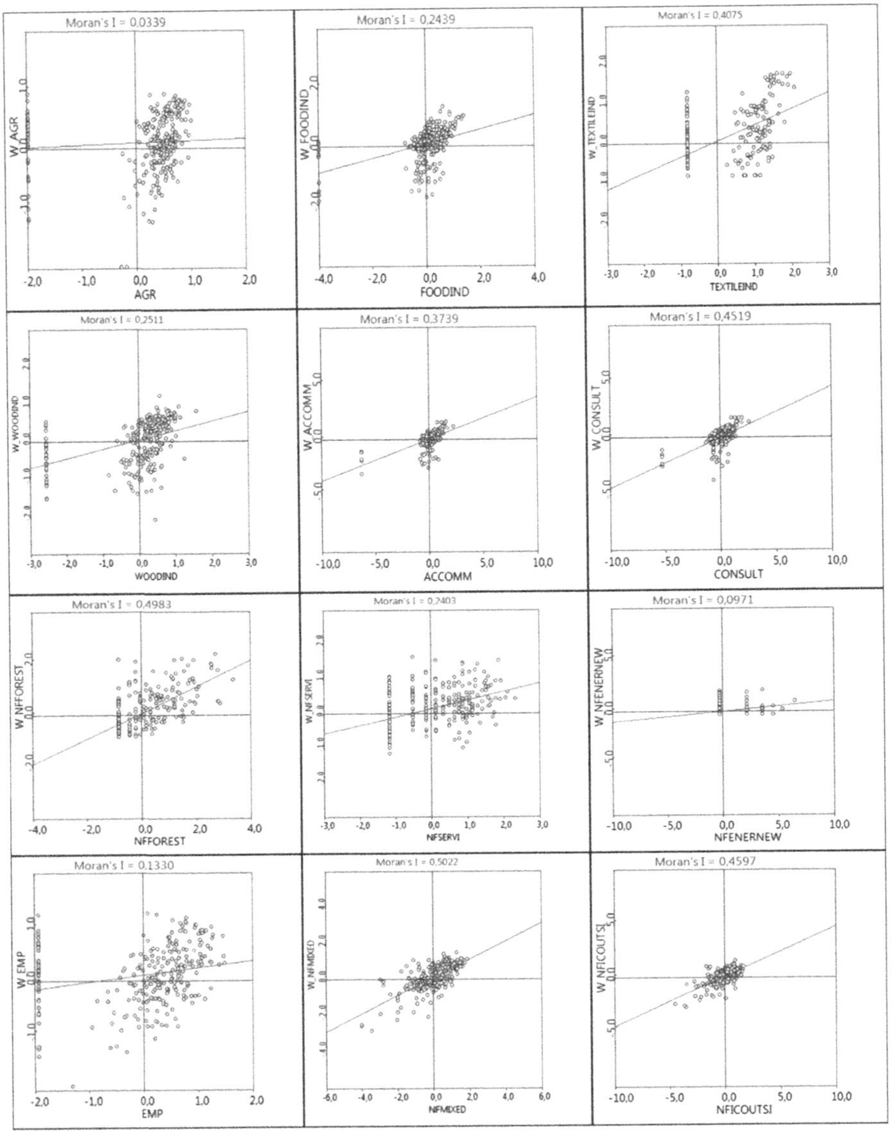


**Fig. 9.3** Global spatial autocorrelation obtained with a queen contiguity matrix, considering one neighbor

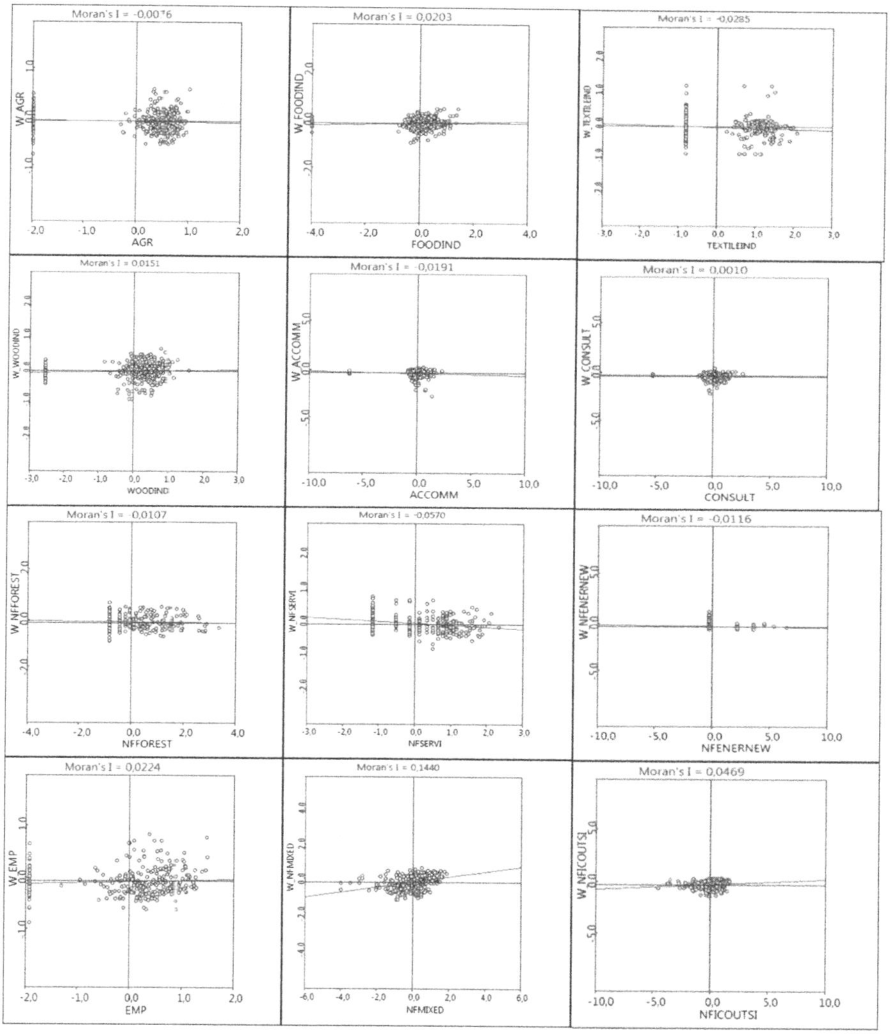


**Fig. 9.4** Global spatial autocorrelation obtained with a queen contiguity matrix, considering five neighbors

# 5 Results

Tables 9.1 and 9.2 present the results which were obtained, through Stata software (2014), with cross-sectional econometric methods and several statistic tests, namely the Breusch–Pagan/Cook–Weisberg test for heteroskedasticity (null hypothesis signifies no heteroskedasticity), the specification Ramsey RESET test using powers of the fitted values (null hypothesis indicates that the model is well specified), and

**Table 9.1** Cross-sectional results obtained among agricultural output, agricultural employment, and the output for the several sectors related with agriculture, for Portuguese municipalities and for the year 2009

| Model | OLS (Robust) | Model | OLS (Robust) | Model | OLS (Robust) | Model | OLS | Model | OLS |
|---|---|---|---|---|---|---|---|---|---|
| Constant | 6.912*<br>(19.450)<br>[0.000] | Constant | 7.265*<br>(22.220)<br>[0.000] | Constant | 6.424*<br>(15.210)<br>[0.000] | Constant | 6.195*<br>(12.740)<br>[0.000] | Constant | 6.906*<br>(19.770)<br>[0.000] |
| Employment | 1.136*<br>(25.890)<br>[0.000] | Employment | 1.224*<br>(25.180)<br>[0.000] | Employment | 1.189*<br>(32.460)<br>[0.000] | Employment | 1.144*<br>(27.650)<br>[0.000] | Employment | 1.143*<br>(27.540)<br>[0.000] |
| Food industry output | 0.083*<br>(2.780)<br>[0.006] | Textile industry output | 0.038**<br>(1.960)<br>[0.053] | Wood industry output | 0.108*<br>(3.440)<br>[0.001] | Accommodations and restaurants output | 0.121*<br>(3.520)<br>[0.001] | Consultant services output | 0.079*<br>(3.100)<br>[0.002] |
| Breusch–Pagan/Cook–Weisberg test for heteroskedasticity | 4.830*<br>[0.028] | Breusch–Pagan/Cook–Weisberg test for heteroskedasticity | 2.830**<br>[0.092] | Breusch–Pagan/Cook–Weisberg test for heteroskedasticity | 3.460**<br>[0.062] | Breusch–Pagan/Cook–Weisberg test for heteroskedasticity | 1.260<br>[0.261] | Breusch–Pagan/Cook–Weisberg test for heteroskedasticity | 0.180<br>[0.674] |
| Ramsey RESET test using powers of the fitted values | 0.320<br>[0.813] | Ramsey RESET test using powers of the fitted values | 1.130<br>[0.339] | Ramsey RESET test using powers of the fitted values | 0.560<br>[0.643] | Ramsey RESET test using powers of the fitted values | 0.470<br>[0.705] | Ramsey RESET test using powers of the fitted values | 0.210<br>[0.892] |
| Moran's I | 1.598<br>[0.109] | Moran's I | 1.453<br>[0.146] | Moran's I | 1.164<br>[0.244] | Moran's I | 1.780**<br>[0.075] | Moran's I | 1.920**<br>[0.054] |

*Note*: *Statistically significant at 5 %; **Statistically significant at 10 %

**Table 9.2** Cross-sectional results obtained among agricultural output, agricultural employment, and the number of farms with other sources of income from both inside and outside, for Portuguese municipalities and for the year 2009

| Model | OLS | Model | OLS | Model | OLS | Model | OLS | Model | OLS |
|---|---|---|---|---|---|---|---|---|---|
| Constant | 8.008* (27.430) [0.000] | Constant | 7.792* (31.190) [0.000] | Constant | 7.570* (14.810) [0.000] | Constant | 7.374* (27.010) [0.000] | Constant | 7.368* (24.540) [0.000] |
| Employment | 1.179* (22.730) [0.000] | Employment | 1.164* (23.800) [0.000] | Employment | 1.243* (13.970) [0.000] | Employment | 1.208* (31.670) [0.000] | Employment | 1.195* (31.060) [0.000] |
| Number of farms with forest | −0.083* (−2.870) [0.005] | Number of farms with service provision | 0.104* (2.070) [0.040] | Number of farms with renewable energies | −0.305** (−1.970) [0.055] | Number of farms mixed | 0.067* (2.030) [0.043] | Number of farms with the income coming principally from the outside | 0.066** (1.710) [0.089] |
| Breusch–Pagan/ Cook–Weisberg test for heteroskedasticity | 0.340 [0.557] | Breusch–Pagan/ Cook–Weisberg test for heteroskedasticity | 1.220 [0.269] | Breusch–Pagan/ Cook–Weisberg test for heteroskedasticity | 0.520 [0.469] | Breusch–Pagan/ Cook–Weisberg test for heteroskedasticity | 1.230 [0.267] | Breusch–Pagan/ Cook–Weisberg test for heteroskedasticity | 1.660 [0.198] |
| Ramsey RESET test using powers of the fitted values | 0.280 [0.840] | Ramsey RESET test using powers of the fitted values | 0.090 [0.965] | Ramsey RESET test using powers of the fitted values | 0.750 [0.5270] | Ramsey RESET test using powers of the fitted values | 0.190 [0.906] | Ramsey RESET test using powers of the fitted values | 0.150 [0.928] |
| Moran's I | 1.527 [0.126] | Moran's I | 1.759** [0.078] | Moran's I | 1.414 [0.157] | Moran's I | 0.818 [0.412] | Moran's I | 1.492 [0.135] |

*Note*: *Statistically significant at 5 %; **Statistically significant at 10 %

Moran's I to evaluate the existence of spatial autocorrelation effects in the regression (null hypothesis means no spatial autocorrelation effects). The values for Moran's I were obtained with GeoDa (2014). The presence of these statistical infractions implies that the results are biased and consequently the conclusions obtained are unadjusted. In some cases there is sign of heteroskedasticity that was corrected with the OLS robust econometric method.

In the two tables the coefficient of the constant varies between 6 and 8 (always with statistical significance), which signifies that there are other variables that influence agricultural output in Portuguese municipalities in addition to those considered (this may be an interesting topic for future studies).

On the other hand the coefficient for agricultural employment is, also, always statistically significant and presents positive values around 1.

In relation to the other variables, only a number of farms with forestry and with renewable energy production have negative effects on the agricultural output (−0.083 and −0.305, respectively). Among the other activities related to agriculture (Table 9.1), the stronger effect comes from the accommodation and restaurants output and also from the wood and cork industry (respectively 0.121 and 0.108). In multifunctional agricultural activities the most important effects come from the number of farms with service provisions (0.104).

In any case the effects of the other activities related with farming and the alternative production that can be developed within farms have a marginal effect over agricultural performance, with values for the coefficients at around 0.1.

The values of the statistical tests (Breusch–Pagan/Cook–Weisberg test for heteroskedasticity, the specification Ramsey RESET test using powers of the fitted values, and Moran's I to evaluate the existence of spatial autocorrelation effects in regression) show that there are no problems with the associated statistical infraction. There are, only, some problems with the heteroskedasticity that was resolved by using the OLS robust.

These data and results show that more concentration upon economic activity is needed, namely those related with agriculture, in the rural zones of the interior and that more capacity to develop alternative activities is also needed, for farming, inside and outside of farms that bring more income to the farmers. To have more positive externalities in agricultural output from industry and services, it is determinant whether these activities are located more in rural zones nearer to the farming sector.

**Conclusions**

The revision of literature related to the issue raised in this study shows that rural development has many problems, with difficult solutions, namely those related with low population density, weak economic activity, and a lack of infrastructures.

(continued)

The integrated rural development, where agriculture can be interrelated with other sectors, seems to be an interesting way to promote territorial branding and potentiating the endogenous products.

The related industries (food, wood, cork, paper, etc.) and services (restaurants, accommodation, consulting services, etc.) can afford an important contribution to this integrated development, but policies are needed to prevent the movement of economic activity and the population from rural to urban zones. The policies must improve accessibility, reducing the costs of transportation and communication, and improving both the basic and nonbasic infrastructures available in these rural zones. However, in Portugal over the coming years and considering the economic and financial crisis this will prove to be difficult, but with some imagination it will be possible to find some solutions.

The landscapes of farms often afford the farmers with enormous potentialities to explore other sources of income, by increasing the multifunctionality of agriculture, namely when the farming activity is not sufficient for the farmer to obtain reasonable earnings for their household. But this often requires some strategies in order to promote well organized alternative activities with significant welfare for society.

Either way, the literature shows that any solution for rural areas must take into account the farmers and the rural economic and social operators, because they know these areas and their dynamics well and can consequently help in the design of adjusted strategies. Several aforementioned studies have been carried out in many European countries which prove this conclusion. Indeed, the local dynamics are extremely specific and must be considered during any successful approach.

The data description shows that the context in Portuguese municipalities is not an exception to those verified in other countries. There is evidence of desertification in rural regions (interior of Portugal) with some congestion in urban areas (littoral, namely north, center, and around Lisbon). Indeed, the concentration for the output of the economic activities considered is greater in the areas around Oporto, Lisbon, and other smaller urban regions of the north and center. It will be important to find adjusted strategies to bring these economic dynamics to the interior so as to promote more positive externalities for agriculture. On the other hand, the greater number of farms with multifunctionality can be found in the interior.

The results obtained in the econometric estimations reveal that the contribution of these activities developed both inside and outside of farms provides a marginal contribution to agricultural performance (when they have statistical significance), but the majority do in fact have a positive effect, which makes for an interesting start.

(continued)

In future research it will be important to test adjusted strategies so as to improve the contexts in the municipalities located around the rural regions of Portugal. The design of these policies must take into account the opinions of the local operators.

## References

Bakri, D. A. (2001). Towards developing a geoscientific approach to sustainable agricultural and rural development. *Environmental Geology, 40*(4–5), 543–556.

Bathrellos, G. D., Gaki-Papanastassiou, K., Skilodimou, H. D., Skianis, G. A., & Chousianitis, K. G. (2013). Assessment of rural community and agricultural development using geomorphological–geological factors and GIS in the Trikala prefecture (Central Greece). *Stochastic Environmental Research and Risk Assessment, 27*, 573–588.

Branca, G., Hissa, H., Benez, M. C., Medeiros, K., Lipper, L., Tinlot, M., et al. (2013). Capturing synergies between rural development and agricultural mitigation in Brazil. *Land Use Policy, 30*, 507–518.

Choisis, J. P., Sourdril, A., Deconchat, M., Balent, G., & Gibon, A. (2010). Comprendre la dynamique régionale des exploitations de polyculture élevage pour accompagner le développement rural dans les Coteaux de Gascogne. *Cahiers Agricultures, 19*(2), 97–103.

Cobb, C. W., & Douglas, P. H. (1928). A theory of production. *American Economic Review, 18* (Suppl), 139–165.

Dibden, J., Potter, C., & Cocklin, C. (2009). Contesting the neoliberal project for agriculture: Productivist and multifunctional trajectories in the European Union and Australia. *Journal of Rural Studies, 25*, 299–308.

Dwyer, J., Ward, N., Lowe, P., & Baldock, D. (2007). European rural development under the common agricultural policy's 'Second Pillar': Institutional conservatism and innovation. *Regional Studies, 41*, 873–887.

Firmino, A. (1999). Agriculture and landscape in Portugal. *Landscape and Urban Planning, 46*, 83–91.

Fleury, P., Petit, S., Dobremez, L., Schermer, M., Kirchengast, C., De Ros, G., et al. (2008). Implementing sustainable agriculture and rural development in the European Alps. *Mountain Research and Development, 28*(3), 226–232.

GeoDa. (2014). *Informatic software*. http://geodacenter.asu.edu/

Granvik, M., Lindberg, G., Stigzelius, K.-A., Fahlbeck, E., & Surry, Y. (2012). Prospects of multifunctional agriculture as a facilitator of sustainable rural development: Swedish experience of Pillar 2 of the Common Agricultural Policy (CAP). *Norsk Geografisk Tidsskrift_Norwegian Journal of Geography, 66*, 155–166.

Groot, J. C. J., Rossing, W. A. H., Tichit, M., Turpin, N., Jellema, A., Baudry, J., et al. (2009). On the contribution of modelling to multifunctional agriculture: Learning from comparisons. *Journal of Environmental Management, 90*, S147–S160.

Hassink, J., Hulsink, W., & Grin, J. (2012). Care farms in the Netherlands: An underexplored example of multifunctional agriculture—toward an empirically grounded, organization-theory-based typology. *Rural Sociology, 77*(4), 569–600.

Hassink, J., Grin, J., & Hulsink, W. (2013). Multifunctional agriculture meets health care: Applying the multi-level transition sciences perspective to care farming in the Netherlands. *Sociologia Ruralis, 53*(2), 223–245.

Heringa, P. W., van der Heide, C. M., & Heijman, W. J. M. (2013). The economic impact of multifunctional agriculture in Dutch regions: An input-output model. *NJAS - Wageningen Journal of Life Sciences, 64–65*, 59–66.

Hildén, M., Jokinen, P., & Aakkula, J. (2012). The sustainability of agriculture in a northern industrialized country—From controlling nature to rural development. *Sustainability, 4*, 3387–3403.

Howells, O., Edwards-Jones, G., & Morgan, O. (1998). Ecozone II: A decision support system for aiding environmental impact assessments in agriculture and rural development projects in developing countries. *Computers and Electronics in Agriculture, 20*, 145–164.

INE. (2014). *Several statistics*. Statistics of Portugal.

Labarthe, P. (2009). Extension services and multifunctional agriculture. Lessons learnt from the French and Dutch contexts and approaches. *Journal of Environmental Management, 90*, S193–S202.

Magnani, N., & Struffi, L. (2009). Translation sociology and social capital in rural development initiatives. A case study from the Italian Alps. *Journal of Rural Studies, 25*, 231–238.

Marsden, T., & Sonnino, R. (2008). Rural development and the regional state: Denying multifunctional agriculture in the UK. *Journal of Rural Studies, 24*, 422–431.

Mettepenningen, E., Vandermeulen, V., Van Huylenbroeck, G., Schuermans, N., Van Hecke, E., Messely, L., et al. (2012). Exploring synergies between place branding and agricultural landscape management as a rural development practice. *Sociologia Ruralis, 52*(4), 432–452.

Moon, W., & Griffith, J. W. (2011). Assessing holistic economic value for multifunctional agriculture in the US. *Food Policy, 36*, 455–465.

Parra-López, C., Groot, J. C. J., Carmona-Torres, C., & Rossing, W. A. H. (2008). Integrating public demands into model-based design for multifunctional agriculture: An application to intensive Dutch dairy landscapes. *Ecological Economics, 67*, 538–551.

Pinto-Correia, T. (2000). Future development in Portuguese rural areas: How to manage agricultural support for landscape conservation? *Landscape and Urban Planning, 50*, 95–106.

Râmniceanu, I., & Ackrill, R. (2007). EU rural development policy in the new member states: Promoting multifunctionality? *Journal of Rural Studies, 23*, 416–429.

Refsgaard, K., & Johnson, T. G. (2010). Modelling policies for multifunctional agriculture and rural development – A norwegian case study. Environmental Policy and Governance, Special Issue: European Society for Ecological Economics 2009 Conference; *Transformation, Innovation and Adaptation For Sustainability, 20*(4), 239–257.

Renting, H., Rossing, W. A. H., Groot, J. C. J., Van der Ploeg, J. D., Laurent, C., Perraud, D., et al. (2009). Exploring multifunctional agriculture. A review of conceptual approaches and prospects for an integrative transitional Framework. *Journal of Environmental Management, 90*, S112–S123.

Rizov, M. (2006). Rural development perspectives in enlarging Europe: The implications of CAP reforms and agricultural transition in accession countries. *European Planning Studies, 14*(2), 219–238.

Rossing, W. A. H., Zander, P., Josien, E., Groot, J. C. J., Meyer, B. C., & Knierim, A. (2007). Integrative modelling approaches for analysis of impact of multifunctional agriculture: A review for France, Germany and The Netherlands. *Agriculture, Ecosystems and Environment, 120*, 41–57.

Shortall, S. (2008). Are rural development programmes socially inclusive? Social inclusion, civic engagement, participation, and social capital: Exploring the differences. *Journal of Rural Studies, 24*, 450–457.

Stata. (2014). *Statistics/Data analysis*. StataCorp, LP.

Unwin, T. (1997). Agricultural restructuring and integrated rural development in Estonia. *Journal of Rural Studies, 13*(I), 93–112.

Wilson, G. A. (2009). The spatiality of multifunctional agriculture: A human geography perspective. *Geoforum, 40*, 269–280.

Yong-fu, C., Zhi-gang, W., Tie-hui, Z., Lei, Y., Guo-ying, M., & Hsiao-ping, C. (2013). Agricultural policy, climate factors and grain output: Evidence from household survey data in rural China. *Journal of Integrative Agriculture, 12*(1), 169–183.

Zander, P., Knierim, A., Groot, J. C. J., & Rossing, W. A. H. (2007). Multifunctionality of agriculture: Tools and methods for impact assessment and valuation. *Agriculture, Ecosystems and Environment, 120*, 1–4.
Zasada, I. (2011). Multifunctional peri-urban agriculture—A review of societal demands and the provision of goods and services by farming. *Land Use Policy, 28*, 639–648.

# Chapter 10
# The Objectives and Priorities for the Azorean Dairy Farmers' Decisions

**Emiliana Silva, Ana Alexandra Marta-Costa, and Julio Berbel**

## 1 Introduction

The single objective of profit maximization has been the classical and neoclassic model for firms' decision making. Nowadays, it is accepted that several and different objectives are most common where the decision is taken at the farm or regional level. That means that profit maximization is a part of the decision models and other objectives must be taken into account in order to be closer to reality. Also, in some cases, firms do not maximize the objectives but rather want to achieve some previously fixed goals (Romero and Rehman 1989). For instance, it is known that familiar farmers must be interested in profit optimization, but also leisure and the farms sustainability have importance (Silva and Berbel 2004).

The recognition of the existence of multiple and sometimes conflictive objectives, since the satisfaction of one implies the underperformance of the other (and vice versa), imposes the multi-criteria methodologies as more suitable to the agricultural reality. Its main objectives are the models development to provide optimal decisions and present the best solutions, reflecting greater adherence to

E. Silva
Centre of Applied Economics Studies of the Atlantic (CEEAplA), Azores University, Rua Capitão João de Ávila, Pico da Urze, 9700-042 S. Pedro, Angra do Heroísmo, Portugal
e-mail: emiliana@uac.pt

A.A. Marta-Costa (✉)
Centre for Transdisciplinary Development Studies (CETRAD), University of Trás-os-Montes and Alto Douro (UTAD), ECHS - Pólo II, Quinta dos Prados, 5000-801, Vila Real, Portugal
e-mail: amarta@utad.pt; http://www.utad.pt

J. Berbel
Córdoba University, Córdoba, Spain
e-mail: Spain.berbel@uco.es



V.J.P.D. Martinho (ed.), *The Agricultural Economics of the 21$^{st}$ Century*,
DOI 10.1007/978-3-319-09471-7_10

reality, taking into account a set of multiple objectives which, being in conflict, cannot be optimized simultaneously. The balance will result in the best combination between them, through a compromise between the solutions, which satisfy as far as possible the proposed targets (Poeta 1994).

This chapter aims to estimate the influence of the objectives in the decision process, using a multi-criteria approach on dairy farmers. This allows to define a surrogate utility function for a dairy farm typology, regarding the different grazing systems. As a consequence the dairy farms' priorities can be provided as well as how they can restrain the decision making.

The study object is the Azores archipelago (Portugal) that produces mainly cow's milk, which represented in 2010 about 30 % of Portuguese milk and 35 % of Portuguese cheese production (INE 2009). More than 27 % of the dairy milk Portuguese quota (2011) was attributed to this region, about 548,000 tons of milk (IFAP 2012), which have 33 % of dairy cows (92,000) of the Portuguese country (INE 2011).

## 2 Multi-criteria Methodologies

There are several techniques that look to support the decision maker in the course of the decision process, with regard to the farmers' priorities. Poeta (1994) uses Rodrigues (1988) to identify two groups of Multi-Criteria decision methods designed to respond to different types of problems: (1) design problems, where the criteria are defined by the objectives and the solutions vary by a continuous mode (continuously variation) and (2) selection problems, whose criteria are defined by the attributes and the number of solutions is finite (discrete variation).

Each one of these problems gives rise to a set of techniques which fall in two major groups (Fig. 10.1): Multiobjective decision techniques (design problems) and Multi-Attribute decision techniques based on Utility Theory (MAUT) developed by Keeney and Raiffa (1976).

Multiobjective decision techniques incorporate the MOP and GP based on conceptual difference between objectives and goals. The objectives represent an improvement of any attribute, through its maximization or minimization. The attribute concept refers to the values of decision maker, related with the objective reality, being capable of mathematical setting, that is, a function of the decision variables.

Moreover, the targets are constraints concerning the mathematical structure and formal appearance. The difference between them lies in the meaning of the second member of the inequation. For the goals, the second member is an aspiration level desired by the decision center that may be or not be achieved, while for the constraints, the second member must be satisfied to find a possible solution.

The MOP is applied when the decision context is defined by a series of objectives to optimize that must satisfy a certain set of constraints. As the simultaneous optimization of all objectives is virtually impossible, the MOP aims to

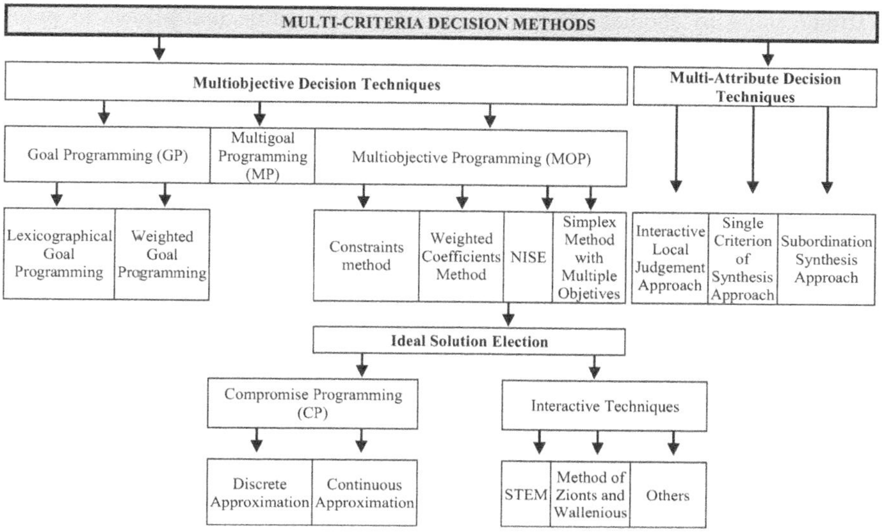


**Fig. 10.1** Multi-Criteria decision methods (Cohon 1978; Zeleny 1982; Romero and Rehman 1989; Romero 1993; Poeta 1994; and Silva 2001)

determine a set of efficient solutions, in a first step, and ideal solutions in a second step, from the first.

If the decision center has to make a decision in a context of multiple goals, then he should apply GP. This optimization program is developed by minimizing the deviations between the actually achieved goals and the aspiration levels set previously.

This minimization process can be achieved by two alternative ways: Lexicographical Goal Programming and Weighted Goal Programming. The first admits that decision maker is able to define all goals and establish priorities among them. The second doesn't consider priorities and the goals are simultaneously embraced on an objective function by minimizing the sum of all deviations between the goals and aspiration levels. The deviations are subsequently weighted according to the importance that the decision center assigns to each goal.

Constraints Method; Weighting Coefficients Method; NISE Method (Non Inferior Set Estimation Method), and Simplex Method with Multiple Objectives are the Multiobjective Programming methods that allow to achieve the efficient solutions.

The first method (Constraints Method) optimizes one of the objectives and the remaining is incorporated in the constraints set. The Weighting Coefficients Method is the combination of all objectives into a single function (aggregated and weighted), associating a weight or weighting coefficient to each one. The NISE Method is a variant of the Weighting Coefficients Method based on the attribution of weights for each objective according to the slope of the straight lines that connect the extreme efficient points. The method of the simplex algorithm with multiple objectives generates the efficient set through a "jump" from an extreme point to another. This method uses a subroutine that allows to prove (or not) the effectiveness of each extreme point.

The MP is hybrid between GP and MOP, which minimizes the deviation variables with a vector such as vector optimization (MOP). It brings together the idea of "meeting" of the GP and the demand for efficient solutions of MOP. It is classified as an interactive method, because it seeks interactively the goals or aspiration levels of the decision center (Silva 2001).

When possible solutions and the efficient set are found, it is necessary to determine the ideal solution, that is, the solution that is closest to the ideal point. There are basically two techniques for the election of the ideal solution within the efficient set: CP and Interactive Techniques.

The CP proposes to reduce the efficient set based on the notion of distance between (possible) solutions and the ideal solution, through discrete or continuous approach. This ideal is a utopian solution but it is also a reference point for the decision maker.

The interactive methods have the advantage of the decision maker intervention, which progressively defines his preferences. The analyst is the intermediary between the model and decision center, that is, the first calculates and the second decides, so there is an interaction between the decision maker and the model. There are various interactive techniques such as STEM and Zionts and Wallenius Methods. Other interactive methods can be found in Silva (2001).

The Multi-Attribute decision techniques are intended to select the options from among a set of predetermined solutions (discrete set of alternatives) through a cardinal utility function, which is a mathematical expression able to order the preferences among different alternatives. To do so, for each attribute value a corresponding function is determined. This system allows to distinguish the three methodologies that are identified in Fig. 10.1, based on discrete variables.

In the Interactive Local Judgement Approach, the process of preferences modeling is based on the dialogue between the analyst and the decision maker. With the calculation process, the analyst must submit an alternative to decision maker that he should enjoy. This cycle of dialogue and calculation ends when the decision maker is satisfied with an alternative that he considers to be the best.

When the preferences modeling is done by a function construction that aggregates multiple criteria is referred as Single Criterion of Synthesis Approach. This technique starts from a discrete number of alternatives and accept certain assumptions about the preferences of the decision maker, being possible to establish the utility function.

Finally, the Subordination Synthesis Approach assumes that preferences are modeled by a binary relation construction, called a subordination relationship, in order to the comparison, indifference, or preference of one of the two alternatives.

## 3 Decision Making Support Models for Agriculture

Although that the methodologies based on the Multi-Criteria decision theory be used in a context of multiple objectives, the fact is that they are associated with specific themes being the pursuit of sustainability in agriculture who has more gained space in the research of decision making. The agricultural sustainability concept, since it integrates the environmental, economic, and social dimension, came to significantly increase the complexity of decision making process, given the multiplicity of objectives involved and the conflict often generated in its optimization (Carvalho 2006). In fact, agricultural farm units are faced, on the one hand, to the maximization of the economic performance and, on the other hand, to the need to preserve and to protect the environment and natural resources, taking into account issues of social equity. Such a challenge requires, among other things, an appropriate consumption of production factors (such as fertilizers and crop protection products), and a readjustment of the used technologies (mainly through the adoption of energy saving measures), without jeopardizing food safety standards that society expects (Marta-Costa 2008, 2010; Marta-Costa et al. 2013).

The first researches that aimed to solve problems with objectives of economic efficiency, environmental quality, social welfare, and economic and regional development were of Neely et al. (1977). In this study, the technique of goal programming was applied, the model being developed in projects dedicated to water resources.

Other works that followed with the application in water management in agriculture, reconciling economic and environmental goals, were the ones of Zekri and Romero (1993), Heilman et al. (1997), Carvalho (2006), Raju and Vasan (2007), and Zhang et al. (2007). However, the planning of the agricultural systems and land use, in order to coordinate multi-sectorial goals, has been the main target of the study by Bartlett and Clawson (1978), Shakya and Leuschner (1990), Antoine et al. (1997), Dunn et al. (1998), Thankappan et al. (2006), and Silvestri et al. (2007), while Mardle et al. (2000) have been dedicated to the management of fish activity and Diaz-Balteiro and Romero (2004b) applied the goal programming for the development of a plan for a sustainable forest management.

Also, the development and evaluation of the effects of regulatory policies or supporting activity have been developed based on the multi-criteria theory. It was the case of Willet et al. (1997), Köbrich and Rehman (1998), Flury et al. (2000), and Rozakis et al. (2001) works. Recently Bartolini et al. (2007) stand out by assessing the impact of various scenarios of agricultural policies and water on sustainability of selected agricultural irrigation systems in Italy.

The analysis of critical framework of methodologies applied in farm planning on the context of multiple objectives (Fig. 10.1) allows to emphasize that under the multi-criteria decision theory, several methodological alternatives can be identified. The assumptions on which they are based as well as the advantages and limitations they present lead to the claim that there is no "better" methodology than another;

there are several factors that affect the use of methodologies in same problems that are intended to solve.

Moreover, the use of various multi-criteria methods are often not done in an isolated or individual way, but integrated or in a combined form, complementing the procedures performed, as evidenced by the work of Zekri and Romero (1991), Poeta (1994), Lakshminarayan et al. (1995), Van Huylenbroeck (1997), Mimouni et al. (2000), Raju et al. (2001), El-Gayar and Leung (2001), Carvalho (2006), Akkal-Corfini et al. (2007), Latinopoulos (2007), Marta-Costa (2008, 2010), and Marta-Costa et al. (2013) where objectives of multiple nature, which included criteria for economic, social, and/or environmental, have been equated.

Other times, the obtained results from the Multi-Criteria decision models allow the development of methodologies for planning, simulation, or evaluation as seen in the works of Prathapar et al. (1997), Nibbering and Van Rheenen (1998), Zander and Kächele (1999), Diaz-Balteiro and Romero (2004a), Meyer-Aurich (2005), and Groot et al. (2007). In the first a multi-criteria hierarchical structure (Salt Water And Groundwater MANagement—SWAGMAN) to identify a profitable use for the land not destined for rice cultivation was developed. Nibbering and Van Rheenen (1998) presented a tool for the analysis of agricultural systems (Quantified Farming Systems Analysis—QFSA), based on the optimal allocation of resources at the farm level (Farm Level Optimal Resource Allocation—FLORA). Zander and Kächele (1999) developed a model based on hierarchically interrelated modules, called Multi-Objective Decision Support Tool for Agroecosystem Management—MODAM, later used by Meyer-Aurich (2005). IMAGES (Interactive Multi-goal Agricultural Landscape Generation and Evaluation System) is the designation of the methodology for land optimization use proposed by Groot et al. (2007), where agronomic, economic, and environmental indicators with indicators of biodiversity and landscape quality are combined. And, through the techniques of Multi-Criteria decision, Diaz-Balteiro and Romero (2004a) have proposed a "Sustainability Index" to assess the sustainability of natural systems, according to a set of indicators, based on the minimization of the distance to the ideal point. Its objectives consisted of a compromise between solutions that promote maximum aggregate sustainability (engineering solution) and the most balanced solutions (green solution).

In the concrete case of the Azores study in regard to the farmers' priorities, the two main approaches showed in Fig. 10.1 can be used in building decision making models. The major difficulty associated with the formulation of MAUT models lies in the high degree of interaction with the decision maker required by this methodology. This is important in agriculture, where cultural background is often the most suitable form undertaken in such interactive process, but it is difficult to apply to agriculture decisions, because there is some interaction difficulty between the analyst and the farmer (low level of education) (Amador et al. 1998). However, Multiobjective criteria lack the theoretical soundness of MAUT, but it can accommodate in a realistic manner the multiplicity of criteria inherent to most agricultural planning problems (Romero and Rehman 1989).

The selection of the relevant objectives and the estimation of the related weights, as alternative of MAUT, present a methodology proposed by Sumpsi et al. (1996), Amador et al. (1998), and Berbel and Rodríguez-Ocaña (1998), which allows the assessment of the farmers' utility function. The proposed method does not rely on interaction with the decision maker, but is aware of the actual behavior demonstrated by the farmers, meaning a utility function consistent with the preferences revealed by the farmers themselves will be obtained.

The utility models have wide applications in agriculture, as confirmed in the works of Rehman and Romero (1987), Gómez-Limón and Berbel (1995), Sumpsi et al. (1996), and Gómez-Limón and Berbel (2000). The use of the weighted-goals program in this sector to estimate the utility function was developed in the last for multiple authors.

Preferences of the decision centers (Heilman et al. 1997; Carvalho 2006) or of the local population (Tiwari et al. 1999) are usually incorporated in Multi-Criteria decision models. However, other studies use MAUT to estimate a surrogate utility function for farmers' decision process (Amador et al. 1998; Gómez-Limón and Berbel 2000; Riesgo and Goméz-Limón 2006; Bartolini et al. 2007), which will be outlined later to face the parallelism with the present work.

Amador et al. (1998) proposes a methodological approach for electing farmers' utility functions (using three functions: separable and additive utility function, Tchebycheff utility function, and augmented Tchebycheff utility function), for observing the actual behavior of farmers. They use this methodology assuming the conflictive objectives (working capital, risk, and profit) of Spanish farmers. Their results showed that multiple objectives are taken in account by farmers' decision, but the traditional objective, profit maximization, is not always the most important in their decisions. This result is very important to understand the decision making process in agriculture and the farmers' behavior.

Gómez-Limón and Berbel (2000) used a weighted goal programming to estimate a surrogate utility function for farmers' decision process. This model allows them to estimate the value of water demand in irrigated crop production and the economic, social, and environmental impact, using as farmers' objectives profit maximization and risk and labor input minimization. Their results show that the water price is not the only tool to reduce the water consumption but also the economic and social impact, which means a negative effect in agricultural income and employment.

Silva (2001) estimated a surrogate utility analysis using the weighted goal programming for Azorean dairy farms. The first step found three types of grazing system, a second step estimates a payoff matrix with the most relevant objectives, and finally, a utility function that reveals the dairy farm objectives for each system grazing was estimated. The results showed that only the less intensive system grazing (low than 1.4 animals per ha) weighted income. The other system grazing (1.4–2.4 and superior to 2.4 animals per ha) has little significance in the objectives of priorities for Azorean dairy farms. It can be explained by the amount of subsidies in total income (around 20 %).

A methodological approach to simulate policy scenarios by using multi-criteria mathematical programming models for simulating the behavior of farmers, in

Spain, was developed by Riesgo and Goméz-Limón (2006). These authors have been chosen MAUT as the methodological framework for model-building at farm level and four objectives (total gross margin, risk, total labor, and working capital) to support the decision making process. The results obtained define a set of relevant economic, social, and environmental attributes related to public criteria. The results show the usefulness of this methodological approach to evaluate the impact of policies. Also it was found the need of water pricing and agricultural policy to be closely coordinated in order to meet the EU's policy objectives for the irrigated agriculture sector.

Bartolini et al. (2007) show the effects of the scenarios on five irrigated farming systems were simulated using multi-attribute linear programming models representing the reactions of the farms to external variables defined by each scenario. The results show a tradeoff between socioeconomic and environmental sustainability. In this research objectives connected with income (net income and profit) and labor (total, family, and external) were used. This emphasizes the need for a differentiated application of the Water Framework Directive at the local level as well as a more careful balance of water conservation, agricultural policy, and rural development objectives.

In Portugal, the cases studies of Carvalho (2006, 2007) can be highlighted for the overall planning of irrigation intervention in the area of Alqueva, taking into account multiple criteria of economic, social, and environmental nature. These works simulated the possible preference of decision centers to face the identified objectives, through the utility function maximizing, with different weighting assumptions to the criteria. Two hypotheses reflected only the economic concerns and risk aversion, while the remaining three considered issues of environmental and social nature.

# 4 Material and Methods

Many authors have demonstrated the complexity of farmers' decision making (Solano et al. 2001; Bergevoet et al. 2004) and stressed the importance of a variety of criteria that are taken into account by farmers when they have to decide. These studies suggest that decision making is driven by other criteria conflictive with profit such as risk, leisure, environmental policies, and others. In the light of these findings, MAUT has been proposed to this chapter as a theoretical approach for the Multi-Criteria decision making programming modeling, which uses not only the classical single-attribute utility function (profit maximization) but also take into account other farmers' objectives in their decision making processes. Riesgo and Goméz-Limón (2006) concisely described this methodology as a calibration procedure developed through a process of weighted goal programming that estimates objective weightings that better fit actual farmers' behavior. The MAUT was used in this model because the other methodologies that allows to estimate the utility function needs in its processes an interaction between farmers and models analyst.

In the case study, the education level of Azores dairy farmers is low and it will be very hard to have a suitable answer. Then, MAUT allows to estimate this function, indirectly.

The data of Azorean dairy farms, for the years 1990–1996, were obtained on the Farm Accountancy Data Network (FADN), complemented with INRA (1988) and the previous research of Berbel and Barros (1993).

Based on the seven production system types of Azorean dairy farms defined by Silva and Berbel (2006), according to specialization (meat, milk, mixed) and intensification criteria (intensive, medium, extensive), only the dairy milk typology was selected for this case study (Type I, II, and III—grazing systems), because these types of farms have a bigger impact on greenhouse gas (methane emissions) in the Azorean animal grazing system. Three groups were distinguished by Silva and Berbel (2006), using FADN, according to its intensification: Group I—medium intensive grazing systems (1.4–2.4 cows per ha), Group II—low intensive grazing systems (less than 1.4 cows per ha), and Group III—high intensive grazing systems (more than 2.4 cows per ha).

The Multi-Criteria methodology used in this research (MAUT) was developed according to Sumpsi et al. (1996) and used by Berbel et al. (1999). It follows four main steps:

1. To establish a set of objectives that can influence the farmers' decision. In this research objectives were defined according to the literature (economic and social) and the new development of CAP (environmental nature). Besides, a survey by inquiry was done to the Azorean dairy farms to point the most important three objectives in their decision making process. Five objectives were found: profit maximization, risk minimization, labor seasonality minimization, leisure maximization, and deviations to the goal of total labor minimization.
2. To determinate the square matrix, according to the number of objectives, that is the "payoff" matrix for above five objectives (five lines and five columns), through the optimization of each objective. The ideal (the best value in the optimization) and anti-ideal values (the worst values in optimization) were also defined in this phase.
3. To obtain the real values for the objective function, through the literature and statistical data research and based on inquiries to the farmers.
4. To obtain the set of weights ($W_j$) that indicates the ranking of the objectives followed by a farmer elicited, which reproduces their behavior and reflects the farmers' preference by solving the weighting goal programming approach.
5. If the weights found in (4) were satisfactory, the process finishes and, finally, the utility function is estimated. If the weights weren't satisfactory, there is a need to search another possible solution.

In order to get a solution, Amador et al. (1998) propose three alternative criteria to get a solution: the $L_1$ criterion and the Manhattan utility function ($\mu$), the Tchebycheff function, and an intermediate criterion (a mix of Tchebycheff and Manhattan). The first was chosen because that criterion is widely used in most agriculture researches and the results obtained using alternative methods are similar. That means that any method can explain the preferences revealed by farmers. This criterion intends to minimize the distance of any point to its ideal, so the sum of negative and positive deviational variables is minimized and it underlines the use of metric 1. This problem can be formulated in terms of goal programming, as following:

$$\text{Min}\sum_{i=1}^{q}\left[W_i\left(\frac{n_i+p_i}{f_i}\right)\right]$$

subject to

$$\sum_{j=1}^{q} w_j f_{ij} + n_i - p_i = f_i \quad i = 1, 2, \ldots, q$$

$$\sum_{j=1}^{q} W_j = 1$$

where $p_i$ and $n_i$ are the positive (over-achievement) and negative deviational variables respectively for each objective. From a preferential point of view, an $L_1$ criterion is consistent with an additive and separable utility function, and permits the estimation of a standard function (Amador et al. 1998). That means weights obtained from the last equation lead to the following function:

$$\mu = \text{Max}\sum_{i=1}^{n} w_i \frac{f_i(x)}{K_i}$$

subject to

$$X \in F$$

$$K_i = f_i^* - f_{i*}$$

where $K_i$ is a normalized factor obtained by the difference between the maximum value—$f_i^*$ (ideal)—and the minimal—$f_{i*}$ (anti-ideal)—of objective $i$ of the payoff matrix. This allows estimating the weights which indicate the ranking of the objectives followed by a farmer elicited.

## 4.1 Multi-criteria Model Definition

The farmers optimize their personal utility function which comprises the objectives taken into account by the decision maker. The optimization of these objectives is limited by certain constraints that need to be met.

Decision variables, objectives, and constraints are the main elements of the model described for Azorean dairy farmers in different systems grazing. In the multi-criteria model, the decision variables can assume any value of the feasible set, and this is defined by constrains of the systems (land, agronomic, feeding, and labor requirements; grazing systems; risk profit; and so on).

In the Azorean dairy farm usually farms have three land pasture altitudes and the animals are fed directly in pasture. The three altitudes allow the feeding of the animals in the different seasons. In winter time the animals stay mainly in low altitude, but in summer time the animals move to high altitude which has more grassland availability. The animals are fed mainly with pasture and in some season they are supplemented with silage and hay. The concentrated feed is the usual management practice in dairy farms as a complement in the period of more production. In Azores, there are two main peaks of milk, spring and autumn, when more green food is available. In autumn it is usual to seed maize and other temporary cultures.

The mathematical model that reflects the Azorean dairy farm, Typology I, is given in the Appendix. The decision variables selected as belonging to the decision making processes of dairy farms were: $X_1$—direct pasture cultivation high altitude (ha), $X_2$—direct pasture cultivation medium altitude (ha), $X_3$—direct pasture cultivation medium altitude and silage (ha), $X_4$—direct pasture cultivation medium altitude and hay (ha), $X_5$—direct pasture cultivation altitude area (ha), $X_6$—direct pasture cultivation low altitude silage (ha), $X_7$—direct pasture cultivation low altitude hay (ha), $X_8$—maize cultivation medium altitude (ha), $X_9$—maize cultivation low altitude (ha), $X_{10}$—annual crop winter medium altitude (ha), $X_{11}$—annual crop winter altitude area (ha), $X_{12}$—annual crop winter medium altitude (ha), $X_{13}$—annual crop winter low altitude (ha), $X_{14}$—concentrated feed (Kg), and $X_{15}$—number of dairy animals.

The model takes into account five objectives—1: profit maximization (Gross margin—MB, €); 2: risk minimization, by Minimization of Total Absolute Deviation (MOTAD, €), developed by Hazel (1971) and presented by Romero and Rehman (1989); 3: labor seasonality minimization (EST, hours), 4: total labor minimization or leisure maximization (MO, hours); and 5: deviations to the goal of total labor minimization (DMMO, hours).

The model constrains are—1 to 4: total cultivation area per altitude (high, medium, low); 5–7: rotational and agronomic considerations (20 % of the area was improved by maize over 5 years); 8–9: different labor requirements concerning six periods and specific activities, and the possibility of finding work in the exterior of farm; 10: risk profit (€) over 7 years; 11: operational constrain; 12–18: feed and animal requirements of energy (UFL), protein (PDIE and PDIN), calcium (CA), and phosphor (P), and dry matter intake (MS); 19: intensity grazing system; 20: no negativity constrains.

## 5 Results and Discussion

The payoff matrix determination for the five objectives and the Real Values achievement for the objective function were estimated for the Azorean dairy farm typology I, whose results are shown in Tables 10.1, 10.2, and 10.3 for each group (second and third step of the methodology). The algorithm began by optimizing each objective individually subject to the same constraints set.

In Group I—medium intensive grazing systems (Table 10.1), the objectives of target of seasonality labor (EST), and total labor minimization (DMMO) were complementary. That means they have similar values (7,823,000 € to seasonality and 7,804,000 € for hired target of total labor minimization). It is observed also in Table 10.1 that Real Value is quite similar to seasonality and target of DMMO, and this can mean that Azorean dairy farms in their decision processes include the labor rationality.

**Table 10.1** Payoff matrix—Group I (1,000 € per year)

| | MB | MOTAD | MO | EST | DMMO | Real value |
|---|---|---|---|---|---|---|
| MB | 8,775 | 3,107 | 3,107 | 7,823 | 7,804 | 6,935 |
| MOTAD | 3,303 | 1,168 | 1,170 | 2,946 | 2,942 | 2,592 |
| MO | 4,242 | 1,517 | 1,470 | 3,835 | 3,882 | 3,405 |
| EST | 359 | 2,365 | 2,412 | 139 | 282 | 478 |
| DMMO | 720 | 2,365 | 2,412 | 47 | 0 | 477 |

*Source*: The author's findings

**Table 10.2** Payoff matrix—Group II (1,000 € per year)

| | MB | MOTAD | MO | EST | DMMO | Real Value |
|---|---|---|---|---|---|---|
| MB | 8,939 | 3,107 | 3,107 | 8,511 | 8,726 | 8,586 |
| MOTAD | 2,826 | 980 | 984 | 2,692 | 2,756 | 2,709 |
| MO | 3,882 | 1,492 | 1,283 | 3,737 | 3,907 | 3,786 |
| EST | 459 | 2,415 | 2,624 | 316 | 386 | 352 |
| DMMO | 25.4 | 2,414.7 | 2,624.2 | 170.6 | 0 | 121.7 |

*Source*: The author's findings

**Table 10.3** Payoff matrix—Group III (1,000 € per year)

| | MB | MOTAD | MO | EST | DMMO | Real Value |
|---|---|---|---|---|---|---|
| MB | 11,171 | 8,466 | 8,520 | 9,954 | 10,021 | 8,303 |
| MOTAD | 3,417 | 2,600 | 2,610 | 3,051 | 3,073 | 2,620 |
| MO | 4,320 | 3,434 | 3,355 | 3,927 | 3,960 | 3,431 |
| EST | 359 | 527 | 605 | 127 | 142 | 530 |
| DMMO | 720 | 526 | 605 | 33 | 0 | 529 |

*Source*: The author's findings

The conflictive and conditioned objectives in the decision processes, in Group I, were profit maximization, risk minimization, and labor seasonality minimization.

In Group II—medium intensive grazing systems (Table 10.2), the risk (MOTAD) and total labor minimization were complementary, as well in Group I. The Real Value (8,586,000 €) was similar to the profit maximization (8,939,000 €), and the decision making process was much influenced by profit maximization. The dairy farms decision of Group II was conditioned by three conflictive objectives: profit maximization, risk, and labor seasonality minimization. The target of total labor minimization (DMMO) seemed to be complementary of profit maximization.

In Group III—high intensity system grazing (Table 10.3), the risk and total labor minimization were complementary too. The Real Value was similar to the risk minimization. In this group the gross margin (profit maximization) reaches the highest value (11,171,000 €) when compared with the other groups. The reality is well represented by the risk minimization.

In any group of Azorean dairy farms the decision making process seems to be influenced by three conflictive objectives: profit maximization, labor seasonality, and risk minimization. The total labor minimization was generally complementary to other objective (MOTAD).

The goal programming formulation was the fourth step of the methodology, related to the weights estimation that should reflect the best farmers' preferences. Using $L_1$ criteria and the Manhattan utility function, the next utilities models for the Azorean dairy farms were obtained.

Group I: $U_1 = -17.6MOTAD_1 - 82.3EST_1 - 4.6 \times 10^{-10}DMMO_1$
Group II: $U_2 = 8.8\ MB_2 - 3.4MOTAD_2 - 65.7\ EST_2 - 25.07DMMO_2$
Group III: $U_3 = -95.9MOTAD_3 - 3.9MO_3 - 0.03DMMO_3$

Groups I and III don't have a weight value for the profit maximization, but Group II (low intensive grazing system) shows a weight value to profit maximization of about 8.8 %. Group I gives more importance (82.3 %) to labor seasonality minimization, and risk minimization (17.6 %), while Group II (low intensive group) attributes more magnitude (65.7 %) to seasonality minimization. Group III (more intensive system grazing) considers the risk minimization as the most significant (95.9 %).

The set of weights is not compatible with a type of a traditional behavior (maximization of profit), except in Group II.

The next step of the methodology estimates utility functions per group of grazing system of Azorean dairy farms. At first the utility function was estimated by the $L_1$ method, the subrogated utility function. Then, the final utility function was estimated using the normalized factors. In these functions the maximization objectives have a positive signal and the minimization objectives have a negative signal.

Standard utility functions of the Azorean dairy farms were:

Group I: $U_1 = -0.8MOTAD_1 - 3.6EST_1 - 2 \times 10^{-11}DMMO_1$,
Group II: $U_2 = 0.15\ MB_2 - 0.02\ MOTAD_2 - 2.8\ EST_2 - 0.97DMMO_2$
Group III: $U_3 = -11.7MOTAD_3 - 0.41MO_3 - 3.9 \times 10^{-3}DMMO_3$

**Table 10.4** Weights of multiutilities functions for the different grazing systems

| | | $W_1$ | $W_2$ | $W_3$ | $W_4$ | $W_5$ |
|---|---|---|---|---|---|---|
| Group I | Research I | $1 \times 10^{-13}$ | −2.521 | 0 | −15.36 | n.a. |
| Group I | Research II | 0 | −0.8 | −3.6 | 0 | $-2 \times 10^{-11}$ |
| Group II | Research I | 20.47 | 0 | −11.7 | 0 | n.a. |
| Group II | Research II | 0.15 | −0.02 | −2.8 | 0 | −0.97 |
| Group III | Research I | $3.77 \times 10^{-15}$ | −0.73 | −2.967 | 0 | n.a. |
| Group III | Research II | 0 | −11.7 | 0 | −0.41 | $-3.9 \times 10^{-3}$ |

*Source*: Research I—The author's findings; Research II—Silva and Berbel (2004)
*Legend*: Profit maximization—$W_1$, Risk minimization—$W_2$, Seasonability minimization—$W_3$, Hired labor minimization—$W_4$, Deviations to the goal of total labor minimization—$W_5$

The normalized utility functions show major importance of seasonality labor in the Groups I and II. The Group II is the only one that shows some importance for profit maximization. The Group III shows a major importance in the risk minimization.

Table 10.4 shows the comparison of this model (namely research II) with a previous research (namely research I) of Silva and Berbel (2004) which had four objectives (profit maximization, risk minimization, labor seasonality minimization, and external labor minimization) in the dairy farm decision making. The actual model includes the same four objectives, as the Silva and Berbel (2004), plus the deviations to the goal of total labor minimization. The results demonstrate less importance in profit maximization (W1) in the research II. Besides this situation, in the research developed by Silva and Berbel (2004), the Group II has a bigger weight in the profit maximization comparing with other objectives but the importance of profit maximization failure in the other Groups (I and III).

The low importance of profit objective maximization is unusual, because it was expected that the traditional objective would be more important. But this situation was already observed in previous works (Rodríguez Ocaña 1996; Amador et al. 1998; Silva and Berbel 2004). It may be explained, in part, by the imperfect Azorean information systems that constrain a risk aversion decision of their dairy farms, and also, because the amount of grant that dairy farms receive in Azores.

The great importance of farming labor can be explained by family farms which generally comprise small areas and there is no alternative labor market in Azores.

The dairy farms' income (including the subsidies received by European Union) can be enough to maintain the farm and family. If the economic objectives are satisfied, then the farmers can satisfy other objectives. Tauer (1995) noted that the main objective that constrains the decision making processes may be the production cost minimization. However, there might be other factors (not economical ones) that constrain the decision making process.

**Conclusions**

Various operative techniques of Multi-Criteria decision with the development of mathematical programming models, which integrate technical and economic data characteristic of regional activities, have been revealed to be "tools" of great importance for the development of decision support systems for managers and farmers.

This observation assumes greater importance when objectives are defined and have a strong degree of conflict among them. This is the case of the Azorean farmer's decision made with conflictive objectives such as profit maximization, risk minimization, labor seasonality minimization, leisure maximization, and deviations to the goal of total labor minimization.

Using $L_1$ criterion and the Manhattan utility function, a surrogate utility function for the Azorean dairy farms that seems to be consistent with the real preferences revealed by farmers was estimated. The three groups selected according to different systems grazing (low, medium, and high intensity) differ in objective weights. Only one group (the less intensity system grazing, characterized by less than 1.4 animal per ha) weight the economic objective (profit maximization). The other two groups, more intensive (animals per ha greater than 1.4), prioritize other objective like labor and land use.

This conclusion is unexpected as profit does not seems to be the priority in the Azorean farmer's decision as already observed by Amador et al. (1998) and Rodríguez Ocaña (1996). However, we can conclude that there might be other factors (not economical ones) that constrain the decision making process.

# Appendix

$$\text{Objective (1)}: \quad \text{MAX MB} = \text{MAX}\sum_{i=1}^{15} X_i \text{MB}_i,$$

$$\text{Objective (2)}: \quad \text{MIN MOTAD} = \text{MIN}\sum_{k=1}^{7} N_k$$

$$\text{Objective (3)}: \quad \text{MIN EST} = \text{MIN}\sum_{j=1}^{6} n_j + p_j$$

$$\text{Objective (4)}: \quad \text{MIN MO} = \text{MIN} \sum_{i=1}^{15} X_i \text{MO}_i$$

$$\text{Objective (5)}: \quad \text{MIN DMMO} = \text{MIN} \sum_{i=1}^{15} n_{1j} + p_{1j}$$

$$\text{Constraint (1)}: \quad X_1 \leq S_A$$

$$\text{Constraint (2)}: \quad X_2 + X_3 + X_4 + \frac{1}{2}X_8 + \frac{1}{4}(X_{10} + X_{12}) \leq S_M$$

$$\text{Constraint (3)}: \quad X_5 + X_6 + X_7 + \frac{1}{2}X_9 + \frac{1}{4}(X_{11} + X_{13}) \leq S_B$$

$$\text{Constraint (4)}: \quad S_A + S_M + S_B \leq S_T$$

$$\text{Constraint (5)}: \quad X_8 + X_9 \leq 0.2(S_M + S_B)$$

$$\text{Constraint (6)}: \quad X_{10} + X_{11} \leq X_8$$

$$\text{Constraint (7)}: \quad X_{11} + X_{13} \leq X_9$$

$$\text{Constraint (8)}: \quad \sum_{i=1}^{15} \left(\text{MO}_j X_i\right) + n_j - p_j = \overline{\text{MO}_{dj}}, \quad j = 1, \ldots, 6$$

$$\text{Constraint (9)}: \quad \sum_{i=1}^{15} \left(\text{MO}_j X_i\right) = \text{MO}_{dj_j}, \quad j = 1, \ldots, 6$$

$$\text{Constraint (10)}: \quad \sum_{i=1}^{15} \left(\text{MB}_{ik} X_i - \overline{\text{MB}_{ik}}\right) + N_k - P_k = 0, \quad k = 1, \ldots, 7$$

$$\text{Constraint (11)}: \quad \sum_{i=1}^{15} \text{MB}_i X_i \geq 3107$$

$$\text{Constraint (12)}: \quad \sum_{j=1}^{6} \sum_{i=1}^{14} \text{UFL}_{ij} \text{MS}_{ij} X_i \geq \sum_{j=1}^{6} \text{UFL}_{15j} X_{15}$$

$$\text{Constraint (13)}: \quad \sum_{j=1}^{6} \sum_{i=1}^{14} \text{PDIE}_{ij} \text{MS}_{ij_i} \geq \sum_{j=1}^{6} \text{PDIE}_{15j} X_{15}$$

$$\text{Constraint (14)}: \quad \sum_{j=1}^{6} \sum_{i=1}^{14} \text{PDIN}_{ij} \text{MS}_{ij} X_i \geq \sum_{j=1}^{6} \text{PDIN}_{15j} X_{15}$$

$$\text{Constraint (15)}: \quad \sum_{j=1}^{6} \sum_{i=1}^{14} \text{CA}_{ij} \text{MS}_{ij} X_i \geq \sum_{j=1}^{6} \text{CA}_{15j} X_{15}$$

$$\text{Constraint (16)}: \quad \sum_{j=1}^{6} \sum_{i=1}^{14} P_{ij} \text{MS}_{ij} X_i \geq \sum_{j=1}^{6} P_{15j} X_{15}$$

$$\text{Constraint (17)}: \quad \sum_{i=1}^{14} \mathrm{MS}_i X_i \geq \mathrm{MS}_{15} X_{15}$$

$$\text{Constraint (18)}: \quad X_{14} - 547,7X_{15} = 0$$

$$\text{Constraint (19)}: \quad X_{15} - 1.4\sum_{i=1}^{13} X_i \leq 0$$

$$\text{Constraint (20)}: \quad X_i \geq 0, \ i = 1, 2, \ldots, 15$$

## References


Akkal-Corfini, N., López-Ridaura, S., Walter, C., Menasseri-Aubry, S., & Bissuel-Belaygue, C. (2007). Integrated analysis of vegetable farming systems. The case of Bretagne, West of France. In M. Donatelli, J. Hatfield, & A. Rizzoli (Eds.), *Farming Systems Design 2007, International Symposium on Methodologies on Integrated Analysis on Farm Production Systems* (pp. 131–132). 10–12 September 2007, Catania (Italy), Book 2 – Field-farm Scale Design and Improvement.

Amador, F., Sumpsi, J., & Romero, C. (1998). A non-interactive methodology to assess farmer's utility functions: An application to large farms in Andalusia, Spain. *European Review of Agricultural Economics, 25*, 92–109.

Antoine, J., Fischer, G., & Makowski, M. (1997). Multiple criteria land use analysis. *Applied Mathematics and Computation, 83*, 195–215.

Bartlett, E. T., & Clawson, W. J. (1978). Profit, meat production or efficient use of energy in ranching. *Journal of Animal Science, 46*(3), 812–818.

Bartolini, F., Bazzani, G. M., Gallerani, V., Raggi, M., & e Viaggi, D. (2007). The impact of water and agriculture policy scenarios on irrigated farming systems in Italy: An analysis based on farm level multi-attribute linear programming models. *Agricultural Systems, 93*, 90–114.

Berbel, J., & Barros, M. (1993). Planificación Multicritério de Empresas Agroganaderas con Bovino de Leche de Islas Azores (Portugal). *Invest. agr. Econ, 8*(2), 197–208. (Multicriteria management of dairy farms in the Azores islands)

Berbel, J., Cañas, J., Gómez-Limón, J., López, M., & Arriaza, M. (1999). *Micromodelos de Gestión de Agua de Riego, análisis del Impacto socioeconómico y ambiental de una política de precios*. Córdoba: Editorial Vistalegre, ISBN: 968-839-544-7 (Micromodels of water management, analysis of socioeconomics and environmental impacts of a prices policy).

Berbel, J., & Rodríguez-Ocaña, A. (1998). An MCDM approach to production analysis: an application to irrigated farms in southern Spain. *European Journal of Operational Research, 107*, 108–118.

Bergevoet, R., Ondersteijn, C., Saatkamp, H., Van Woerkum, C., & Huirne, R. (2004). Entrepreneurial behaviour of Dutch dairy farmers under a milk quota system: Goals, objectives and attitudes. *Agricultural Systems, 80*(1), 1–21.

Carvalho, N. S. (2006). Agricultura Sustentável em Regadio e o seu Planeamento Face aos Desafios Económicos, Sociais e Ambientais (O Caso da Futura Zona Irrigada de Intervenção de Alqueva). In *Actas do 5° Congresso Ibérico "Gestão e Planeamento de Água"*. 4–8 December 2006, University of Algarve - Faro, 10 p.

Carvalho, N. S. (2007). O Planeamento Agrícola Face aos Actuais Desafios Ambientais, Sociais e Económicos (Uma Aplicação da Programação por Metas Lexicográficas ao Caso da Futura Zona de Regadio de Intervenção de Alqueva). In *Actas do V Congresso Nacional da Associação Portuguesa de Economia Agrária "Globalização, Agricultura e Áreas Rurais"*. 4–6 October 2007, UTAD - Vila Real, 10 p.

Cohon, J. L. (1978). *Multiobjective programming and planning* (Mathematics in science and engineering, Vol. 140). San Diego, CA: Academic Press.
Diaz-Balteiro, L., & Romero, C. (2004a). In search of a natural systems sustainability index. *Ecological Economics, 49*, 401–405.
Diaz-Balteiro, L., & Romero, C. (2004b). Sustainability of forest management plans: A discrete goal programming approach. *Journal of Environmental Management, 71*, 351–359.
Dunn, E. G., Keller, J. M., & Marks, L. A. (1998). Integrated decision making for sustainability: A fuzzy MADM model for agriculture. In: S. A. El-Swaify & D. S. Yakowitz (Eds.), *Multiple objective decision making for land, water, and environmental management. Proceedings of the First International Conference on Multiple Objective Decision Support Systems (MODSS) for Land, Water, and Environmental Management: Concepts, Approaches, and Applications* (pp. 313–322). Florence, KY: Lewis Publishers.
El-Gayar, O. F., & Leung, P. (2001). A multiple criteria decision making framework for regional aquaculture development. *European Journal of Operational Research, 133*, 462–482.
Flury, C., Gotsch, N., & Rieder, P. (2000). The effects of alternative direct payment regimes on ecological and socio-economic indicators: Results of a spatial linear programming model for a Swiss Alpine region. In *Proceedings of Fourth International Conference on Chain Management in Agribusiness and the Food Industry*, 24–26 May, Wageningen, 9 p.
Gómez-Limón J., & Berbel J. (1995). Aplicación de una Metodología Multicritério para la Estimación de los Objetivos de los Agricultores del Regadío Cordobés. *Invest. agr. Econ, 10* (1), 103–123 (Application of a multicriteria methodology to estimate the objectives of Cordoba farmers).
Gómez-Limón, J. A., & Berbel, J. (2000). Multicriteria analysis of derived water demand functions: A Spanish case study. *Agricultural Systems, 63*, 49–72.
Groot, J., Rossing, W., Jellema, A., Stobbelaar, D., Renting, H., & Van Ittersum, M. (2007). Exploring multi-scale trade-offs between nature conservation, agricultural profits and landscape quality – A methodology to support discussions on land-use perspectives. *Agriculture, Ecosystems and Environment, 120*, 58–69.
Heilman, P., Yakowitz, D. S., & Lane, L. J. (1997). Targeting farms to improve water quality. *Applied Mathematics and Computation, 83*, 173–194.
IFAP (Instituto de Financiamento da Agricultura e Pescas). (2012). *Regime de Imposição sobre os Excedentes no Leite (Quotas Leiteiras)*. Retrieved September 10, 2012 from http://www.ifap.min-agricultura.pt/portal/page/portal/ifap_publico/GC_quotleite
INE (Instituto Nacional de Estatística). (2009). *Estatísticas Agrícolas 2008*. Retrieved September 17, 2012 from http://www.ine.pt/
INE (Instituto Nacional de Estatística). (2011). *Recenseamento Agrícola 2009. Análise dos principais resultados*. Retrieved September 17, 2012 from: http://www.ine.pt/
INRA (Institut National de la Recherche Agronomique). (1988). In R. Jarrige (Ed.), *Alimentation des bovins, ovins & caprins*. Paris: INRA; ISBN 2-7380-0021-5. (Feeding bovines, sheep and goat).
Keeney, R., & Raiffa, H. (1976). *Decisions with multiple objectives: Preferences and value tradeoffs*. New York: Wiley. ISBN 0521438837.
Köbrich, C., & Rehman, T. (1998). Sustainable agriculture and the MCDM paradigm: The development of compromise programming models with special reference to small-scale farmers in Chile's VIth Region. In S. A. El-Swaify, & D. S. Yakowitz (Eds.), *Multiple Objective decision making for land, water, and environmental management. Proceedings of the First International Conference on Multiple Objective Decision Support Systems (MODSS) for Land, Water, and Environmental Management: Concepts, Approaches, and Applications* (pp. 557–569). Florence, KY: Lewis Publishers.
Lakshminarayan, P. G., Johnson, S. R., & Bouzaher, A. (1995). A multi-objective approach to integrating agricultural economic and environmental policies. *Journal of Environmental Management, 45*, 365–378.

Latinopoulos, D. (2007). Multicriteria decision-making for efficient water and land resources allocation in irrigated agriculture. *Environment, Development and Sustainability*. doi:10.1007/s10668-007-9115-2. Retrieved from: http://www.springerlink.com/content/v8j2h44j4w02g443.

Mardle, S., Pascoe, S., Tamiz, M., & Jones, D. (2000). Resource allocation in the North Sea demersal fisheries: a goal programming approach. *Annals of Operations Research, 94*, 321–342.

Marta-Costa, A. (2008). *A Tomada da Decisão no Planeamento da Exploração Agrária no Contexto da Sustentabilidade: o caso da Produção de Carne Bovina Maronesa*. PhD Thesis, vol. I. UTAD: Vila Real.

Marta-Costa, A. A. (2010). Application of decision support methods for sustainable agrarian systems. *New Medit, IX*(2), 42–49.

Marta-Costa, A. A., Manso, F., Tibério, L., & Fonseca, C. (2013). Ecological-economic modelling for farming systems of Montemuro Mountain (Portugal). In: A. Marta-Costa, & E. Silva (Eds.), *Methods and procedures for building sustainable farming systems: Application in the European context* (Chapter 6, pp. 207–217). New York: Springer, ISBN 978-94-007-5003-6 (eBook); ISBN 978-94-007-5002-9 (Hardcover).

Meyer-Aurich, A. (2005). Economic and environmental analysis of sustainable farming practices – A Bavarian case study. *Agricultural Systems, 86*, 190–206.

Mimouni, M., Zekri, S., & Flichman, G. (2000). Modelling the trade-offs between farm income and the reduction of erosion and nitrate pollution. *Annals of Operations Research, 94*, 91–103.

Neely, W. P., North, R. M., & Fortson, J. C. (1977). An operational approach to multiple objective decision making for public water resources projects using integer goal programming. *American Journal of Agricultural Economics, 59*(1), 198–203.

Nibbering, J. W., & Van Rheenen, T. (1998). The development of a quantitative method for setting research priorities: A critical assessment. *Agricultural Systems, 56*(2), 145–165.

Poeta, A. (1994). *A Tomada de Decisão no Planeamento da Exploração Agrícola num Contexto de Objectivos Múltiplos*. PhD Thesis. UTAD: Vila Real.

Prathapar, S. A., Meyer, W. S., & Madden, J. C. (1997). SWAGMAN options: A hierarchical multicriteria framework to identify profitable land uses that minimize water table rise and salinization. *Applied Mathematics and Computation, 83*, 217–240.

Raju, K. S., Duckstein, L., & Arondel, C. (2001). Multicriterion analysis for sustainable water resources planning: A case study in Spain. *Water Resources Management, 14*, 435–456.

Raju, K. S., & Vasan, A. (2007). Multi attribute utility theory for irrigation system evaluation. *Water Resources Management, 21*, 717–728.

Rehman, T., & Romero, C. (1987). Goal programming with penalty functions and livestock ration formulation. *Agricultural Systems, 23*, 117–132.

Riesgo, L., & Goméz-Limón, J. A. (2006). Multi-criteria policy scenario analysis for public regulation of irrigated agriculture. *Agricultural Systems, 91*, 1–28.

Rodríguez Ocaña, A. (1996). *Propuesta Metodológica para el Análisis de la toma de Decisión de los Agricultores: Aplicación al caso de Regadío Extensivo Cordobés*. PhD Thesis. Escuela Técnica Superior Ingenieros Agrónomos y Montes, Universidad de Córdoba.

Romero, C. (1993). *Teoria de la Decisión Multicriterio: Conceptos, Técnicas y Aplicaciones*. Madrid: Alianza Editorial.

Romero, C., & Rehman, T. (1989). *Multiple criteria analysis for agricultural decisions* (Developments in Agricultural Economics, Vol. 5). Amsterdam: Elsevier. ISBN 0-444-87408-9.

Rozakis, S., Sourie, J.-C., & Vanderpooten, D. (2001). Integrated micro-economic modelling and multi-criteria methodology to support public decision-making: The case of liquid bio-fuels in France. *Biomass and Bioenergy, 20*, 385–398.

Shakya, K. M., & Leuschner, W. A. (1990). A multiple objective land use planning model for Nepalese hills farms. *Agricultural Systems, 34*, 133–149.

Silva, E. (2001). *Análisis Multicriterio da la Eficiência Económica de las Explotaciones Agroganaderas de las Azores (Portugal)*. PhD Thesis. Universidad de Córdoba.

Silva, E., & Berbel, J. (2004). *A decision support model for dairy farms. Quality assurance, risk management and environmental control in agriculture and food supply networks* (Vol. B, pp. 583–591). Bonn: Universitat Bonn-ILB.

Silva, E., & Berbel, J. (2006). An Azorean farms typology. *New Medit, VI*(1), 51–54.

Silvestri, N., Andreoli, M., & Bellocchi, G. (2007). Assessing Agricultural management via multi-criteria analysis: Case-study on maize systems. In: M. Donatelli, J. Hatfield, A. Rizzoli (Eds.), *Farming systems design 2007, Int. Symposium on Methodologies on Integrated Analysis on Farm Production Systems*. 10–12 September 2007, Catania (Italy), book 2 – Field-farm Scale Design and Improvement, pp. 189–190.

Solano, C., León, H., Pérez, E., & Herrero, M. (2001). Characterising objective profiles of Costa Rican dairy farmers. *Agricultural Systems, 67*(1), 153–179.

Sumpsi, J., Amador, F., & Romero, C. (1996). On farmer's objectives: A multicriteria approach. *European Journal of Operational Research, 96*, 64–71.

Tauer, L. (1995). Do New York dairy farmers maximize profits or minimize cost? *American Journal Agricultural Economics, 77*, 421–429.

Thankappan, S., Midmore, P., & Jenkins, T. (2006). Conserving energy in smallholder agriculture: A multi-objective programming case-study of Northeast India. *Ecological Economics, 56*, 190–208.

Tiwari, D. N., Loof, R., & Paudyal, G. N. (1999). Environmental-economic decision-making in lowland irrigated agriculture using multi-criteria analysis techniques. *Agricultural Systems, 60*, 99–112.

Van Huylenbroeck, G. (1997). Multicriteria tools for the trade-off analysis in rural planning between economic and environmental objectives. *Applied Mathematics and Computation, 83*, 261–280.

Willet, K., Zhang, T., Mcternan, W., Sharda, R., & Rossman, E. (1997). Regulation of pesticide discharge into surface and groundwater under uncertainty: A model for environmental risk-profitability tradeoffs and policy selection. *Environmental Modeling and Assessment, 2*, 211–220.

Zander, P., & Kächele, H. (1999). Modelling multiple objectives of land use for sustainable development. *Agricultural Systems, 59*, 311–325.

Zekri, S., & Romero, C. (1991). Influencia de las Preferências del Centro Decisor y de los Incentivos Economicos en la Reduccion de la Contaminación por Sales. *Invest. Agr. Econ, 6* (2), 223–239 (Influence of decision making preferences and economic incentives in reducing pollution).

Zekri, S., & Romero, C. (1993). Public and private compromises in agricultural water management. *Journal of Environmental Management, 37*, 281–290.

Zeleny, M. (1982). *Multiple criteria decision making* (McGraw-Hill Series in Quantitative Methods for Management, 563 p.). New York: McGraw-Hill.

Zhang, Q., Maeda, S., & Kawachi, T. (2007). Stochastic multiobjective optimization model for allocating irrigation water to paddy fields. *Paddy Water Environment, 5*, 93–99.

# Chapter 11
# Final Conclusions

Vítor João Pereira Domingues Martinho

This handbook is an original contribution to international literature related to agricultural economics and is a useful publication for farmers, policymakers, politicians, and researchers. The following will show the main conclusions obtained from this handbook throughout its several chapters.

The preoccupation with sustainability is at the top of the agenda for many countries, when discussing agricultural economics within the context of globalized economies, where the pressures from international organizations, namely the World Trade Organization, have their given weight. On the other hand, despite the increase in productivity, for agriculture in the United States of America (and its associated advantages and disadvantages), this was not sufficient to avoid the reduction in volume for the farming output within the economy. Consequently, there are, as expected, some environmental problems in agriculture, due to the volumes of methane and nitrous oxide emissions produced by this sector. However, the reduction in volumes of fossil fuel energy consumption reveals concern for the environment and sustainability in this country.

In the context of the European Union the values of some agricultural economic indicators and the results obtained show the importance of some countries, such as France, and the relevance of some variables in the explanation of the agricultural output, such as employment. On the other hand, the spatial autocorrelation must be taken into account in the design of new agricultural policies.

The economic reality, across the different 27 former European Union countries, is strongly diverse. Another finding is that the manufacturing sector, namely that based on agriculture and fishery, is not sufficiently developed in order to exploit opportunities that come from the spillover effects, externalities, endogeneity of the factors, and learning by doing effects.

V.J.P.D. Martinho (✉)
Agricultural School, Polytechnic Institute of Viseu, 3500 Viseu, Portugal
e-mail: vdmartinho@esav.ipv.pt



V.J.P.D. Martinho (ed.), *The Agricultural Economics of the 21st Century*,
DOI 10.1007/978-3-319-09471-7_11

The review of literature reveals that there are many determinants for agricultural output with various sources, namely, economic, social, environmental, and biological. In the group of European Union countries having larger dimensions and those that had financial help from International Institutions, such as Portugal, Ireland, and Greece, the statistical information indicates that the economic problems of countries such as Portugal and Greece will indeed last for some years.

The reality of the BRICS countries is, also, indeed very different in many variables across several dimensions. The statistical data shows that, namely India has many economic and social fragilities and, in some cases, so too does Brazil. In terms of agricultural performance, China and India have a lower farming productivity whereas South Africa and Russia demonstrate the best performance.

From the variables considered, related with sustainability in the Portuguese context, only the population density presents a negative impact upon the economic performance of the whole economic dynamic and the agricultural sector. These conclusions may be an important indication for public institutions in the definition of their public policies, namely when searching for a sustainable development.

The evolution of the productivity growth rate among the Portuguese NUTs III and the several groups of manufacturing considered is not uniform and there are some regions where this variable, on average, presents negative values such as in the Algarve, Açores, and Madeira. The variables considered related to the environment have little impact on these relationships.

The review of literature shows that rural development has many problems, with difficult solutions, but the possible solutions must take the farmers and the rural economic and social operators into account, because they are the ones who know these areas and their dynamics well. In Portuguese municipalities there is evidence of desertification from rural areas with some rise in congestion in urban areas.

The manufacturer's authorised representative in the EU is Springer Nature Customer Service Centre GmbH, Europaplatz 3, 69115 Heidelberg, Germany. If you have any concerns regarding our products, please contact ProductSafety@springernature.com

Printed and bound by CPI Group (UK) Ltd, Croydon, CR0 4YY
30/09/2026
02225665-0009